STRICT RULES

THE ICONIC STORY OF THE TOUR THAT SHAPED
MIDNIGHT OIL

ANDREW McMILLAN

People of Aboriginal or Torres Strait Islander heritage are advised that this book contains names of people who are deceased or may be deceased.

This edition published in Australia and New Zealand in 2017
by Hachette Australia
(an imprint of Hachette Australia Pty Limited)
Level 17, 207 Kent Street, Sydney NSW 2000
www.hachette.com.au

First published as *Strict Rules: The Blackfella – Whitefella Tour* in 1988
by Hodder & Stoughton

10 9 8 7 6 5 4 3 2 1

Copyright © Andrew McMillan 1988
Copyright Foreword © Rob Hirst 2008, 2016
Copyright Epilogue © Peter Garrett 2016

This book is copyright. Apart from any fair dealing for the purposes of private study, research, criticism or review permitted under the *Copyright Act 1968*, no part may be stored or reproduced by any process without prior written permission. Enquiries should be made to the publisher.

National Library of Australia
Cataloguing-in-Publication data:

McMillan, Andrew, 1957–2012, author.
Strict rules / Andrew McMillan.

9780733638084 (pbk)

Midnight Oil (Musical group)
Warumpi Band.
Concerts–Northern Territory.
Rock concerts–Northern Territory.
Aboriginal Australians–Northern Territory.

Cover design by Luke Causby, Blue Cork Design
Cover photographs courtesy of Ken Duncan
Map design by Sarah Novinetz and Niblock Publishing
Text design by Bookhouse, Sydney
Typeset in 10.5/13.5 pt Minion Pro by Bookhouse, Sydney

FOREWORD

One day turns into the next out here.

Big city words like 'Reconciliation' and 'Intervention' get sucked up in willy-willies and spun around and around, before getting snagged in the branches of a poverty bush, or impaled upon spinifex needles.

Urban fiascos involving corrupt councils, dodgy tunnel deals and plummeting share markets seem ludicrous, irrelevant, ephemeral.

In the Western Desert of Australia the land takes hostages. Freedom is regained slowly, often imperceptibly: vanities must be shed, wisdom must be drawn, humility learned. Time moves forward, but only in grinding tectonic shifts, unnoticed by squinting intruders with too much noise in their heads.

Thirty years ago the young men in Midnight Oil were held hostage by the land. It was only for a month, but none of us was ever the same again. With a manager and a couple of crewmen we journeyed from the surf to the centre. At first, we played too loud, too fast. Our audiences were small – depleted by those who'd fled to play footy on the red dirt ovals of distant towns.

Gradually, however, with the Warumpi Band as guides, and Charlie McMahon as wise counsellor, we learned how to use space in our music, to breathe the slower rhythms of the desert. In other words, to fill the gaps between the beats, notes and words with what Charlie referred to as 'The Great Quiet'.

Andrew McMillan noticed this. A keen observer and compulsive storyteller, he'd been out bush before. Like us, Andrew was equally amazed and appalled by the sights, sounds and smells of the outback communities. Skinny legs sprawled in the dust, he hammered away on his primitive laptop, as cool, cloudless days gave way to freezing nights, and biblical sunsets accompanied by soundtracks of guitars, drums and didjs made way for immense heavens full of celestial fireworks.

Then came the Top End leg of the so-called Blackfella-Whitefella Tour. Travelling now by light aircraft, Andrew accompanied the band as we were engulfed in a much wilder world – one of swamp jockeys and saltwater cowboys, killer crocs and giant barramundi, land councils, cattle stations, mineral leases and massive uranium mines. Crazed-eyed pilots parachuted into our gigs, booze barges docked and were drunk dry within hours, band members would disappear after gigs then reappear without explanation, several days later, and manager Gary Morris – tanned, fit and shirtless – swaggered around with a python wrapped around his neck. Meanwhile, two dazzling new colours were added to the rust-red hues of the centre: the turquoise of an implausibly clean, clear tropical sea; and the grey/gold of the world's last unspoilt coastlines. The total effect was intoxicating – in every sense of the word.

In 2008 much has changed, much has stayed the same. Neil Murray, Warumpi's band leader, guitarist, songwriter and bush poet, is a (still unsung) national treasure, even though his songs such as 'My Island Home' and 'Native Born' are de facto national anthems. Warumpi guitarist Sammy Butcher opened and operates a recording studio in Papunya, releasing his own album, the beautifully entitled *Desert Surf Guitar*.

Charlie McMahon toured overseas with Midnight Oil, and continues to travel the world solo or with Gondwana, using his legendary didjeribone and 'face bass'. Midnight Oil hit the road with a vengeance following the release of the desert-inspired *Diesel and Dust* album – propelled by successful international singles such as 'Beds are Burning' and 'The Dead Heart' – and continued to write, record and tour until late 2002, when vocalist Pete Garrett left for a career in federal politics, and the remaining band members forged new alliances, pursued other dreams.

Meanwhile, an Aboriginal band from Yirrkala, Yothu Yindi, who also toured the USA with Midnight Oil, had a smash hit with the danceable, political, land rights song, 'Treaty'.

As for Andrew McMillan, the city kid who fell for the bush stayed on, making the Northern Territory his adopted home, his obsession, his life. Andrew's knowledge of the history and cultures of the Top End, and of East Timor to the near north, was without peer (his *An Intruder's Guide To East Arnhem Land* has recently been republished). He was a multi-talent, writing late into the hot nights for books, theatre, magazines and his band, the notorious Darwin's 4th Estate. He was an author with a passion, too busy to eat but never too pressed for a chat and a smoke. He was a thinking man's drinking man, off solids for 40 years and still searching for the truth. The man had strict rules.

Rob Hirst
Sydney, 2008, 2016

For my mother,
who bought me a typewriter and guitar . . .
my father,
in the wish that we could've spent another weekend
in Tara . . .
and the people who pick up hitch-hikers . . .

CONTENTS

Foreword		iii
PROLOGUE – 1985	Boots	ix
ONE	Alice Springs	1
TWO	Uluru	24
THREE	Docker River	52
FOUR	Warakurna	77
FIVE	Kintore	98
SIX	Papunya	125
SEVEN	Yuendumu	141
EIGHT	Funnel Webs in the Bedroom	159
NINE	Maningrida	182
TEN	Galiwin'ku	194
ELEVEN	Yirrkala	210
TWELVE	Groote Eylandt	225
THIRTEEN	Numbulwar	241
FOURTEEN	Barunga	257
FIFTEEN	Wadeye	269
SIXTEEN	Nguiu	280
SEVENTEEN	Cooinda	290
Epilogue		300
Acknowledgments		307
About the Author		308

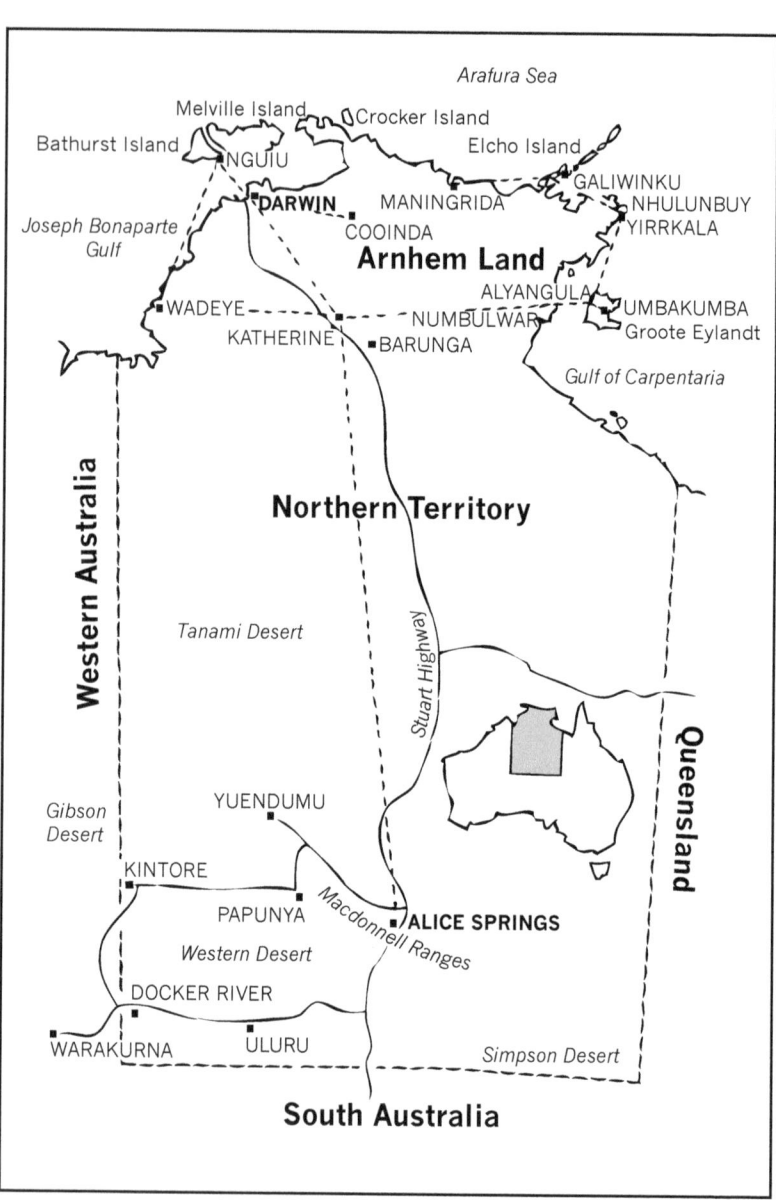

PROLOGUE – 1985
BOOTS

In the end, Gordon Tjapanangka Butcher wanted boots as black as his skin.

For most of his life, he'd happily gone without. The spinifex country of the Western Desert was hot and dry and hard, and over a period of twenty-three years the soles of his feet had grown claypan cracked and pale.

But when the Warumpis looked like becoming a 'king band', he splashed out and bought a new pair of boots.

An initiated man, he'd grown old in a couple of decades, and yet still he seemed young. His torso was as solid and scarred as a river red-gum's trunk, and he had a smile that flashed across his face like a flood. His eyes were deep and dark, and when he was happy they sparked like coals in a fire. But when he was troubled, they'd do an eight-ball roll in their sockets and drop right out of sight.

He conversed primarily in Luritja, one of twenty-three surviving languages of the desert, and would stumble into English only when his shyness among whitefellas was momentarily overcome.

He'd grown up in Papunya, a government settlement for Aborigines 150 kilometres north-west of Alice Springs, which has been variously described as 'like something out of the Third

World' and 'like Beirut after the bombing'. Before the coming of the Europeans, it had been known only as a site of the Honey Ant Dreaming.

His mother, whose name (like his father's) can no longer be mentioned because she has now 'finished up', was married in the tribal manner and had her first child at the age of 15. Gordon was her fifth, though only three had survived until his birth. (The parents neither drank nor smoked, but both 'finished up' before they were 50.)

His brother, Sammy Tjapanangka Butcher, eighteen months older than him, turned out to be an inspired guitarist. And Gordon was an excellent drummer, though he spent more time mending fences than hammering away at the kit. Together they formed the rhythm section of the Warumpi Band, an outfit that hoped to do much for the esteem of their people.

Although the brothers were born in Papunya, such were the conditions of the settlement at the time that the Deputy Registrar of Births, Deaths and Marriages can find 'no record' of Sammy's arrival.

Unlike most of their countrymen, who rarely stray from the lands of their Dreaming, Gordon and Sammy had been to the cities. Sydney and Melbourne – fast places with too many cars and too many houses, places Gordon approached with a mixture of fear and curiosity, neither of which may have shown because of his strong sense of reserve. He had the shyness so characteristic of the desert blacks, and a sense of instinctive survival. When he saw the old men in Sydney's Taylor Square tossing breadcrumbs to the pigeons, he presumed that they were only luring them close enough to capture and eat.

He had no great rapport with the blacks from the cities, for they were, by and large, detribalised people who'd lost their language and, with it, the intrinsic spirit of their culture. They'd experienced rites of passage in the urban environment that were utterly different from his own. They were angry and bitter for they had no land to call home. They didn't belong to the land; nor did it belong to them. They wanted to hoist the Aboriginal flag on to the stage when the Warumpis played, and get the band to make statements about Land Rights. But Gordon's grasp of politics wasn't that keen: besides, the cross-cultural chasms his own soul had to bridge by their very nature would have been incomprehensible to the urbanised blacks. He just wanted to play – to blacks and whites alike – and see everybody having a good time. After that he could go home with a few dollars in his pocket and 'siddown' with his family for a time.

His visits to the cities were brief, a week or two for recording or a series of showcase concerts, and then he'd return to his own country, to his wife and his family and his friends. There, he'd take a fencing job within 60 kilometres of his home, and, no doubt, promise never to leave again.

It was in the city that Gordon Tjapanangka Butcher bought the boots, a pair of R.M. Williams' finest. They had leather soles and Cuban heels, suede uppers and elastic sides. In an impulsive moment, he'd forked out over a hundred bucks for them.

But they weren't black; they were brown. So after a couple of weeks he tossed them into the back of the bus and there they lay, discarded among the soggy towels, the mouldering t-shirts and the half-eaten burgers, until the hitch-hiker tried them on.

CHAPTER ONE
ALICE SPRINGS

We bailed out of Sydney at dawn, flying west over the mountains and drifting across the plains, touching down outside Bourke to refuel and again in Birdsville for more Av-gas and beer. Strapped into a string of light aircraft we chased the sun across the driest continent on the planet and still didn't see Alice 'til dusk.

Keyed up like schoolkids on the eve of a summer camp, we were embarking on a tour that had never been tackled before. We were heading into an ancient land where tribal law stood at odds with the modern world.

Out in the deserts of Central Australia, the razorback ridges of the Macdonnell Ranges split the plains like a wedge, splintering the earth with shards of granite and sedimentary deposits. A glowing, primeval spine from the air, they crease the desert like the ceremonial scars on an old man's chest.

For thousands of years the region was the domain of tribes like the Eastern and Western Aranda, nomadic hunters and gatherers whose relationship with the land was so deeply spiritual that to harm the country of their ancestors would have resulted in unspeakable retribution.

In 1788 tall ships arrived on the coast almost 1700 kilometres to the south-east, and using the legal fiction that the continent was uninhabited, white settlers claimed sovereign title to the land.

The continent they'd claimed in the name of King George III was, unbeknown to the newcomers, criss-crossed with Dreaming tracks, the paths taken by the ancestral beings that had created the land and the lore. With extraordinary speed, the newcomers built dreaming tracks of their own: a network of roads and bridges and railway-lines linking their cities and farms and towns and mines.

For almost a century, the Aranda and their neighbours remained blissfully unaware of such developments. They wandered from rock-hole to rock-hole, hunting kangaroo and possum and goanna, and gathering bush tomato, sweet potato and bush banana. They travelled and camped in extended family groups and maintained a complex social order, observing the responsibilities of a complicated kinship system and 'looking after' the country in which they roamed. They burnt patches of land every few years to promote regeneration, and set aside conservation zones around their sacred sites, decreeing that even in the driest seasons the animals and plants within those areas were not to be harmed. Theirs was, the anthropologists now argue, part of the oldest existing culture in the world.

In the 1860s, the newcomers moved into the region, fencing off the waterholes, clearing tracts of land and introducing horses and cattle and goats to keep themselves alive. They shot out the roos and the emus that were eating the vegetation and chased the Aborigines away from their sacred sites. In their ignorance, the pastoralists rearranged the physical face of the land, altering the delicate balance of an ecology that had been nurtured for thousands of years.

In the 1870s, a telegraph station was established within sight of the Macdonnell Ranges. It was built above a waterhole the newcomers called Alice Springs.

Jammed up against a pass known as Heavitree Gap, Alice sprawls along the sandy bed of the Todd, a watercourse that's inundated so rarely that the annual boat race is conducted on foot.

Corrugated iron glints in the noonday sun, four-wheel-drive Toyotas hum on the tar and vacancy signs peel in the heat. Alice is, the tour operators will tell you, a couple of days' drive from the nearest beach. If you're an asthmatic, it's an ideal place to dry out.

The Alice averages less than 250 millimetres of rain a year, which is hardly enough to settle the dust. It's so dry that in summer, when the thermometer gets up around 42 degrees Centigrade in the shade, even the crows take an hour or two for siddown time.

The town itself is a small one, with a population of just 23,000. Many of the people are public servants; others seek to make a living from the tourist trade. Like any bureaucratic country town, its social life revolves around interdepartmental rivalries and factional groupings. Everyone seems to know everybody else's business, and the range of social opportunities is limited. Life is so slow, it is said, that the town's inhabitants will accept you as a local just as soon as you've seen the Todd flow three times. Not that there are too many people who want to pack their bags and move into a town like Alice.

There's a feeling that the newcomers are still afraid of the country they've conquered; that they feel belittled by its emptiness, disturbed by its isolation, and suspicious of its original inhabitants who've survived in its harsh environment and learned to live in harmony with the land the newcomers are still trying to tame.

Since the earliest days of the Flying Doctor, Alice has held a special place in the hearts of urban Australians. The popular image has been of an outpost, a wild frontier town full of rough diamonds pitting themselves against the rigours of life in the outback: tall, bronzed men driving herds of cattle to the rail-head, hoary old Afghan camel drivers saddling up for another expedition, and drunken blacks sleeping it off in the bed of the Todd.

The first time the hitch-hiker saw Alice was in the late winter of 1978. Slipping out of the desert, the town swam through the grimy tinted windows of a Greyhound at dawn. He'd been on the bus out of Darwin for twenty-three hours, a trip that had drained his last 55 bucks. If he'd had the sense to check the weather reports, he never would've climbed aboard. Far better to have stayed on the tropical beaches of Darwin for another month or two and then made a run for it just before the Wet. In Alice it was minus 6 degrees and the mercury hadn't yet bottomed out.

In the kit he had neither jumpers nor a jacket, just grubby shirts, a stack of paperbacks and the badly distorted recording of a new Sydney band called Midnight Oil. (On the road outside Charters Towers, a Queensland cop, with an air of childlike curiosity, had unravelled the cassette, dribbling shiny streamers of tape into the dust while he watched the wheels go round.)

It was Rodeo Week when he arrived, and the town was bustling with gaudily clad tourists and black stockmen in from the sprawling pastoral leases of the Centre. He'd never seen so many Aborigines before. Spilling out of the parks and the pubs in boots that squeaked on the tar, the stockmen would yell 'Gidday' to everyone they met, flashing broad grins beneath even broader brimmed hats. Rolling down the footpaths, they chatted and laughed and sang along to the music that leaked into the cool dry air. The loud speakers along Todd Street crackled with Elvis and Slim Dusty and Ted Egan, but mostly Elvis, his voice blistering around the edges, thin and wasted as if it was coming out of the rusty depths of a 44-gallon drum being hammered by sheets of rain.

Alice was a low-slung town then, a slow place with dusty streets and noisy bars. The cars had Commonwealth plates and roo bars and a sun-baked veneer of fine red dust. And those that weren't so attired had left-hand-drive signs across the rear dash – big Yank tanks shipped in for the American intelligence personnel working beneath the radomes of Pine Gap.

By 1986, Alice had lost much of its outback charm. The population had almost doubled, a set of traffic lights had been installed, and what the termites hadn't eaten the developers had bulldozed in the hunt for the tourist dollar. Fuelled by speculation that hordes of international visitors would descend on the Centre to view the passing of Halley's Comet, the town had succumbed to a building boom. But by the time the comet had passed, many of the flash new motels had gone to the wall.

Despite the frenzied construction of multi-storey carparks and motels, Alice was still a sleepy place. Even something as disruptive as a police road-block at Heavitree Gap, which brought much of the town's traffic system to a standstill, could escape the attention of the local media for a week or more.

Just a block from the GPO on Railway Terrace, you can scamper through the spinifex and the shattered footloose stones that grip the sides of Anzac Hill. At the lookout, you can join busloads of Japanese tourists taking in the panorama of lunchbox supermarkets, caravan parks, corrugated-iron workshops and pressed-metal fences. You can see the brick and fibro houses with air-conditioning units that bubble from their walls and roofs like warts. You can see the garish signs of the video stores and the gnarled trunks of the river red-gums hanging over the Todd. You can gaze in the direction of the town camps like Ewyenper-Atwatye, Yarrentye-Arltere and Aper-Alwerrknge – fringe settlements where the original inhabitants of the region, deprived of their traditional lands or attracted by the booze, now reside. You can look out over the golf courses and the casino and up to the treacherous bluffs of the Macdonnells.

Beyond that lies the desert.

> What is missing at the moment is an account of where we go from here. It may be that the present scenario is that of a people waiting for the barbarians. It may be that already some group has been out into the desert, and is about to come back with a message. But what that message will be, no one at the moment is even daring to guess.
>
> MANNING CLARK, *THE BULLETIN*, 29 JANUARY 1980

Midnight Oil hadn't spent much time in the desert.

A powerful rock 'n' roll band who, according to Mark Mordue of *RAM* magazine, 'occupy a critical and central position as the most widely heard radical voice for young people in Australia', they'd drawn their earliest support from the ranks of Sydney's beachside surf culture.

They'd been around for about nine years, and in that time had transcended the boundaries of what could reasonably be expected from a bunch of rock 'n' rollers.

From the outset, the Oils had been different. Eschewing the clichéd excesses of sex and drugs and rock 'n' roll, they'd developed a low-key but strict code of behaviour. While many of their contemporaries were burning themselves out in two or three years, the Oils seemed to be working to a long-term plan. Circumstances changed, opportunities arose, tactics were altered and the Oils rolled on. They maintained a low and private profile, working behind the scenes in setting things up and appearing only when they considered the contribution to be valid. And when the chits came down, they were arguably the cleanest outfit in the country.

Even as an almost unknown band, they'd steadfastly refused to play the music industry's game. In order to break the monopoly of the established booking agencies, they booked their own gigs and blacklisted venues with heavy bouncers or high prices. They wouldn't launch their records with extravagant media receptions and refused to appear on 'Countdown', the country's most influential rock television show.

When a Sydney pub barred patrons wearing t-shirts, the band bought hundreds of collared surf shirts and gave them away at the door. The no t-shirts rule was subsequently revoked. They gave up their time and resources to play in a women's prison on New Year's Eve and to stage regular benefit concerts that drew attention to the issues they'd investigated. They rejected the efforts of international record companies to tame the political and overwhelmingly Australian nature of their lyrics. They turned down an offer of 70,000 dollars to play at an outdoor festival because the promoters wouldn't give a percentage of the gate takings to a project aimed at providing musical facilities for the unemployed of Sydney's western suburbs.

They were an '80s band with a social conscience, an enigma in an era in which so much pop music was devoid of integrity, in which bands were manufactured and moulded for a market. By the winter of 1986, they'd sold over a million records in a country with a population just sixteen times that number.

The reason for their popularity, of course, was that they were an incredibly dynamic band. Their shows were wild and noisy affairs, bristling with tension, excitement, and an exhilarating sense of power. Their lyrics had always had a political edge, but instead of just singing about the issues that affected them, the Oils sought solutions and backed up the rhetoric with irrefutable deeds.

'There's a feeling in Midnight Oil,' said their singer Peter Garrett in a 1985 interview, 'that the band should be involved in doing these things, or lending itself to doing these things, that it should not be unaware. There's a feeling that to have the kind of audience and long-term success that this band has had is a privilege: it's not a right. And I believe that with that privilege comes certain responsibilities, which is to give as good as you've got according to your view and your vision and the sort of things that you've been singing about. And Midnight Oil would be a bunch of hypocrites if it didn't jump up on its box and preach and also didn't give out the money now. You can't preach it and then not deliver the goods.'

Described by one journalist as 'a one-band community service organisation', they'd raised, by 1986, around a million dollars for those causes in which they'd developed a passionate interest. Through their fans, Midnight Oil was funding refuges for the homeless, rehabilitation centres and projects for the unemployed. They were supporting anti-nuclear campaigns, non-political peace and disarmament activities and drawing attention to environmental and conservation issues.

In late 1985, for instance, they released the EP *Species Deceases*. It sold 50,000 copies in two days and debuted on the national singles charts at number 1. All royalties were channelled into a trust fund for peace and disarmament activities. Coinciding with the release of the EP, the band embarked on a twenty-five date national tour that saw them performing before 130,000 fans. Profits from the sale of t-shirts, singlets and badges (90,000 dollars in all) were given to the Open Family Foundation in Melbourne for distribution to band-selected youth refuges throughout the country. The tour ended with a Wilderness Society benefit in front of 13,000 people at the Sydney Entertainment Centre. The proceeds from that show were used to finance *Islands of the Green Dinosaurs*, a film focusing on North Queensland rainforests that had been threatened with destruction.

The Oils' unparalleled profile didn't go unnoticed by the Federal Labor government. In early 1986, Garrett, a law graduate and former Senate candidate, was appointed to the committee examining the 'Individual and Democratic Rights of Australians under the Nation's Constitution'.

'We're providing the signposts the politicians aren't providing,' said the vocalist. 'We're showing kids where to put their feet.'

It was getting to the point where almost anything Midnight Oil involved itself in was guaranteed to attract some degree of national attention.

Even when their activities were centred on some place like Alice...

Alice Springs is so far removed from mainstream Australia that it's more likely to host a press conference for the opening of a new car yard than the arrival of a visiting rock band. For Midnight Oil, an exception was made.

It was the first weekend in July, 1986, and the Oils were about to embark on a tour unlike any ever attempted by a white band; a tour that would see them visiting Aboriginal communities like Mutitjulu, Docker River, Kintore, Papunya and Yuendumu in the Western Desert, and Maningrida, Galiwinku, Yirrkala, Umbakumba, Numbulwar, Barunga, Wadeye and Nguiu in the subtropical wetlands of the Top End.

They were setting out on a trip that would, they hoped, 'promote closer ties between black and white Australians', and enable them to gain 'a better understanding of [Aboriginal] communities' needs, aspirations and lifestyles'.

Shortly before 4 pm (Central Standard Time) media representatives from around the country rolled into the Oasis Motel on Gap Road and set up their equipment. News crews from the radio and television divisions of the Australian Broadcasting Corporation planted their microphones in front of the potted palms. The *Centralian Advocate* sent a reporter to feed the wire services. The Melbourne *Age* flew in a journalist and a photographer. And the ABC's documentaries department was represented by a four-man crew from 'A Big Country'.

Amidst the tape-recorders, cameras and television lights lay copies of a press release issued twenty-four hours earlier by the Federal Department of Aboriginal Affairs:

> Popular Australian recording groups Midnight Oil and the Warumpi Band leave today to begin an historic tour of Aboriginal communities in the Northern Territory.
>
> Announcing this today, the Minister for Aboriginal Affairs, Mr Clyde Holding, said he congratulated Midnight Oil on organising the tour.
>
> 'The Government, through the Department of Aboriginal Affairs, was delighted to join with Midnight Oil and the Warumpi Band in facilitating the tour,' Mr Holding said.
>
> 'Thousands of people in remote Northern Territory communities will now be able to see, for the first time, live performances by Midnight Oil and the Warumpi bands.
>
> 'But apart from the music, Midnight Oil want the tour to be a bridge-building exercise for Aboriginal and non-Aboriginal Australians. The group has already expressed its wish to help expand community understanding of Aboriginal aspirations.
>
> 'Midnight Oil is itself meeting a considerable component of the tour's cost, with assistance from my Department under its Public Awareness Program.'

Behind the microphones, peering into the glare of the television lights, sat two members of the band.

The first thing that strikes you about Peter Garrett is his enormous height. Then you're caught by the clear blue eyes, the gaunt features, and maybe the way the top of his left ear sweeps up towards a point. He shaved his head in 1976 or 1977, either because of a scalp irritation or because, as a keen bodysurfer, he was tired of his long blond hair flicking into his eyes. The reasons have never been fully explained because, as far as he's concerned, 'it's not an issue.'

He's got such a striking presence that people who, having written him off as a publicity-seeking crank, see him interviewed on television and remark on the honesty in his face, the openness of his body language, and the sense of conviction with which he speaks.

He's one of the most commanding speakers in the country, and when he's firing in debate you almost feel sorry for his adversaries. (After a series of exchanges over the Australia Card in 1987, television critic Peter Luck was moved to describe Garrett's opponent, Senator Susan Ryan, as 'the Government's sacrificial anode. She's like a canary in a coal mine . . . they send her in to see whether she comes out alive or not.')

In Alice, Garrett was in his fireside-chat mode:

> 'I'm Peter Garrett and this is Rob Hirst. We're from Midnight Oil. We're talking to you today, basically, to let you know what we're doing over the next three weeks.
>
> 'We feel that if we're going to truly reflect feelings and issues and matters which are of concern to Australians and are part of the Australian ethos in 1986, then we need to go out there and see them first-hand and be a part of it, if you like.
>
> 'We're less inclined to believe what we read and what we see on the box than we are to go out and experience first-hand, and I think that Midnight Oil's always had a direct relationship with the people that it's played to anyway.

> 'These people out here won't often get an opportunity to hear or see a band like this, so one way of actually overcoming that is to lob in that area, in the backyard, so to speak, and do it.'

The backyard of which Garrett spoke is a big one. The Northern Territory covers 1,346,200 square kilometres and supports a population of just 130,000, 25 per cent of whom are Aborigines. Since the introduction of the *Land Rights Act* (NT) of 1976, Aborigines have been granted inalienable freehold title to almost 35 per cent of the Territory: 19.72 per cent was transferred from the existing Aboriginal reserves and the other 14.35 per cent was Crown land that has been successfully claimed under the terms of the Act.

The *Land Rights Act*, introduced by the Whitlam Labor Government and enacted by Fraser's Liberal regime, was a radical piece of legislation, allowing Aborigines to claim Crown land from which they'd been dispossessed by the white settlers.

When claiming land, Aboriginal people have to produce evidence of their connection with the land. That involves tracing their tribal ancestry back to before the coming of the Europeans, pointing out their sacred sites and explaining their significance, repeating the songs and the stories that show their spiritual attachment to a particular piece of country, and outlining the tribal bonds, customs and beliefs that link them with that land. If successful, they win inalienable freehold title to the land, which means that while Aboriginal people can lease their land out for mining or pastoral activities, they can never sell it. Controlled by the Federal government (as opposed to an autonomous State government) the Northern Territory is, at the time of writing, the only place in the country in which Aboriginal people have been given such an opportunity.

In 1983, the Hawke Labor Government was elected on a platform that included the promise that laws would be introduced allowing Aborigines in other parts of the country to lodge similar claims.

Clyde Holding, Hawke's first Minister for Aboriginal Affairs, had proposed a five-point package for uniform national Land

Rights legislation: inalienable freehold title; protection of sacred sites; Aboriginal control over mining; access to mining royalty equivalents; and negotiated compensation for lost land. That proposal, however, was bitterly opposed by the giant mining companies and a number of the State governments, including those of Holding's political persuasion. As a result, the Hawke Government, much to Holding's discomfort, put the Land Rights issue on the backburner.

Frustrated, Holding recognised the need to overcome the anti-Land Rights propaganda campaigns being mounted by the mining companies. Surveys conducted for the Department of Aboriginal Affairs by Australian National Opinion Polls showed that some of the strongest support for Land Rights rested with the under 25s. Holding felt the need to mobilise that support, hence the connection with Midnight Oil.

The Oils had long been supportive of Land Rights, of the need to recognise that land had been taken away from the Aboriginal people, though their raising of Aboriginal issues had been limited to a couple of songs ('Kosciusko' and 'Jimmy Sharman's Boxers' from *Red Sails In The Sunset),* and a few statements by Peter Garrett reflecting the view that white Australians didn't own the land and that the question of Aboriginal sovereignty needed to be addressed.

In 1983 the band had their first contact with a tribal community when they were invited to perform in an Aboriginal settlement in eastern Arnhem Land. It was an experience that had a profound effect on the band and led to their interest in doing more shows of a similar nature.

Two years later, a couple of heavyweight promoters from Melbourne started checking out the feasibility of staging a massive televised concert at Uluru (Ayers Rock). The concert, with an international satellite link-up, would coincide with the passing of Halley's Comet. Among the acts they hoped to attract were Dire Straits, Sting and Midnight Oil.

When the Oils' manager, 29-year-old Gary Morris, was approached, he sought the opinion of Aboriginal Arts Board director Gary Foley. Foley told him to can the proposal. If the Oils wanted to do something, said Foley, they should do it in conjunction with the relevant Aboriginal community – the Pitjantjatjara and Yankunytjatjara people of Mutitjulu.

Keen to at least get the ball rolling for the Oils, Morris flew to Alice Springs for meetings with the Central Land Council and then headed to Uluru to meet with the community elders. At the time, the Mutitjulu community, with the assistance of Film Australia, was working on *Uluru, An Anangu Story*, a film celebrating the return of Uluru to its traditional owners. Perhaps, the community's representatives suggested, the Oils would like to write a song for the soundtrack.

Morris returned to Sydney and the Oils wrote, recorded and submitted 'The Dead Heart', 'Beds Are Burning' and '40,000 Years Come Home'. 'The Dead Heart' was accepted for the soundtrack and the idea of the Oils embarking on a desert tour was floated.

After further meetings with Foley, during which the idea of a tour was discussed, Morris met with Clyde Holding in Canberra and put forward the tour proposal. Holding, seeing merit in the idea of getting the Oils involved in the Land Rights debate, asked for a budget and requested a meeting with Peter Garrett.

The budget, for a tour of remote communities in which Midnight Oil could gain first-hand knowledge of the aims, aspirations and lifestyles of Aboriginal people who were living on their traditional tribal lands, came in at 85,000 dollars. Holding took the money from his department's Public Awareness Program and loaned it to the Oils. (By November 1987, 26,000 dollars had been repaid through royalties from the Oils' single, 'The Dead Heart'.)

The Aboriginal Arts Board contributed a further 15,000 dollars so the (predominantly Aboriginal) Warumpi Band could join the tour.

In order to televise the tour, the Australian Broadcasting Corporation set aside another small fortune so that the film crew from 'A Big Country' could accompany the bands. The Melbourne

Age also spent 8,000 dollars to cover the costs of getting a journalist and a photographer to join the expedition.

'In some ways,' Neil Murray would concede, 'I guess the other guys in the (Warumpi) band are really politically naive, in terms of the overall Australian thing; that doesn't take away from the fact that they can grasp very quickly the issues and things and also make a statement about them, which happened a few times in Sydney.'

As the Warumpi Band's guitarist, co-lead singer and principal songwriter, it was Neil who could claim much of the credit for what success the group had enjoyed.

The predominantly Aboriginal band had initially come to the attention of urban rockers in late 1983 with the independent release of their debut single, 'Jailanguru Pakarnu' (Out From Jail). Recorded in Alice Springs and produced by the Warumpis and the Central Australian Aboriginal Media Association (CAAMA), it was the first rock 45 to have been recorded in an Aboriginal language.

Midnight Oil had invited the Warumpis to Sydney on a couple of occasions, giving them the opportunity to play in front of large audiences they would not have otherwise reached. Now, as the Warumpis saw it, they were returning the favour by giving the Oils a chance to perform before small audiences that had never seen a white rock 'n' roll band before.

Coming out of Papunya, the Warumpis were essentially a settlement band struggling for recognition; recognition that only Neil Murray and the band's manager, David Cooke, seemed overtly concerned about. Murray and Cooke were whites from the east coast who'd reaped the benefits of reasonable schooling and, in different capacities initially, had moved into the desert to work with Aboriginal people.

The rest of the band, conversant in English only as a second or third language, had, like the vast majority of Australian blacks, been poorly served by the non-Aboriginal education system.

The Warumpis' financial position was reflected succinctly in the title of their first album, *Big Name No Blankets,* and their first single, 'Jailanguru Pakarnu', stands as testament to their familiarity with the rigours of incarceration.*

When they weren't touring, they took jobs driving graders and mending fences, and loved nothing better than heaping hot coals over a freshly killed goanna.

The saga of their on-again off-again career was littered with tales of tours that had failed to eventuate, with stories of the pressures felt by an Aboriginal band trying to make an impression with the whitefellas' music. The conflicts were of a variety that no city-based rock 'n' roller would ever comprehend: conflicts between the old ways and the new, between the traditional teachings of the Dreaming and those of Christianity, between the priorities of family life and those brought on by spending weeks or months on the road.

Despite their familiarity with such trappings of the modern world as electric guitars, videos and discs, the Warumpis were still deeply influenced by ancient cultural traditions; traditions that were destined to affect the Blackfella-Whitefella Tour even in such day-to-day things as calling someone's name. Under the laws of Aboriginal culture in the Northern Territory† when a person dies his or her name cannot be mentioned for at least a year. To mention a dead person's name, it is believed, is to disturb that person's spirit when it is in the process of returning, to the place of its Dreaming. In respect of that belief, in Central Australia all other people going by the same name are referred to as *Kumanjayi* or No Name.

---

* According to statistics released by the Australian Institute of Criminology, although Aborigines comprise only 1.07 percent of the population they represented 10.6 per cent of the national prison population in 1985. Throughout Australia, Aborigines are imprisoned ten times more than any other ethnic group. In Western Australia the figure is twenty times higher.

† When the Muirhead Royal Commission into Aboriginal Deaths in Custody was convened in November 1987, the names of the NT dead were deleted and replaced by the dates of their deaths. The names of the dead from other States, where the custom of not naming the dead is no longer culturally appropriate, were retained.

Consequently, because the Warumpis' singer, George Rurrambu 11 Burrarrawanga, shared the same Christian name as Sammy and Gordon Tjapanangka Butcher's father, who 'finished up' around the time the tour was announced, he was to be called *Kumanjayi* or Rurrambu.

It was a custom that David Cooke first found out about when Neil Murray introduced him to the other members of the band as 'Cookie'. When the newcomer tried to explain that he preferred being called David, he was quickly silenced. A man from Papunya called David had died, and out of respect for the dead the Warumpis have never addressed Cookie by his Christian name.

Although aspects of their participation in whitefella society were governed and, at times, restricted by traditional Aboriginal values, the Warumpis were using the whitefella medium of rock music to address problems within their own society. In songs like 'Wima Juta' (All the Kids) they sang, in the Luritja dialect, of the need to ensure that children were given an adequate, nutritious diet: *Mangarni tjukarrurru ngalkunytjaku*, (Should eat good food)/ *Ngalkura tinarringkunytjaku miinta wiya*, (to grow up without sickness)/*Yuwara wiima tjuta mangarri tjukarurru*, (If you give the kids)/ *Palunyangurunya tjana palya nyinanytjaku*, (proper food they will live healthy).

They used their own language within a Western rock format to highlight the benefits of people like the Pintupi returning to their traditional lands ('Kintorelakutu') and to emphasise the problems associated with the abuse of alcohol ('Nyuntu Nyaaltjirriku').

Throughout their homelands of the Western Desert, people responded enthusiastically to the fact that the Warumpis were making it in the white man's world. And in Alice Springs they were immensely popular.

On the eve of the Blackfella-Whitefella Tour, just hours after the Oils had held their press conference, the Warumpis took to the stage at Bazzo's Farm, a town camp on the outskirts of Alice, to headline a show that had been organised as a major part of the 'Beat the Grog' campaign.

Initiated by CAAMA, the Beat the Grog campaign was essentially an educational exercise aimed at fostering awareness among the Aboriginal community of the problems brought on by alcohol abuse.

In a town that was once swamped by images of drunken blacks bottling each other with flagons in the sandy bed of the Todd, it's a vital and successful campaign, which thrives on the high-profile support of acts like the Warumpi Band.

Throughout Alice, the streets were festooned with hand-coloured, photocopied posters:

> WARUMPI BAND
> Ilkari Maru & Isaac Yama
> presented by
> Beat The Grog

The venue for the performance was a makeshift stage that bounced all over the place and, as the band chopped through songs like 'Breadline', smoke billowed from the surrounding fires. Held beneath the clear desert skies, it was an open-air show that had attracted a thousand people, the sort of audience for whom the Warumpis rarely get to perform.

The Warumpis' singer, Kumanjayi Rurrambu, was a skinny Top Ender from Elcho Island, a delightful spot off the coast of Arnhem Land. He'd studied linguistics at Batchelor College, met his wife Suzina and moved to the desert in the late 1970s. But in the desert he was, literally, like a fish out of water. He never really fitted in. He was older than anyone else in the band, but he hadn't been through the necessary rituals of initiation to become a *wati*, or man, and would never, therefore, command the respect of the desert.

His idol was Little Richard and he wanted desperately to be a star. He had it in him, too. He had a way with women and could charm the socks off anyone who might help him up the ladder. And unlike his desert-bred compatriots, he loved to show off, to wear loud shirts and gyrate his hips on stage. In that regard he was the perfect foil for the other members of the band, who were so shy they'd rarely move on stage, preferring to fade into anonymity and the darkness of their amplifiers.

Out front, under the lights at Bazzo's Farm, Rurrambu is in his element. He's wearing a synthetic black jacket decorated with red and yellow bands across the chest. Of all the blokes who've passed through the band, he's most keenly aware of the symbolism of the Land Rights struggle, wearing jeans patched with Aboriginal flags and t-shirts with a similar motif. He has wavy, shoulder-length black hair and the beginnings of a moustache. And despite the cold, he's cutting loose. His wife never comes to the shows in Alice because, as Cookie once said, 'If she did he'd get embarrassed and wouldn't do any pelvic thrusts or anything like that. He'd just sort of stand there.'

Behind Rurrambu, with his back to the audience and his ear to the amps, stands Sammy Butcher. He's wearing a Papunya 'Warriors' windcheater in the home-team colours of green and gold, and his playing is, as always, inspired.

Sammy, like his brother Gordon, is a fine musician, but the idea of being a professional rock 'n' roller isn't one that appeals. They like playing and getting paid for doing so, but neither has any ambition to be in a 'king band'. They are happy staying close to home, getting jobs mending fences and looking after their families. Getting either of them to embark on tours, even at the best of times, is invariably a difficult proposition.

Tonight, Gordon is nowhere to be seen. Yesterday morning he bought himself a car. In the afternoon he sold it. Now, from what Cookie can gather, he's sitting out at Haasts Bluff, 200 Ks to the west, waiting for a lift to the gig. This morning Cookie gave someone 70 dollars for fuel to go out and collect him. But as yet he hasn't made it in and, for tonight's show at least, his drumkit's being handled by a whitefella from Alice. Rusty after a six-month break and trying to work around a new drummer, the band is as shaky as the makeshift stage.

The boulder-strewn ridge surrounding the stage is a stunning natural backdrop that's been brought to life with a couple of arc lights. Hundreds of Aboriginal people – the Eastern and Western Aranda of the Alice Springs region and the Warlpiri, Luritja, Pintupi, Pitjantjatjara and people of other regional language groups who've come into town – stand back in the shadows. They shiver under blankets and West German army jackets, garments eagerly sought because of their red, yellow and black sleeve patches that so many people associate with the Aboriginal flag.

Cutting through 'Blackfella-Whitefella' and bouncing across the stage, guitarist Neil Murray, himself a recent convert to army surplus clothing, is sporting a four-day growth of ginger stubble. He's just driven from Sydney, a journey of 3,000 kilometres, in an HQ panel van laden with guitars, a Fender twin, a 38-centimetre bass bin, his swag and a pile of luggage. Since the Warumpis' last show, supporting Midnight Oil at a Wilderness Society benefit for the Daintree Rainforest at the Sydney Entertainment Centre in December 1985, he's been living with a girlfriend in Elizabeth Bay, an up-market harbourside suburb of Sydney.

If it hadn't been for Neil, it's unlikely that anyone outside the communities of the Western Desert would ever have heard of the Warumpi Band. He grew up on a property in the Western District of Victoria, headed to Melbourne to do his teacher's training, and ended up teaching, driving trucks and sinking bores around Papunya and Kintore. It was he who, following the band's loose formation in 1980, introduced the whitefella concepts of touring and recording and doing things of which Aboriginal people throughout the country could be proud.

In spite of his best efforts, Murray still has his fair share of detractors. Aboriginal activist Gary Foley, for example, believes that if Neil 'hadn't been involved with Aboriginal people he'd probably still be strummin' a guitar on some street corner in Alice Springs.'

Tonight, he's got a lot on his mind. He's about to kick off an important tour with the Oils and his drummer hasn't turned up for the first gig. He's going to have to work with Martin Hardie, a guy he doesn't get along with, who's now been appointed as the

Oils' tour manager for the Blackfella-Whitefella exercise. And to make matters worse, his nose is still tender after an argument he had with Foley before leaving Sydney.

While the Warumpis are playing, Midnight Oil and their Sydney entourage climb into a string of hire cars and head out of town. Aware that the Oils have never performed in Alice, the organisers of the Rock Without Grog show have invited the band to make an unannounced appearance.

A couple of Ks up the Stuart Highway, out towards Mount Nancy, the fleet of gleaming Toyotas pulls into Bazzo's Farm. As they swing into the camp, their crews are bitten for a two-dollar fee.

'No,' comes a voice from the glow of the dashboard lights. 'We're with Midnight Oil. We've come to give you something else.'

The last time the Aboriginal communities of Alice Springs staged a concert, a Coloured Stone gig at Amoongana in May 1985, drunken fights resulted in four stabbings and eight arrests. So tonight's show, with its strict rules of 'No Grog, No Drunks', is an important one. The responsible Aborigines of Alice are out to prove that they can stage and police a family show, a concert that's free of alcohol and violence.

And if some whitefella band from Sydney think they can just march in and upstage the whole event, then, the gatekeepers argue, they're in for a rude shock. 'No, we're not going to give you two dollars,' comes the voice again. 'We're going to give you a show like this place has never seen.'

Blissfully oblivious to the ill-feeling generated by such a response, unaware that the reply has been construed as predictable arrogance from a bunch of gammon whitefellas from the city, a bunch of upstart pop star blow-ins who think they can just roll into town and take over, the Sydney crowd heads towards the stage.

There, rugged up against the bone-chilling cold in jumpers and jackets and heavy boots, the Oils and their companions huddle around the fires that blaze behind the stage, cupping mugs of tea and blowing steam at the light. Beside them, the Warumpis are chugging through 'My Island Home' as the podium rolls like a boat at sea.

It soon becomes obvious, amidst the chaos that surrounds the stage, that some people involved in the organisation of the show are less than impressed by Midnight Oil's gesture of turning up to give a free show. The attitude expressed at the front gate has filtered back to the powers that be, and the pervading attitude is that the Oils can go jump. So, when CAAMA director Freda Glynn climbs on stage, thanks everyone for coming, and bids them 'good night', Martin Hardie has to explain that Midnight Oil are here too and would like to contribute to the evening's festivities.

From the moment they climb aboard, the stage starts bouncing like a trampoline.

Since they first broke into the Sydney pub scene in 1978, climbing through the ranks with Cold Chisel and The Angels, Midnight Oil have proved themselves to be perhaps the wildest and brightest band in the country. Their shows – whether before a few hundred punters in a sweaty pub or 12,000 in a booming stadium – are intense, dramatic affairs in which the band's stagecraft is shown to its greatest advantage.

But for the first time in years the Oils are performing without the standard life-support system of a finely tuned PA, a crack fold-back system and banks of pretty lights. Jim Moginie's got no keyboards, and during the first song, 'Hercules', Rob Hirst battles on without a snare drum. To complicate matters, they've got a new sound engineer, a lanky tattooed character named Pat Pickett who boasts that he's never listened to an Oils album the whole way through. With the equipment provided and the brevity of the notice, there's little he can do to salvage the sound.

But instead of degenerating into an unmitigated shambles, the gig starts working, and by the time they hit 'Only the Strong' the band are firing on all five cylinders. At the end of the song, the sixth is introduced.

'Well we brought a friend along with us to play on this tour,' says Garrett, wiping the sweat from his skull, 'and maybe you'd like to welcome her on stage. It's Glad from Sydney, and as you can see she plays a pretty mean violin, so just watch out and be careful. Ah, this one's called something or other about I don't know what.'

And with that auspicious introduction they swing into 'Sleep' and Glad Reed and her trombone make their debut with Midnight Oil. Shortly before the tour was announced, Glad was plucked from the relative obscurity of Just a Drummer, an inner-city band that had failed to achieve more than minor cult status, and invited to join the Oils as a guest sessioneer. For someone whose dreams were more concerned with developing her musicianship than flitting around with the stars, the opportunity came as something of a surprise.

In recent months, the Oils have spent much of their time in the studio developing demos for their sixth album. So fighting the chill factor of the bitter desert air is an enervating experience. With inadequate fold-back (the sound the band hears on stage), the playing is rough. As the crowd down the front, a curious mixture of white hippies and blanket-clad blacks, dances furiously against the cold, dust rises and mixes with the smoke to swamp the stage.

After a thirty-minute set that includes the Oils' first live performances of 'Dead Heart' and 'You May Not Be Released' the band prepare to retire.

'We'd like to thank the No Grog people for putting on a really good night tonight,' says Garrett. 'It's been excellent. And to all you folk for coming along and making it just one of those special occasions it's very difficult for us to describe to you, because normally we play surrounded by concrete.' Pete keeps glancing around, marvelling at the setting while the drums keep patting out the rhythm for 'The Power and the Passion'. 'And if you don't reckon you should have a nuclear target about ten minutes' drive away from where you live then you should come out tomorrow morning to Pine Gap on the South road and have a go with us, all right!'

The band members are all grinning, the amps are teetering on the back of the stage, hundreds of Aborigines are fading into the shadows and down the front the whites are dancing in the dust.

For here, on the outskirts of Alice Springs, out here in the Dead Heart, the Oils have been reduced to the level of a settlement band, a bunch of strangers in a strange land with only their wits and their songs to get by on.

CHAPTER TWO
ULURU

The hitch-hiker stands on the side of the road, his boots drinking in the dust. A felt Akubra shades his head and beads of sweat roll cool and ticklish down his ribs.

The last time he tackled a decent hitch was a year ago when he knocked out 2,300 kilometres between Perth and Broome. The trip took him close to a week, and when he arrived, Gordon Tjapanangka Butcher stood on a fine old mango-shaded verandah with a look of incredulity in his eyes, as if he couldn't believe that the hitch-hiker hadn't faked it and jumped on a plane.

The hitch-hiker was mystified by his surprise, until he realised that a blackfella like Gordon wouldn't have had a hope in hell of hitching that distance in that space of time. People just wouldn't have picked him up.

In a rattling explosion of wind and dust and grit a road train rips past the hitch-hiker, three trailers bouncing across the tar, and by the time the third has passed he's off and running, leaping over the shredded tyres and shattered stubbies – glistening chips of amber sparkling in the clay – chasing his hat as it rolls and tumbles through the spinifex.

You can wander off the road in these parts and never return. Walk 50 metres and you'll lose sight of the road. In the heat of day or dead of night you can walk around in circles and never find the track. For there's nothing out here: not a tree, not a hill, not a landmark – nothing by which to take a bearing. Just the endless saltbush plains shimmering in the heat. He'd read of people who'd left their cars to take a piss and died days later with bloated tongues; people who'd died within 200 metres of the water quietly stewing in the radiator. Whole families, perishing in the desert, so close to help it didn't bear thinking about.

When he felt really bored, zapped by the heat and sick of the flies, the hitch-hiker would wander off the road, 20 or 30 metres, and stand in the middle of a spinifex ring, spinning like a ragged punchdrunk ballerina on the toe of his boot. His eyes shut tight, spinning around and around and around until his balance failed, and he'd go sprawling in the hard red dirt.

When the plains stopped pitching and rolling, he'd stand up, dust himself off and try to work out where he was. And when he was totally bamboozled, utterly defeated by the space and the sheer monotony of it all, he'd search out his carefully exaggerated boot prints in the dust and retrace his steps. Sometimes they'd take a while to find, and that's when the fear really started rising, when doubt overpowered logic and his heart started pounding a little faster.

Over the last eight years or so he'd managed to cover most of the country with his thumb, picking a point on a map and reaching it with a pocketful of promises and a head loaded with stories.

In recent months, he'd taken to hitching on to Oils tours, lobbing into places like Grafton and Dubbo and joining up for a couple of days until he ran into some town like Coffs Harbour that took his fancy and seduced him for a week or more.

The Oils would've been the first to admit that they weren't the most relaxed people in the world. They kept to themselves and liked to protect their privacy. But the Blackfella-Whitefella Tour was one ride the hitch-hiker didn't want to miss. There were too many questions he wanted answered; questions, he had no doubt, which were shared by the Oils.

Like the Oils, he'd been city born and bred. He'd grown up in Brisbane, a place his father had always sworn 'should be given back to the blacks'. As a schoolboy he'd read books about Aborigines hunting with boomerangs, dancing in corroborees and sleeping in *gunyas,* about children splashing around in creeks and people building fish traps and bird traps and paddling around in their dugout canoes. But the books were all written in the past tense . . . and the only Aborigines he ever came across were those who tried to bludge 'two bob' or a cigarette down by the Roma Street railway-yards.

He had childhood memories of an old neighbour who'd worked on the railways and told him, 'The Abos aren't so bad. The ones who work anyway. But any bloke who works, he's got nothing left at the end of the week 'cos all the others hang 'round and bludge off him. Even though they live in the city they've still got these tribal obligations, so anyone who's got any money has to share it with everyone else. So the bludgers just hang around waitin' for the pay packet to come walking out the gates. You'd be bloody amazed how many old "uncles" these blokes've got. 'Specially when they've got a quid in their pockets.'

On his last trip into the desert the hitch-hiker met plenty of Aborigines. But communication had been limited by the culture shock and the language barriers. He'd spent forty or fifty days with the Warumpi Band and he'd come away more disturbed than fulfilled. The boys from the desert spoke Luritja among themselves, breaking into English only to ask for cigarettes or a light, though more often they'd restrict even these requests to Luritja words like *puyu* and *waru.* He'd picked up a few other words, too, most notably *kungka* (girl) and *kundawiya* (no shame).

But in the same intolerant way in which his father had cursed the Greeks and Italians of his native Melbourne for not speaking fluent English, so the hitch-hiker felt frustrated by the Warumpis and those other Aboriginal people he came across in the bush for not speaking the language of his country. And it wasn't until too late that he realised that the problem lay not in them failing to speak his language, but in his intolerance of the languages of their country.

He came away from that tour shocked by the violence and deprivation he'd witnessed, confused by the pressures, and appalled by the injustices. But when he tried to discuss it with people in the city, they'd relate their own tales, their own urban perceptions. They understood less than he did, and that left him even more confused, prompting him to flee to Tasmania.

He'd spent the most memorable months of his life on the road, his thumb on the breeze and his eyes on the tar, camouflaging himself at night, bunking down in gullies beside every major highway in the country. And what he couldn't get over was the concept, the alien idea, that it wasn't his country, that it belonged to people who'd been here for 40,000 years or more.

They knew the country, he realised, so much better than he ever would. They were so attuned to it, so critically in touch with it that they were aware of every change. They knew the moods of the land and the weather and all the creatures they shared it with. It was knowledge that was so utterly perfect, so damned intuitive that he couldn't accept it. It spooked him that people could read the bush – his land, their land – far more sharply than he could read even the city . . . and yet, in the end, it wasn't guilt or shame for their losses that he felt, it was almost contempt for their knowledge, for their ignorance, for their superstitions and their inability to embrace the culture that had been forced upon them. And that conclusion disturbed him even more.

The Oils, he figured, were taking a gamble. And the hitch-hiker wanted to be there to watch the pennies spin.

In the past they'd shouted loud and long, holding the banners high for all to see. For almost ten years they'd been embarking on flag-waving exercises, conducting rock 'n' roll campaigns, getting involved in issues and when their time had come, picking up the ball and running with it. But this time they were dealing with something so close to everyone as engrained prejudice and ignorance, so threatening as giving land and support to the blacks.

Four hundred kilometres south-west of Alice Springs, Gary Morris Vasicek pushes his hired Toyota Landcruiser down the highway towards Uluru.

Midnight Oil's manager, he is, as the sixth member of the band, credited for his mastery of telephones, telexes and negotiations. In more succinct moments, he sees himself as the band's 'facilitator'.

When the Oils were at university pursuing their degrees, Gary was out riding the waves. His father was a QANTAS engineer, and Gary spent his formative years in the highlands of New Guinea. When he met the Oils at the Royal Antler on Sydney's northern beaches, he was 20 years old. He'd already earned a hot reputation as a surfer, pro golfer, successful real-estate agent and brown belt martial artist.

At 29, he's powerfully built and deeply tanned. A man who can recite large tracts of the Bible while he's out hunting pigs with a bow and arrow, he thrives on the power and speed of big bikes and fast cars. Hyperactive, impulsive, generous, forthright, and uncompromising in the projection (and protection) of his bands, he's been described in the *Bulletin* as 'the extremely tough manager [who] makes the average, able multinational executive look like a sissy'.

When it comes to ideas (of which he has no shortage), Morris has never been stingy. He likes to work on the big canvas, developing ambitious concepts that present his vision for the future. And if the nuts and bolts technicalities of following those ideas through happen to traverse the bounds of feasibility, then at least they've been presented and therefore stand as a future possibility. (Such an idea presented itself when he first entertained the idea of staging a concert at Uluru. Why not light up the Rock so that it glows through the night! That Uluru is so large that it's visible for 60 Ks or more seemed to be of little import.)

As he's bolting down the road to Uluru, foot flat to the floor, his mind pacing the speedometer, he happens across a stranded truck surrounded by blackfellas. In the back, shivering against the cold, is a family wrapped in dusty blankets.

Dropping the anchors, the Oils' manager pulls over to see what the problem is.

'We got flat tyre,' comes the reply.

Without a second thought, Gary pulls the spare out of the hire car and bounces it up to the truck. 'Try this one for size.'

With characteristically ill-fated timing, the Oils' road crew – stage manager Michael Lippold and sound engineer Pat Pickett – arrive on the scene, rolling up in their gleaming new Landcruiser. After introductions are made – the Aboriginal party includes members of the South Australian band Ilkari Maru – Lippold and Pickett land the job of changing the wheel.

'Gary, it won't fit!' says Pickett.

'Yes it will.'

'But Gary, wheels for Landcruisers aren't made for Donald Ducks! They're the wrong bloody size!'

'That's okay Pat, it'll work. Just try it.'

'Gary, the hire company's gonna want to know what happened to their spare Jack Dyer.'

'Pat, it's on toast. We'll get another one in Alice.'

Across the road, some kids are squealing and jumping about. Scooping up handfuls of stones they start pelting them at the ground.

'Hey what's up with you mob?' asks Gary.

'Snake! Snake!'

Morris grabs a forked stick and goes after it, pinning it down in the crevice of a rock and moving closer to take a better look at it. He stretches its head out, fascinated by the symmetry of the scales, by the fluidity of its movement.

'Hey, watch out,' calls one of the blacks. 'That one dangerous. Him deadly.'

'Don't worry about the Joe Blake,' calls Pickett. 'It's that bloke you should be worried about. He's mad! Loony! A few bob short of a quid!'

Gary edges closer. 'She'll be right.' The snake arches its neck and strikes. Gary doesn't flinch, just stands there watching it.

Back at the truck, Lippold and Pickett force the Landcruiser's wheel on. It's too big for the truck, but it'll get them to Uluru. And probably beyond.

Satisfied with his nature study, Gary lets the snake go. It slithers into the crevice and disappears.

The whitefellas bid the blackfellas farewell and the Oils' manager resumes his spirited dash to the Rock.

'It was as if,' his assistant, Stephanie Lewis, recalls, 'it was only natural that someone should stop and give them a new tyre. Like it was nothing unusual. We wouldn't expect that sort of thing if we broke down, but to them it was only natural. That was our first contact with the Aboriginal concept of sharing.'

As he drives, Gary breaks into one of his inspired raves. He's instigated this Blackfella-Whitefella adventure, planned it all the way through. 'There's a general consensus in this country,' he tells his passengers, 'that the Aboriginal people should have a land to live on, and it should be a land they can cohabit on and it's a land that should allow them to preserve their culture which, even now, is becoming internationally recognised in a very, very strong way. There's a lot of people in this country who can see that there is a sophisticated art form and culture and society in these people who've got a very historical relationship with the land that modern Australians don't have. And you can't become one of the scars in history by your actions today, saying that those people don't have a right, just as the Tasmanians who obliterated the black race down there have it as a scar in history for what they did then. So Australians themselves have gotta really check themselves out in what their attitude is. I believe there's a lot of Australians out there who would want a genuine reconciliation that enabled both races to live harmoniously. And I believe that's the attitude of the majority of Australians.'

It's almost 9 o'clock when the Oils swing off the highway and into the tourist complex at Yulara. Tucked away in the sandhills 18 kilometres from Uluru, it's a mini-city that can, according to the brochures, accommodate up to 5,000 people. Grabbing their bags the Oils hike up the path and through the revolving doors of the Sheraton.

In the lobby, beneath rows of Stars and Stripes flags, there's a red, white and blue noticeboard: *WELCOME TO AMERICA DOWN UNDER All This Week*. The Oils look at each other in disbelief. They've spent the morning at a demonstration outside the American intelligence installation at Pine Gap, and now they've come to *this!*

At the bar in the Ernest Giles Tavern, the Oils' bass guitarist, Peter Gifford, settles down to a beer. The least politicised member of the band, and the only one accustomed to sinking a few ales, he's insulted by the idea of Yulara: by the red, white and blue bunting hanging over the bar, by the American flags hanging in the lobby of the Sheraton, by the infliction of the concept of 'America Down Under', by the emphasis that's been placed on the Fourth of July celebrations.

In the morning, Pat Pickett takes the steps three at a time, loping down the stairwells in a pair of baggy tracksuit pants and an eyecatching gaudy blue parka, his red beret riding high on his head.

'A great way to start the tour,' he grins, 'late for a briefing with Mister Charisma and the Egg Shell Blond.'

In the Sheraton's lobby, Gary Morris and Peter Garrett pace back and forth across the carpet. Nodding his apologies, Pickett takes his place beside Lippold, stretching his lanky frame across a couch beneath the bunting and the Stars and Stripes flags that hang from the ceiling.

Surrounded by twenty people whose average age is 29 – musicians, roadies, support personnel, journalists, photographers and film crews – Garrett and Morris set to work, hammering out the day's itinerary, arranging transport, co-ordinating the film crews and the band, and organising preparations for the concert. They gesticulate and pace the floor, striking firm eye contact, ensuring that all details are understood.

Quick and bright and highly efficient, theirs is an alliance between two headstrong personalities whose clear focus and sense of united vision is, at times, offset by a volatility that would see lesser mortals harbouring unworkable grudges. Over the next few weeks there'll be enough public brawling to keep onlookers amused, arguments that belie the strength of their rapport.

As slabs of sunlight slip throught the plate-glass windows of the lobby, the crew take notes, nurse the odd hangover, and endeavour to keep up with instructions.

'Any questions?' Their bright eyes sweep the gathering for a response. 'Okay, let's go.'

Twenty kilometres and about 40,000 years away lies the Rock. Uluru: a primeval beast that rises from the spinifex plains. So vibrant it seems alive. Its colours resonate against the sky, pinks and mauves, day-glo orange and fire-engine reds. It's constantly changing, iridescent. From any angle it's so sharply defined against the sky it's like a massive chromakey screen, a video image that predates the technology by millions and millions of years. Throbbing in the heat. Breathing . . .

Wrinkled with deep inviting gorges stained black by the water that gathers, bursts and tumbles in the rains, its shoulders are pitted with caves splattered white with the droppings of wedge-tailed eagles that soar and circle on the thermals, reaching such an altitude that when they drop their beaks and start to plummet, the dominant image beneath them is that of an inverted dingo's paw quivering in the heat.

To sit on a sandhill and watch the Rock is to believe that the Kuniya of the *Tjukurpa* – the great carpet snakes of the Dreaming – still reside inside it.

People come from all over the world to scale it, to sit on its back and take photographs, and return home wearing t-shirts that proclaim *I Climbed Ayers Rock.*

To the local *Anangu* (Aboriginal people in the Pitjantjatjara language) such behaviour is indeed strange. To climb the rock is, they reason, culturally inappropriate.

When the blackfellas' humour is high they indulge in time-lapse cinematography. And when the reels are played back the scenes are of buses zooming in and out, disgorging hundreds of ants, diesel-powered explorers who scurry up and down, snapping Nikons and bolting, rarely pausing to feel the earth move beneath them, to sense the great snakes writhing in their sleep.

The first of the tourists to climb the Rock, back in the 1870s, was Gosse. With characteristic disregard for the notion that the monolith may already have had a name for a few thousand years, he named it after the Governor of South Australia, Henry Ayers.

But the surrounding desert was so disagreeable, even to the pastoralists who'd taken up much of the land south of Alice Springs, that the Pitjantjatjara and Yankunytjatjara people of the region were left almost undisturbed until well into the twentieth century.

In 1920 the Commonwealth government declared the South West Reserve, which included Ayers Rock and the neighbouring Olgas, as a sanctuary for the nomadic people of the desert. Isolated by hundreds of kilometres of red sandhills, the region was accessible only by camel. The only European intruders were prospectors inspired by Lasseter's tales of gold, dingo scalpers and the occasional missionary.

In the '30s, things started to get shaky. Aborigines died after eating kangaroos that had taken the baits laid down by dingo scalpers. And in 1934, an Aboriginal man, who'd escaped after being charged with spearing cattle, was shot dead by a police party at Maggie Springs, a waterhole at the base of the Rock. In the wake of those incidents, the nomadic Pitjantjatjara people cut down on the frequency of their visits to the Rock. It was becoming too dangerous.

There followed a period of assimilation, when the Government and the Lutheran Church, under the impression that Aboriginal society was collapsing, tried to move the people to welfare settlements and missions where they could be clothed and fed and educated in the ways of the Europeans.

To the chagrin of the Native Affairs Branch, the people kept moving around. Some seemed quite happy to stay on the missions for a while, until they'd satisfied their curiosity and, in times of drought, their hunger. And then they'd go walkabout, visiting their kin and returning to the sites of their Dreaming, observing the rituals and passing on the legends of their culture.

After the first track was bulldozed through to Ayers Rock and the Olgas in 1948, the invasion of the tourists began in earnest. In 1958 the Government took back the land around Ayers Rock and the Olgas, removing it from the 'native reserve', and turned it into a national park.

But the Pitjantjatjara people seemed to have no respect for the sensitivities of the tourists. They continued to hold their Red Ochre ceremonies in the region, and by the mid-'60s the Native Affairs Branch was becoming acutely embarrassed by their antics as they sought to take advantage of the influx of visitors by peddling artefacts.

'At night,' wrote Patrol Officer D.A. Stewart in an October 1965 report to his superiors, 'Aboriginals have run into the roadway with burning sticks waving down cars with spears and boomerangs etc clutched in their hands . . . tourists . . . receive quite a shock and think they are being attacked.'

In 1968, in an effort to attract the Aborigines away from the Rock, the Government established a settlement at Docker River in the Petermann Ranges, 200 kilometres to the west. But still Pitjantjatjara people kept returning to Uluru and Kata Tjuta (the Olgas) to conduct their ceremonies and observe the responsibilities of protecting their sacred sites.

Sacred sites, it should be explained, are an important focus for what the people of the Western Desert call *tjukurpa*. Roughly translated, *tjukurpa* means Dreaming, though much is lost in the translation. Essentially it refers to a person's spiritual connection with the land.

The basic belief is that when a person dies, their spirit goes away and dwells in these secret places. That person's spiritual entity is, therefore, symbolised and represented in these locations. If a person says, for instance, that he or she is 'of water dreaming place', then it will be of the utmost importance to that person that the obligations they have to that site – be it a rock-hole or a soak – are adhered to.

In order to uphold their obligations to the maintenance and protection of that site, the people associated with it will perform certain ceremonies over time. By preserving the song-stories associated with that place and by protecting it from damage and treating it with reverence, when they die, their spirit will know where to go. But if a person doesn't follow their Dreaming when they're alive, if they don't carry out those ceremonies and pass on those stories, if they allow that site to be desecrated, then when they die their spirit will be lost forever.

It's a concept that's not far removed from the basis of Eastern and Western religions, in which people practise their religious beliefs while they're alive in the belief that their souls will be saved when they die. If you don't, so the theory goes, you'll end up in Hell or Limbo.

'In Aboriginal culture, the strength of the belief is so significant,' says Neil Murray, 'that people will die. They'll just fade away and die if their sacred sites are desecrated.'

In 1985, after a protracted legal battle, the Pitjantjatjara people won the right to protect and observe their sacred sites when they were granted freehold title to the land around Uluru and Kata Tjuta.

In an historic hand-over ceremony by the old Ininti store, the Rock was returned to its traditional owners – a misnomer, to be sure, and one that begs the question of whether it's the people who own the land or the land that owns them.

In the process, they were given a controlling interest in the management and protection of the National Park. Consequently, Uluru is one of the only national parks in Australia in which Aboriginal people are still living, where the traditional custodians of that country are still alive and tuned into the land.

'PEEEEETER!'

As a tourist-laden chopper hovers into the neighbouring heliport, Peter Garrett steps into the shadow of the sails floating on an azure blue sky above the entrance to the Sheraton Ayers Rock Hotel.

'PEEEEETER-R-R!'

Young whites hanging out on Yulara Drive call his name as, black leather shoes hitting the ochre-red pavement, he strides towards the revolving doors that spin him into the lobby.

Inside, porters slip across polished marble floors. Guests, unable to take their pets for walkies, trail squeaking mobile suitcases in their wake, and receptionists select keys and swoop on purring telephones. Safari-suited lawyers, seeking a respite from the rigours of a convention, lie back in the plush couches, scanning copies of *The Bulletin* and *Australian Business*.

Throughout the lobby, people glance up at the tall figure striding across the floor. Cupped discreetly in his hands are the shards of a broken stubby he's retrieved from the footpath outside. (In Sydney, or anywhere else for that matter, it's not uncommon to see him scooping up litter as he walks down the street, carrying it unselfconsciously until a suitable receptacle can be found.)

Among the tourists – especially those from the camping ground who can't afford the expense of the Sheraton or the Four Seasons – the Oils recognition factor is high . . . almost as high as Garrett's desire to lead by example.

Inside the complex, the other band members relax by the pool. Yulara is so removed from the rugged touring that lies ahead that the Oils are well advised to take advantage of it. They're here for a couple of days, to do some filming and a show at Mutitjulu, and they're making the most of the break. It's a family affair, a brief sojourn before facing the gruelling rigours of the desert. Among the women, babies dominate the conversation. The Oils are hitting their early 30s now, and marriages to long-time sweethearts have been the order of the day. (That three of the Oils are now married to the same girlfriends who accompanied them to gigs ten years ago says much about their stability – a rare factor in the life of rock 'n' roll.)

The Sheraton is an extraordinary place: a red-walled garrison totally enclosed by plush units facing a courtyard. All marble and chrome and desert pink walls, spotless glass doors, brilliant blue pools, manicured lawns, rock gardens, solar panels and those majestic white sails from Switzerland. To get to the rooms you've got to walk along balconies that wrap themselves around the outside of the complex. Just a couple of metres away the blazing red sand dunes rise up, blinding your vision: a wall of sand poised to sweep across the verandah, through shag-pile carpeted rooms, over plant-shaded patios and down into the courtyard, swamping the pools and the bars, the art galleries and restaurants, drifting across polished marble floors, crashing through massive plate-glass windows, scratching the chrome and jamming the revolving doors, until all that could remain is a vision of tattered sails whipping the spinifex shards.

The whole of the Yulara complex presents an intriguing vision of the future. Here, in the middle of the desert, this mini-city that takes its water supply from neighbouring bores is powered by diesel generators and stacks of solar panels, imports all of its foodstuffs, is serviced by a major airport, and provides a standard of living that's unparalleled in many other parts of the world. There could, conceivably, come a time when the vast arid expanses of this country are pin-pricked with hundreds of such communities.

Until the opening of Yulara in 1984, the plains to the east of the Rock were cluttered with shabby motels with names like the Ayers Rock Chalet, the Red Sands, the Inland and the Uluru. All have since been demolished, one of them prematurely by an irate truck driver who charged up his rig and took out a couple of tourists in the front bar.

There was also the Ayers Rock Camping Ground, a place that may have been forgotten had it not been for the celebrated tales of a dingo and a baby. Oddly enough, the rather colourful coverage of the inquiries and the trials that followed Azaria Chamberlain's disappearance didn't include any reference to *Mamu*, the ultimate Dreamtime foil for such a tale.

Mamu was perfect: the great spirit dingo that haunts the deserts of Central Australia and steals the life from young children who stray from the light of the campfires.

Mamu, it was said, would slink up to the camps and prey on the children. And when the people moved on, *Mamu* would creep into the logs around the old camp, hiding and waiting for their return. But the people knew about *Mamu* and they were too smart to fall into his trap. So when they returned to the region they'd always make camp in a different place, a place that *Mamu* hadn't recognised and infiltrated, a place where *Mamu* wasn't lying in wait.

To those who take Aboriginal legends and endeavour to relate them to the modern world, *Mamu* made wonderful sense. For *Mamu* was dysentery and disease. *Mamu* was the germs that bred among the litter and the rubbish, the discarded skins and bones and human waste that lay scattered around the old camping grounds. And if people returned to those sites, it was the children who were the most vulnerable, whose immune systems were the least resistant.

It's that camping ground in which baby Azaria was last seen which is now the site of the Mutitjulu Community, a collection of houses and humpies that have sprung up in the dust around the petrol pumps of the old Ininti store.

The Warumpis camped there in 1985, just a few metres from where Azaria disappeared. During the afternoon crows hacked through their Koolite eskies, spreading sugar and flour and tea across the earth. At night, as the flames of the campfire flickered back to glowing piles of embers, the dogs moved in, skulking about the camp and scavenging for scraps by the fire.

These days, Mutitjulu is off-limits to the tourists. Tired of having pocket instamatics poked in their faces, sick of the lenses invading the privacy of their humpies of corrugated iron and torn canvas, bloodwood boughs and flattened petrol cans, the community has imposed a set of strict guidelines. Entry is restricted and photography forbidden. Any exceptions must be authorised by the community council.

At dusk, in a billowing plume of dust that lingers and drifts and settles over the mulga and spinifex plains, a convoy of Toyotas bumps off the main road and rumbles into the settlement. Young kids with blazing red and white-blond hair and bodies as dark as night gather in front of the store, watching as the Landcruisers and the trucks glide to a halt in the dirt, ejecting ten, twenty, thirty whitefellas who set to work unloading boxes – black ones, blue ones, fire-proof silver ones, plastic boxes and wooden boxes and boxes of reinforced metal. Boxes of shapes and sizes that the kids have never seen before: boxes wrapped with belts, boxes with buckles and clips and latches with tight little springs. And from the boxes they remove more boxes, wedges, guitars, drums, cameras, tape recorders, mixing desks, microphones, tripods, mike-stands and lights. And for the kids, whose parents need little more than a blanket and a billy when they go away, it's overwhelming.

The community hasn't seen this much activity, this much equipment, this much energy being expended since the hand-over ceremony nine months back. And what a time that was! Cameras and television crews and politicians everywhere, as if the whole of the outside world had suddenly descended on the desert. Biggest mobs! Blackfellas, yellafellas, whitefellas all over the place – click click click, talk talk talk, clap clap clap. And when it was over, when the dust had settled and the people had gone home, the traditional owners figured they'd be happy if they never saw another camera again.

For Midnight Oil, though, they've made an exception – albeit with certain reservations.

The Oils provided the community with 'Dead Heart' for *Uluru – An Anangu Story*, so they're allowing the band to film a video clip on their land. The Central Land Council has explained that 'to help get the Land Rights message out' Midnight Oil are being accompanied by a film crew from 'A Big Country' and a journalist and photographer from the *Age*.

But there's a limit to everyone's tolerance, and the Mutitjulu Community has decreed that it be a closed gig, that there be 'no whitefella publicity prior to the show'; media access is to be restricted to those people travelling with the band, and the tourists from Yulara are not to be encouraged to come to the concert. The only publicity for the show will be broadcast on the Pitjantjatjara chatter frequency on the Short Side Band radio transceivers that link the Aboriginal communities with their out-stations and people further out in the bush.

For the 'Big Country' crew from the ABC it's been a hectic week. Negotiations between Gary Morris and the executive producer of the series had been progressing for weeks, unbeknown to the crew. Five days ago they were advised to pack their bags and prepare for a trip. Three days ago they were told where they were going. Today they're trying to catch the band against the Rock before they lose the light.

Lights, action, and dancing in the dust. Six cameras hover around the stage – a low flat mound of red dirt – shooting the Oils miming against the silhouette of the Rock, so sharp against the sky you'd swear it'd been cut out with a razor-blade and glued to the sunset.

A few metres away, the Oils' camp co-ordinator, Charlie McMahon, gets a couple of fires blazing – one for cooking and the other for heat. 'No sign of that Warumpi mob, eh?'

Martin Hardie, the 26-year-old who's been hired to act as Tour Manager for the trip, huddles over the flames and shakes his head.

'*Wiya*. Cookie called through from Alice a few minutes ago and reckons they're about to leave.'

'They got Gordon?'

'Guess so, but we won't see 'em for what? Five hours? Six?'

'No show for them tonight then, eh?'

Hardie shakes his head, cups his hands around a steaming mug of tea and looses a shiver.

Hardie was hired by Gary Morris to assist him in coordinating the tour. As a former Sydney agent for the Warumpis, he was the only person around the Oils' office who'd had any previous experience in the Territory. Working in the office, he seemed to enjoy the gig, flaunting the local idioms, sprinkling his dialogue with his smattering of words from the Luritja dialect, poring over Army survey maps, and punctuating his conversations with 'over'. He seemed to relish the power and the mobility of working with an organisation like the Oils, but there was a deep-seated fear in the back of everyone's mind that he was way out of his depth. And now he's shuddering at the thought of the potential nightmares that lie ahead, at the ramifications of his own bitterly intransigent relationship with the two whites from the Warumpi Band with whom he had worked earlier in the year.

It's cold, so bitterly cold the choices are down to squatting by the flames or dancing like a maniac. There are fires all over the place, dozens of them, surrounded by snarling dogs and people wrapped in blankets, their faces so dark that only the whites of their eyes and teeth show through the smoke.

The gig is wild. Ilkari Maru fill in for the Warumpis, doing a couple of sets, and then the Oils take to the stage. They're so cold they're thrashing through it. Every time Garrett moves, he kicks up soft clouds of dust that roll and billow towards the blinding white lights planted in the dirt. The Oils are all power and light and movement, a swirling circus, leather jackets and woollen beanies and heavy leather boots, clanging guitars and booming drums and vocals choked with dust and smoke.

But the reaction is . . . subdued. There are too many cameras. There's a veritable circus of whitefellas milling around. The Oils' music is so quirky in its use of different rhythms that these people brought up on the songs of the Dreamtime and country and western tapes don't know what to make of it. The lights are blindingly bright and people fall back into the shadows. And the music is so hideously loud . . . it bounces back off the Rock, booms across the desert, and crashes down around the sensitive ears of people who've rarely heard anything louder than a dog fight.

Back at Yulara, the unattached members of the touring party seek refuge in the centrally heated tavern, conducting a post mortem over cans of beer and the incessant pulse of the disco. Yeah, it was too loud, too bright, too agitated for the people of the desert. And too bloody cold.

As thirsts are quenched, tongues loosened and flesh thawed, the resident disc jockey plays a couple of Oils songs back to back and offers snide thanks to the band 'for playing for the whites'. It's an attitude that, since the tour was first mooted, has been finding favour among the more narrow-minded throughout the country: 'What have they ever done for the blacks before? They're just jumping on another bandwagon.' 'Why are they going out and doing twenty shows for the blacks when they've done so few for us lately? It's reverse racism!'

An hour or so later, the Oils' two crew members, Michael Lippold and Pat Pickett, walk in. After pulling down the gear and packing it back into the truck, they're understandably tired and cold and thirsty. If you've ever seen the Oils in action, then no doubt you've also seen Lippold. He scampers across the stage, replacing mikestands, taping leads to guitars, rearranging the drumkit, dodging and scurrying between the band members as the lights dip and he spots a gap in the proceedings.

A veteran of the celebrated Old School of roadies, he's been Midnight Oil's stage manager since the pub-rocking days of 1980. He joined the band at a time when, as drummer Rob Hirst puts it, 'We desperately needed someone who wasn't about to sit down and have an intelligent conversation with some drunk punter who was going to slam a beer glass into his face. He'd just knock 'em over the head with his wombat basher and that'd be it.'

When the band is off the road, Lippold is occasionally called in to act as Garrett's minder, keeping photographers at bay and getting his charge in and out of potentially uncomfortable situations. He scrubs up pretty well, too, and it's generally a pleasure to watch him work. In any situation he's got 100 per cent dedication to his gig, keen senses, and a firm understanding that he's there to protect the act. The flip side is his temper.

He's got a fierce reputation for dealing with problems by punching walls, kicking trees, smashing telephones and loudly abusing people. Later in the piece, when he's simmered down, he'll usually apologise while making it clear that whatever transgression it was that offended him should never be repeated. But by that stage, it's often too late. Around him, people – even his crews – tend to walk on eggshells.

He grew up on the streets of Melbourne and he's developed a finely tuned sense of the streetfighter's bluff, an astonishingly effective weapon in those situations in which it's required to enforce the peace.

He lives in a tent in the mountains north of Sydney, just him and his dog and a Coolgardie safe. His kitchen's the tailgate of an old Dodge pick-up, the showerbag hangs from a tree and he has to cart his own water from the creek. When the Oils give the word, he climbs into his battered amber Toyota truck and returns to the city, picking up where he left off, preparing the gear and the crews for the tours.

'Hey Parrot!' he calls to the hitch-hiker. 'How long have we got before closing time?'

'Dunno. You got the time, Pat?'

Pat Pickett, a veteran of tours with AC/DC, The Models, Strange Tenants, *The Rocky Horror Show*, Spy V Spy and countless other acts, is like a walking billboard, covered in tattoos and adorned in an obnoxious pair of red pants and a brilliant blue jacket.

'Nah, I left me Gordon & Gotch in me Goldsborough Morts.'
'Pardon?'

'He means,' explains Lippold, 'that he left his watch in his shorts.'

'Are the staff 'round 'ere dog 'n' boned or what?' says Pickett with disgust. 'I'd kill for a pig's ear in the Ray Milland.'

The hitch-hiker looks to Lippold for a translation. 'He reckons the staff are stoned and he wants a beer in his hand. Shop!'

The first time the hitch-hiker caught up with the Oils on tour, the room he crashed in was Lippold's. The crew returned from the gig at around two in the morning and retired to an adjoining room to wind down. And for a couple of hours they got down to the serious business of dominoes. Money changed hands, beers were sunk, tapes played, jibes thrown and laughter reigned. It was the first night of the tour and Lippold, the team captain, the Oils' longest serving roadie, was geeing his new crew up. He was building up the team spirit, the gang mentality, that sense of teamwork and mateship so vital for a good working crew.

Tiles clattered across the table, slapping the deck amid the shouts and the groans. And when it was over, the hitch-hiker confessed that he hadn't played dominoes for maybe fifteen years, that his childhood interest in that game had given way to an obsession with Scrabble.

'Scrabble's no good here, mate. You've gotta be able to spell to play that. And most of these boys didn't get that much school, y'know. But dominoes! It's just colours 'n' dots, so nobody feels any more superior than anyone else.'

But out here, there'd be no room for late nights, no room for the sort of pranks for which Lippold's renowned. The whole operation's been stripped back to absolute basics and there's no margin for error. At the last minute, he found that the generators he'd ordered wouldn't fit into the planes and the size of his crew was reduced from three to two. He's heading into the most rugged tour he's ever embarked on. The whole party is top heavy with management and media personnel, and he's got serious doubts about the capacity of his tour manager, Martin Hardie. If the tour is to proceed without further hitches, he's going to have to rely on the untested Aboriginal crew travelling with the Warumpi Band ... if they ever arrive.

Just before closing time, David Cooke strolls in and orders himself a beer. Like a cattle dog, Lippold leaps down his throat. 'Where the hell have you been? You guys didn't turn up for the show! You were supposed to supply two luggers! And now you've got the bloody hide to come in here for a drink without even apologising! Without even asking if there's anything you can do!'

Cookie's exhausted, so tired that a look of utter defeat and dismay sags across his face, and he slumps toward the bar as though he's just had the wind knocked out of him. Getting the Warumpi Band to tour has never been easy. A series of shows at the Sydney Opera House in 1984 was almost cancelled because Sammy Butcher was under pressure to stay home with his sick child. A 1985 tour had been in doubt because Gordon's young wife wanted him to stay in Papunya with the family. And now, in 1986, three tour proposals have already been blown out for similar reasons.

That Lippold has, at this stage, little comprehension of the difficulties involved in getting the Warumpis on the road is understandable. Few people who haven't worked with Aboriginal people, particularly those from the bush, can fully appreciate the differences in priorities. Cookie was more aware than most.

For reasons that defy logic, and perhaps even border on the masochistic, he's been tour managing the Warumpis since 1984. Unable to comprehend just why the band seemed to have such difficulties in getting things together, he shifted from Sydney to Alice in January 1985, clocked on to the dole and set up an office. By the end of the *Big Name No Blankets* tour that year he'd become a physical wreck. At 27, he was a burnt-out shell of a man who didn't have the commonsense to get out while he was still alive.

He stuck it out in the hope of achieving something, in the hope of breaking down racial barriers on the rock 'n' roll scene. But when the opportunity finally arose with the Blackfella-Whitefella

Tour, he felt as though he'd been left out in the cold. The tour had presented nothing but headaches since he first heard about it.

The Warumpis' priorities being somewhat different from those of any other act in the country, they'd demanded a six-month gig-free break so they could concentrate on their football commitments. The annual Yuendumu Sports carnival is coming up in August, and the Papunya Warriors are keen to take out the premiership.

Within a week of hearing about the tour, Cookie covered 1,000 kilometres, boring across the Western Desert in an effort to find his band. In mourning after the death of their father, Gordon Butcher was out at Haasts Bluff, and his brother Sammy was at Papunya. The roadies were scattered all over the desert, and vocalist George Rurrambu was back in his own country, living on his out-station in north-eastern Arnhem Land.

Cookie had to find them and sit down with them, telling them what little he knew about the trip and breaking the promise of a tour-free winter.

The band was 5,000 dollars in debt and there were fears that their gear had been wrecked by petrol sniffers. To make matters worse, Cookie was having communications difficulties with the Oils' office.

On Thursday, 26 June, just ten days before the tour was due to kick off, he lodged a verbal complaint with the Department of Aboriginal Affairs in Alice Springs, citing his frustration at his lack of involvement in the organisation of the tour. Not only had the Warumpis not been consulted, he said, but they hadn't been given any written notification of the tour, nothing the band members could read and discuss and show their families. The complaint was duly passed on to the Minister.

'Gary Foley,' Hardie noted, 'wanted to kill him. And some people from the Central Land Council couldn't believe it. They wanted to string him up in the middle of Alice Springs.'

He'd developed an 'Us versus Them' mentality, a parochial attitude germinated, no doubt, during his days working with

4ZZZ in Brisbane when southern bands would rock into town demanding the world.

On Saturday night, the first show of the tour at Bazzo's Farm, Cookie was feeling used and abused. The biggest band in the country had suddenly moved onto his turf, rolling into town with journalists and a film crew and an entourage of 'friends and neighbours', and there was Cookie, tearing his hair out, working his butt off and trying to hold it together on the dole. He was wound up so tight his work effort bordered on panic.

He'd given a friend of the band 70 dollars for fuel and sent him out to Haasts Bluff to collect Gordon. But the guy spent the money on grog and failed to return with the drummer.

Today, Cookie's had to drive 1,000 kilometres, trekking out to Papunya and Haasts Bluff, picking Gordon up, returning to Alice and then belting down the highway to the Rock. And now, having arrived with a full contingent – a miracle in itself – he's got to contend with Lippold doing his block.

Shaken by the ordeal, Cookie retires to his room to lick his wounds. But even there, in the comfort of his room, he can find little joy. The band has been booked into the Sheraton but they've got no money, not even enough for a feed. The charge for a hamburger is 13 dollars and that's about all they've got between them. There's a definite sense of *déjà vu* here.

A week after the release of their aptly titled debut album, *Big Name No Blankets,* in March 1985 the Warumpis embarked on a tour. Yulara was the first stop, and the band was given permission to sleep on the floor of a gymnasium.

In booking the gig, Cookie had come to an arrangement with various businesses in the complex that they'd each chip in a certain amount of money to cover the costs of a performance in the amphitheatre opposite the entrance to the Sheraton.

The band had cinematographer Patrick O'Neill on board to shoot a film clip for *(Living On the) Breadline* and permission to get some footage by the Sheraton's pool was requested and duly granted on the proviso that the name of the resort be featured prominently.

The hitch-hiker's fondest memory of that session was the sight of George Rurrambu sitting on the edge of the pool, dangling his feet in the chlorinated water and cleaning the dirt from between his toes. He'd do it on the banks of a lagoon in Arnhem Land, so why not on the paved edge of a million-dollar swimming pool?

After the amphitheatre show – a fine performance that had both tourists and staff up dancing – Cookie went around to collect the band's fee. All was going smoothly until he reached the Sheraton. There, the duty manager informed him that the 100 dollars earmarked for the Warumpis' performance had instead been donated to the Chilean Earthquake Relief Fund.

A few minutes later his contempt for Yulara was further reinforced when the white-run Aboriginal arts and crafts shop refused to stock copies of the Warumpis' cassette.

Just before dawn, bedside telephones bleat in darkened rooms, and the Oils and their film crew arise. Toyotas are gunned into life under freezing conditions and the convoy descends on the sand dunes that surge like waves towards the base of the Rock. But directions and arrangements are confused, and valuable time is lost while the troop carriers plough through the desert in search of each other.

As the long cold fingers of the dawn creep across the landscape, an argument erupts between Garrett and Morris. Up with the early bird, *Age* journalist Janet Hawley catches it: the sight of Garrett naming witnesses and times, of Morris yelling 'Don't you Mister Barrister me!' and Garrett striking back 'Don't you motormouth me!'

'I've seen better fights between prime ministers,' she says later.

The argument dies as quickly as it was ignited and everyone gets back to the business of completing the film clip for 'Dead Heart'. Cameras roll, band members mime, and behind them Uluru stirs.

It's a symbol for white Australia, perhaps even as much as it is for black. An enormous fold of sandstone in the centre of the country, which lives and breathes and exudes so much energy it's a vital force, a magnet. A monument to creation and existence, it inspires the most fanciful ideas.

But it's a symbolism that's been harnessed, projected and reinforced by advertising agencies flogging banks and soft drinks and petroleum products. An energy that's been recognised and exploited by those who would seek to reap the dollar by playing on national pride.*

A year ago the Warumpi Band spent a couple of days filming out here. But to look at the clips, you wouldn't recognise the Rock. They painstakingly avoided the cliches, the postcard shots of Uluru, anything that would demean a place that was so intrinsically significant that they refused to even climb it.

They were filming at Maggie Springs, a waterhole sunk deep into the folds of the Rock and a regular destination for the coach tours, when a party of American tourists strolled up the track.

A few minutes later, as the Warumpis' gear was being loaded back into the bus, the tourist party reappeared. They stood back, jumbling up on each other by the front of the bus. And then a woman plucked up the courage to ask George Rurrambu if they could perhaps take his photo.

'Yo,' George grinned. 'You mob can take my photo.'

'See,' said one of the women. 'The man at the bureau was wrong. They're not fierce at all.'

The hitch-hiker sat at the poolside bar and pulled on another rum. Maybe he'd had too many already but he knew he wouldn't see another for a week or more. He looked out across a forest of tubular metal chairs and beige gauze umbrellas. The Oils were reclining

---

* In August 1987, the traditional owners who control the Uluru National Park banned commercial filming in the Park on the grounds that it was demeaning and culturally inappropriate.

on deck-chairs, their wives sipping exotic milk-shakes and shading their babes from the sun. Tomorrow, most of the women would be returning to Sydney and the Oils would be heading west into an old world in which such opulence had never been dreamt of.

The Oils' only contact with Aboriginal communities had been an overnighter in Numbulwar, an idyllic settlement on the Gulf of Carpentaria where food and water were in plentiful supply and the people had little to fear. And from that evening in 1983 the fantasies had blossomed; fantasies that might wither and die in the desert.

The hitch-hiker had been through this land before, and his principal memories were those of the sadness of a people dying to survive. Of petrol sniffers, wide-eyed and drooling, as they staggered through the dust. Of cars, sliding in the dirt and rolling over and over, left buckled and twisted and burned out on the sides of the tracks to be stripped and transplanted. Of sniffer patrols cruising through the night with spotlights searching for the victims. Of old men who were so distraught at the cultural suicide their own sons were committing that they'd mutter about tragedy and loss in the most poetic of terms as tears swelled and trickled from burntout eyes that had seen too much and couldn't stand to see any more. He'd heard too many tales of death and destruction, rape and annihilation. Of languages that had been lost, tribes wiped from the face of the earth by poison and disease. Of sacred waterholes and soaks that had been churned to putrid mud by the horses and the camels of Europeans who had no respect ... no respect for land or life or God. He'd been through this country before and he'd seen little sense of hope. He'd seen people who'd been so devastated by the teachings of the Church they didn't know which way to turn, whether to renounce the Dreaming as the devil's work or to embrace that which their fathers had held to be so sacred. People who just ended up wasted and dazed and confused. Stricken with grief and soul-destroying confusion, trying to straddle that impossible gulf between the modern world and the traditional way, clinging to phantoms and falling, reeling into the chasm. He'd seen the walking dead, their faces pressed against the windows of the night. He'd seen young teenagers with fencing wire protruding from their eardrums and jam tins full of petrol splashing off their chests. He'd seen people who were painfully aware that what they had lost could never be replaced . . .

CHAPTER THREE
DOCKER RIVER

It was a Monday night in late January 1978 when Charlie McMahon first heard Midnight Oil.

An unlikely fruit picker (he blew much of his right arm off making rocket fuel when he was 16), Charlie had just arrived back in Sydney after a few weeks working in the orchards of the South Coast. Walking up Oxford Street, he heard a frenetic noise pounding out from the depths of a subterranean wine bar called French's, and, his curiosity aroused, he trotted downstairs to investigate.

In his left hand he was carrying his bag. It was full of clothes and, wrapped in a blanket, a didgeridoo a friend had brought back from Alice. He kept the log in the blanket not so much to protect it as to hide it, because he was getting tired of people stopping him on the streets and asking him to give it a blow. Which is precisely what drummer Rob Hirst did when he spotted Charlie between sets and, out of curiosity, enquired about the contents of the bag.

French's wasn't too crowded that night, though there were perhaps a hundred people getting hot and sweaty and blitzed on the bar's staple libation of head-cracking cider.

Charlie had blown his didgeridoo to the accompaniment of a couple of acoustic guitars before, but he'd never played with a full-tilt rock 'n' roll band. And he'd certainly never heard his log amplified through a PA. So he suggested that if Rob wanted to hear him play, it should be with the band in full flight.

In those days, as a little-known outfit from Sydney's northern beaches, the Oils could afford to take such chances. The results were electrifying, producing a rumbling, wailing, droning fusion of energy and sound that raised the hair on the backs of a hundred necks and kicked off a relationship that would endure for years.

'I got stood on that night,' Charlie recalls, ''cos I was sitting on the stage. After that, I developed the forked microphone technique so I could stand up and play.' At the time, Charlie was in a bit of a bind. An economics and sociology graduate, he'd been sacked from his job as a tutor at Sydney University after inspiring his class to brighten up their dingy room with a few cans of paint. In 1978, shortly after his first brush with the Oils, he headed out to Alice and scored a job with the Department of Aboriginal Affairs. He was sent to Papunya, and spent three months reporting on and assessing local efforts at self-determination. 'But,' he says, 'I always wanted to grab a crow bar and a shovel and join in, not stand around with a pen and a clipboard taking notes.'

Quitting the DAA, he took a job as a community advisor for the Pintupi tribe, sinking bores at Kintore, supervising the construction of airstrips and the building of the shop at Kiwirrkurra. In the process, he earned the affectionate nickname of Marra Hook (*Marra* meaning hand).

Since then he's divided his time between the people of the desert and the increasing demands of his musical pursuits in Sydney. Between stints in the bush, he's joined the Oils as a guest didgeridoo player on tours of the 'motel land' of America and the Australian east coast, and has won considerable acclaim with his own band, Gondwanaland. He's played with the London Philharmonic Orchestra and worked on numerous film soundtracks, including *Mad Max – Beyond Thunderdome*.

Of such stark differences in the nature of his lifestyle he says, 'There's one very funny thing, y'know. Whatever I've been doin' in the bush, I've never pined for music. But when I've been doin' music, I'll often pine for the bush.' Now, having been hired as the camp coordinator for the Central Australian leg of the Blackfella-Whitefella Tour, he's able to combine both pursuits.

Soon after hearing about the Blackfella-Whitefella Tour, he left a handwritten note on Gary Morris's desk:

Sacred Places:
1. If you want to go off road and you want to know if it's okay by the locals, ask if the place is *milmilpa* (meaning sacred and dangerous to the uninitiated). All country is sacred but not *milmilpa* sacred.
2. If it gets very wet never go off road to avoid water on the road, because you might sink in uncompacted soil.
3. All communities have medical services and stores.
4. Avoid driving over mulga wood for flat tyres.

He also pointed out the need for swags and good tucker boxes and the benefits of using diesel-powered vehicles in country in which petrol sniffing is rife.

'I was a bit worried when I first heard about this tour,' Charlie recalls, 'because no one had bothered to ask me to come out and supervise things. But we got that sorted out.'

At Gary's behest, he shifted back to Alice a couple of weeks in advance and set about organising the camping equipment for the tour and preparing food and utensils for the tucker boxes.

'There,' says Charlie as he slams home the bolt on the back of his Toyota, 'that should do it, eh!'

'You have got it down to an art, mate,' Rob Hirst replies.

Charlie's Toyota is an old workhorse that's been around the clock four times in the five years since he bought it. Seemingly held together with fencing wire and gaffa tape, its canopy-covered tray is stacked with tucker boxes and swags, camp ovens, jerry cans, billies, tools and the most essential item – an SSB radio for emergencies.

What's missing from the ensemble is Charlie's dog, Danger. A wild mongrel that tore Rob's dog Sprint apart during a foray into Sydney a couple of years ago, Danger lost it under the back wheel of a Landcruiser.

As they pull out of Yulara and rumble towards the Olgas, Charlie clasps his metal hand around the steering-wheel, reaches into the pocket of his vest, withdraws a tin of tobacco and proceeds to roll himself a smoke. 'Kata Tjuta!' he shouts, nodding towards the Olgas. 'Beautiful eh?!'

Thirty Ks west of Uluru, Kata Tjuta waits. Crouches in the desert like a squadron of rusty Dakotas, waiting for the order to scramble. Lines of wind-sucked eaves pock-mark the fuselage walls ... portholes on the flight-deck of some futuristic space station.

The sand-blasted texture of the rocks is similar to that of Uluru; their shades of orange and pink and purple resonate under a clear blue sky. Beneath the spinifex plains, their ancient engines rumble.

There are a number of important women's Dreaming sites here but, significantly, none have been fenced off. A couple of sites at the base of Uluru are surrounded by low fences and signs requesting the tourists to respect the wishes of the traditional owners by not trespassing on the sacred ground. Around Kata Tjuta, the approach has been taken that by not fencing the sites off, their sanctity will be preserved through their anonymity. Tourists are unlikely to wander off the beaten track and trespass on sacred places, so the argument goes, if attention is not drawn to those places.

The domes on the western side, it is said, are the camping sites of the Pangkalangka: hairy giants who eat human flesh and are, it seems, still very much alive today.

Weeks later, upon his return to the desert, the hitch-hiker swam naked through the icy waters of Redbank Gorge, a crevice west of Alice so narrow that with each breast stroke his fingers, cold and blue and brittle, almost touched the golden walls that towered above. Cold and foolhardy and a little nervous – for it was another solo venture – he made it through four chasms before turning back. The water was so chilling that he was losing strength, the muscles in his arms and shoulders were threatening to seize up, his flesh had shrunk, skin had turned purple and his brain felt as if it was about to explode. And even when he was within 15 metres of the point at which he'd plunged in, he feared he wouldn't make it. When he finally emerged he shivered uncontrollably for almost an hour.

'Pangkalangka,' was Neil Murray's explanation when the hitchhiker recounted the story. 'Aboriginal people never swim up there. Pangkalangka lives there. He was trying to get you.'

From Kata Tjuta the convoy strikes west, half-a-dozen Toyotas and an ex-army truck barrelling through the dust towards the settlement at Docker River.

'Up to about fifty million years ago,' Charlie yells above the hum of the motor, 'this was a very big forest. This flat land,' he says, sweeping his goanna skin-clad metallic arm across the harsh, dry spinifex plains, 'used to be big river valleys. See, all this flat land is the dust and the sand that's been blown by the arid hot winds that have been blowing across Central Australia for the last five million years. And this sand has moved in to cover up the old river valleys. But if you care to drill down through that layer of earth and into the first layers of rock, you'll find that under a lot of the ground there are vast amounts of water. And those ancient rivers, they're still flowing . . . underground! Because when the rain hits this ground it goes straight through the sand, down to the aquifers below, and moves off to all sorts of places: places that we still don't know exist underground.'

Leaving the boundaries of Uluru National Park in a lingering cloud of dust, they head into the Petermann Reserve, a region to which Aboriginal people have been given inalienable freehold title under the *Land Rights Act* of 1976.

'The main thing about this country out here,' Charlie says, 'is that the people are here. They're on it. And it's going to stay as part of Australia. I think probably one of the biggest arguments for Land Rights at the moment is the fact that at least it's not going to be sold to some big real estate company in Los Angeles or Tokyo or whatever . . .'

Under the Land Rights legislation introduced by the Fraser Federal Government in 1976, to the consternation of future Northern Territory governments, inalienable freehold title to vast chunks of land in the south-west and the Top End of the Territory was given to the Aborigines who lived there. It's their land and over that land they retain absolute control.

There are various autonomous forms of authority operating out here, some of them beyond whitefella's law.

In order to administer the land that's been returned to Aboriginal people, the Central Land Council (CLC) and the Northern Land Council (NLC) were set up. The CLC represents 15,000 Aboriginal people in the desert regions, while the NLC looks after the interests of 17,000 in the Top End. The Land Councils are made up of representatives elected from each community and have a staff of lawyers, anthropologists, journalists and consultants who advise on such matters as mining, protection of the environment, pastoral ventures, commercial interests and tourism.

'The Land Councils,' says Charlie, 'are meant to set up land trusts, to represent Aboriginal people in negotiations with outside interests – both in government and private enterprise – and to see that the people get a good deal.'

Since their inception ten years ago, the Land Councils have added to the bureaucratic tangle of Aboriginal affairs. Mining companies and conservative politicians complain that they move too slowly and that they're unwieldy organisations with too much political power. There's an argument that, rather than exerting control over such issues as mining exploration, the Land Councils should simply operate as letterboxes for the individual communities, acting as intermediaries for the traditional owners, and thereby allowing each community to make decisions that are relevant to its own circumstances.

Conservative politicians make election pledges promising to dismantle the Land Councils, a move that, presumably, would create a situation in which only the richest communities would survive, because they'd be the only ones able to afford the consultants and the advice to facilitate the decision-making process. Until the educational opportunities in the bush communities are improved dramatically, such a move would be disastrous.

'The Land Councils,' says Charlie, 'are also there to make sure that the *Land Rights Act is* adhered to as regards permits of entry into Aboriginal lands by outside people. And the permits issue really only relates to non-Aboriginal people.

'If you were to look at the equivalent – a piece of European-owned country like a cattle-station – you'd have similar laws which prevent the access of people on to that land.

'Basically the permits are there because that is Aboriginal land. And the Aboriginal people, in a lot of cases, find themselves unable to deal with random outsiders, whether they be tourists or surveyors. And everyone, even government people, are meant to have permits to go on the land.*

'In some instances, the permits issue has created more fear and loathing than it should have, as regards outsiders. But you can understand that people don't want a four-wheel-drive club going through their sacred sites.'

To enter the Petermann Reserve, for example, you have to apply for a permit, showing cause as to why you want to enter Aboriginal land and how long you're likely to stay. Alcohol is forbidden on the Reserve, and offenders are liable for hefty fines. The seizure of vehicles used to cart liquor has been automatic since 1982.

•

---

* When police were hunting the killer of five tourists in the Kimberleys in June 1987, they were able to report with confidence that he hadn't escaped onto Aboriginal land because, even in communities that hadn't heard of the manhunt, any stranger without a permit would've been reported.

The road to Docker River, apart from a couple of washouts, is in reasonably good condition. It's about four lanes wide; four lanes of fine red dust that's been bulldozed from the plains. Twenty years ago, vehicles using this track were lucky to cover more than 16 kilometres an hour. Today, they can bolt along.

It wasn't always so easy. It was in this region that Harry Bell Lasseter perished in 1931. Searching for his reef of gold, he was stranded when his camels bolted. He tried to make it back to the Olgas, 140 kilometres to the east, but despite the aid of an Aboriginal family, he died within the shadow of the Petermann Ranges.

On the way through to Docker River the convoy stops off at Lasseter's Cave, a small hole in the base of a rocky hill. It was here in the summer of 1931 that the prospector spent twenty-five days, seeking shelter from the blazing desert sun, rationing out the last of his meagre foodstuffs and scribbling his tragic last notes in a diary.

'A gold reef!' Charlie almost spits the words out. 'You know that's all bullshit, eh! There's no gold out here. No, the thing this country's got which is even better than gold these days is clear air and lots of space. And that's the modern gold, I reckon. That's the modern scarce thing.'

A few kilometres further west lies Docker River.

The Mission at Docker River was set up for the Pitjantjatjara people in 1968. The official reasons for its establishment included the provision of education for the children and employment for the adults. Though it may well have been that the Native Affairs Branch (as it was then called) was getting peeved by the number of Pitjantjatjara people hanging around Ayers Rock and the Olgas, trying to sell artefacts to the tourists. They were, said Native Affairs Branch patrol officers, 'nuisance itinerants'.

It also seems the Native Affairs Branch was concerned about the number of Red Ochre ceremonies being carried out in the region, and when such things started getting in the way of tourist developments – well what choice did they really have, except to round the people up and truck them to a new settlement where they'd be out of sight and couldn't really bother anyone.

As further pressure to get people to move to Docker, pastoralists to the east of the Rock were advised to stop giving clothes and rations to Aborigines camping on their properties.

From the south, Yankunytjatjara people were transferred to the new government settlement, as were Pitjantjatjara people from the west.

The move from the west, while having nothing to do with the interests of pastoral or tourist ventures, was brought about by government fears that nomadic Aboriginal people would wander on to the flight path for rockets being fired from Woomera in South Australia. A no-go zone had been established that extended from Woomera for 1,200 kilometres to the north-west, a missile range corridor that ran from just above Spencer Gulf right through to the Western Australian coast. So, in the interests of safety and the progress of the arms race, people were taken off their land and sent to Docker.

It was an experiment that wasn't wholly successful. People from different tribes and language groups were put together with extremely limited facilities, and ordered to live a sedentary existence far removed from their traditional lifestyles.

Little consideration was given to the traditional religious interests of the people, either. A hospital was built without consulting the people about its placement. The site chosen by the builders happened to be sacred, and the establishment was demolished before its completion.

Twenty years later, the biggest problem facing the people of Docker and neighbouring communities to the south is petrol sniffing. In places like Amata, Fregon and Ernabella in the Pitjantjatjara lands of South Australia, petrol sniffing has reached crisis proportions. (By March 1987, petrol sniffing had become so widespread in Docker River that the community's petrol sales were suspended indefinitely.)

'With people who are caught in an enormous schism between the old world and the modern world,' says Charlie, 'there's bound to be disastrous things. And petrol sniffing represents that enormous schism between the old world and the new world.'

Scattered beneath the barren hills of the Petermann Ranges, canvas and corrugated-iron humpies melt into the dusty red floor of the valley. Few of the trees have enough foliage to provide shade, and down by the community store the petrol pumps are housed within big sniffer-proof metal cages. It's a desolate landscape littered with abandoned cars, sheets of tin, buckled wheels, hunks of cardboard, rejected clothes and cans and sheets of plastic that have been turned brittle by the relentless dry heat.

Up until about twenty years ago, these people were nomadic. They'd spend a month or two in a place where seasonal water or hunting was good. During that time they'd burn the dead trees for heat and cooking, gather yams and berries and hunt the roos and lizards and possums and birds that lived in the area. And then they'd move on. They'd allow the land and its resources to regenerate and wouldn't return to that area until its stock had been replenished by nature and the evidence of their previous inhabitation had been erased.

It's only in recent years that they've been encouraged to live in one place. Consequently, the settlements are so foreign to their traditional way of life that little care has been taken in the maintenance and regeneration of the land. The game has been hunted out, the trees turned into firewood and the areas transformed into massive dust bowls. Problems with sanitation have resulted, and communities have been crippled by such health problems as trachoma, respiratory ailments, hearing deficiencies, influenza, gastric epidemics and malnutrition,

The first time the Warumpi Band hit Docker River was back in late March 1985. Cookie pulled the Toyota Coaster into the clearing by the petrol pumps and climbed out, wiping a fine layer of red powder from his green aviator shades as he stretched his legs in the dust.

The air was breathlessly still. In the river red-gums and the coolibah trees down by the dry sandy riverbed, crows nagged at the heat. Behind the store a dieseline generator chugged and hummed. Cookie stood there for a minute or two, shuffling his boots in the dust and toying with a cigarette until a couple of the locals strolled in.

'You mob want petrol?'

'No, Warumpi Band,' said Cookie. 'We've come to do a show.'

'Got to talk to Council,' said one of the blacks. He thought about it for a while and then said, 'Very hard to look for Council around here.'

'Yeah,' said Cookie. 'I got in touch with the Council two months ago. Three months ago.'

'Yeah, we heard it. If Council say it's all right to organise it, I can organise it from here. No problem.'

'Where would we play?' asked Cookie.

'The Council too slow,' said one, passing over the urgency of the whitefella's question. 'Anything that's busy busy they too slow. They don't organise anything. We do. I'll go tell Council. We want concert.'

'Council,' the other nodded, 'lot of times too slow.'

Docker River and its surrounding out-stations are controlled by the Kaltukatjara Nguratjaku Community Council, a homelands council that looks after the 300 people who live in the settlement and the 300 who live on the seventeen out-stations (or bush camps) that are scattered across the south-west of the Northern Territory and the neighbouring regions of Western Australia.

'The communities out here,' Charlie explains, 'are incorporated associations. The community is a properly instituted and incorporated association which submits an audited account of all of finances every year to the Federal government and whoever they're financed by for the different works that they undertake. Their basic works are their own administration, their own areas of water and power and things like that.

'The local community council, which is elected by all the people in the place, is responsible for all aspects of the community which relate to the community and its surrounding area. It's responsible for the store managers, the community advisors and for the essential services control of these places.

'Authority in Aboriginal communities traditionally does not give proper administration. It's a big problem. The elections tend to be a farce. People come up and they get voted for. And then there'll be *hey*, cheers, y'know. But I've seen some elections and they've been total farces. It's very difficult.

'A lot of people don't understand this form of government because in traditional Aboriginal culture no-one has overall authority over people. The main authority that traditionally lies in Aboriginal people is spiritual authority. And every person's responsibility towards the other person is defined according to their kinship relations.

'Everyone has a 'skin name' and that defines their relationship to every other person in that community. There's eight male names and eight female names. Now this system, this family system, does not translate very well into a modern system of administration. After all, us whitefellas have only barely gotten out of nepotism over the last hundred years or so anyway.'

The issue of skin names gives an indication of the apparent complexity of Aboriginal society and the strength of kinship or extended family bonds. When dealing with the Warumpis, for example, Sammy and Gordon Butcher have the skin name of Tjapanangka. One can therefore ascertain that their sister's skin name is Napanangka (and they're not allowed to marry anyone of that skin), and that their father's skin name was Tjapangati (and that he wasn't permitted to marry a Napangati). Whole families can be traced through skin names.

John Hobson of the Institute for Aboriginal Development's Language Development Group writes:

> Most individuals in Central Australian Aboriginal society are members of a subsection or 'skin' group. Membership of a particular subsection is determined by parents' skins,

although there is scope for a skin to be assigned to an outsider or European.

The skin system is essentially a broad grouping of kin, including many people who are only distantly or notionally related. Through the skin system it is possible to calculate one's notional relationships with others, and each skin collects together a particular set of relations. Thus, for example, one's own skin group includes one's brothers and sisters, father's father (and his brothers and sisters), son's children, and brothers' sons' children. The skin system also broadly determines social relations: proper behaviour (avoidance, respect, familiarity etc.), rights and responsibilities, as well as ceremonial and land tenure relationships.

'Authority,' says Charlie, 'moves fluidly through Aboriginal communities. For different purposes different people have authority. Through an Aboriginal person's life, they will have different authorities as they go, different responsibilities to different people. For instance, one of a man's most important responsibilities is the observance of his obligations to his mother-in-law. He's not allowed to see her. He's not allowed to talk to her, right. But he's got to ensure that she doesn't go hungry. If anything goes wrong with her, as regards her welfare, he's got to really stand up for her and her rights. But he's got to be totally deferential. That's how authority works.'

Under the skin system, a man's female cousin is classified as his mother-in-law. Presumably developed as insurance against incest, the traditional law means that a man cannot sit in the same room as his female cousin. Nor are they permitted to talk to or look at each other.

Nor are brothers and sisters allowed to talk privately. A brother cannot ask his sister about her personal life. He can find out about it, but he's not permitted to discuss it with her.

For a woman, another aspect of the system is that her sister's children are automatically considered to be her own and she must, therefore, accept responsibility for their welfare.

'Authority works over spiritual things,' Charlie explains. 'In initiation ceremonies, certain people are responsible for the initiation of certain other persons. Over the passing on of stories about the country, or the teaching of different skills, that's where the authority lies.

'There's authority over medicine, over people's health. Certain people have very strong spiritual powers and you'll find that an outstation group won't move to an area unless they feel that there is someone who is *ngankari* way, meaning a medicine man. That *ngankari* person will have strong powers to combat *kadaitcha*, who are the evil spirits.'

And then there's the authority that's beyond the reach of the law – the authority of the Red Ochre Men.

It was March 1985, and the Warumpi Band were due to kick off a tour. In his cramped office in the wings of the Araluen Arts Centre in Alice Springs, David Cooke relayed messages on the radio-telephone through to the remote desert communities of South Australia.

Through the howling of the transponders the operator's voice sounded as though it was being bounced out of the bowels of a scrap metal factory, all grinding and sparks and distant eerie echoes. 'Onnnne Fooooour Seven-n-n?'

Another voice, that of an Aboriginal woman, erupted through the static. 'Yes?'

'Oh, good morning,' the operator crackled. 'I have a call for you.'

'Yes.'

'Hello Amata! This is David Cooke from the Warumpi Band calling, over.'

'Yes.'

'Ah, we will not be able to play at your community because of 'business' on the road, over.'

'Yes, okay.'

'Okay then, thank you very much.'

'Seeya.'

'Bye bye.'

He put the phone down, fumbled for a cigarette, and stared at an Army survey map of the Petermann region on the wall. Word had come through that the 'business' trucks were moving north, tearing up the dust of the Pitjantjatjara homelands and roping in every eligible Aboriginal man in sight. For Cookie, it meant that the settlements he'd booked gigs at in South Australia – Amata, Fregon and Ernabella – would be virtual ghost towns, utterly devoid of males over the age of 14. It also meant that unless the Warumpis were to be roped in to fulfil their tribal obligations – upsetting their touring itinerary completely – they'd have to take another route south, travelling at night, taking the back roads in an effort to avoid the trucks.

The 'business', he knew only too well, was serious stuff: an annual ritual of secret initiation ceremonies. Aboriginal men are rounded up and taken into the depths of the desert – far away from the women and children – to learn and perform the sacred songs and dances and ceremonies that will instill in them the knowledge and the discipline required of a man.

The night before, he'd been out at Papunya. There, George Rurrambu's wife had asked him if he'd seen any Red Ochre Men on the road. Just the way she said it made Cookie tremble at the prospect of returning to Alice – along 200 kilometres of dirt road at night.

The Red Ochre Men are essentially a traditional form of law enforcement, tribal elders who've been chosen to uphold the traditional values. And when the 'business' is on the move it's their duty to round up the other initiated men and the boys who've come of age and escort them to the site of the ceremonies.

It's said that when the Red Ochre Men approach a community the birds stop singing, the dogs stop barking, and the women cover their heads with blankets.

The idea of running into the Red Ochre Men – of being flagged on to the side of the road by men wearing blood-red headbands and plastered with red ochre, waving shotguns and upholding the strictest of rules – was not one that appealed to Cookie. They wouldn't have harmed him of course, for he was white and therefore beyond involvement. But he was travelling through Aboriginal land and there's no doubt they would've checked the car to ensure he wasn't carrying anyone they wanted.

In the centre of Alice, George Rurrambu, a Top Ender who hasn't been initiated into the ways of the desert people, was pissed and scared. 'They're comin' through to-day!' he cried when he saw Hardie and the hitch-hiker. 'Right after this Fri-day!'

'Who?'

'The "business" mob!'

'From where? From Amata?'

'Yeah! They'll be comin' up right after Fri-day! I saw them! And I met them! And I had a talk with them, all the mob, you know?! Business! They had a red stripe right on the . . .'

'Around the hair?'

'An' I was talkin' to them and they said the "business" will be finished Fri-day. This road will be blocked for to-day! Some people just arrived to-day! I asked the bloke who was in "the business" . . . all the business mob comin'. Some people just 'rived to-day . . . some people 'rived just last night, some people on the road again, and they still coming. More people coming! If they could have, there be a shoot up! We'll get shot! I'm telling, don't go. Are we? We will wait, you know. I don't wanna get shot! I want to wait until Fri-day. Cancel everything, and we wait until Fri-day, until all the road is going to be clear. Right?'

'How do they block the road?'

'It's the "business" mob coming! I'm telling you truth! And I got message from the old people, they just 'rived from the "business", you know. I ask them, and they say road will be open on Fri-day. Not to-day. Blocked. They told me like that. Simple as anything, you know. But if anybody don't believe it, we'll get, I'll get shot! So we have to wait until Fri-day!'

In those places where whites congregate you hear strange tales about the Red Ochre Men. Tales of the executioner's song, laced with cordite, torn plastic rounds, spent cartridges and the trickle of oily black smoke across a sky so clear you can hear the reports for miles. There's the tale of two youths who so feared the rites of circumcision and subincision associated with initiation that they tried to dodge the 'business' in 1978 by grabbing a car and heading out towards Papunya. Once the order was given, so the story goes, their hours were numbered. Shots rang through the night. Such tales, like that of a bunch of Aboriginal kids across the border in South Australia. Out for a joy ride, they came across a big bunch of parked cars and went looking for the party ... But the party was ceremonial and they never made it back to the car.

The Red Ochre Men generally appear in the summer, riding north from South Australia. But in the winter of 1987, they made a move that surprised everybody. Without warning, they appeared at the annual Yuendumu Sports competition, which, in the middle of the preliminary football final between Ti-Tree (NT) and Ernabella (SA), was abandoned immediately.

According to one spectator, a whitefella named Bob Gosford, 'all the players turned to one man who ran on to the field just as a truck-load of people pulled up on the other side of the field ... the players stopped in their tracks as the man shouted a warning and raised his hands, and a visible shudder ran through the crowd. The man on the mike said *What's happening?*, then, as he spied the contents of the truck that had pulled up beside the tower on which he stood, he promptly dropped the mike and fled. The Ti-Tree players sprinted faster than they had during the game towards the safety of their cars and countrymen on the eastern side of the ground. The 500 or so supporters sitting nearby got up almost as one body and ran screaming and shouting in fear. The picture was echoed all around the ground ... what had been a couple of thousand people sitting watching a peaceful football match was now a scattered, screaming mob, running for cars, trucks, any means of transport AWAY FROM THERE.

'Football was forgotten, one thought only ... get as far away as possible from the RED OCHRE MEN that had turned up and achieved maximum effect. All this happened within the space of two or three minutes . . . maybe less.

'Within a few minutes the town was empty and silent but for the retreating sound of unmuffled engines racing away through the scrub. Apparently the Red Ochre Men involved were from South Australia. They certainly picked their moment. Unlike their northern counterparts, who strike equal fear into all who see them, the fellows from the south have, as one man from Lajamanu said, 'Licence to kill, those blokes. Kill anybody, policeman, *kardia*, anybody who sees them, they can kill . . . licence to kill! That's why everybody is so scared of those blokes.'

'Apparently there were a couple of pay backs that were due in Yuendumu. Nobody expected the blokes to turn up during sports weekend, but if the time is right and the chosen victim is around, then who's going to tell a bunch of clever men that they can't carry out their wishes. Even the cops run away with everyone else. It's just too serious for them and would be a major transgression of their patiently built-up trust to try to step in . . . if you could find any coppers stupid or ignorant enough to try.

'An hour or so out from Yuendumu a Ford XW sits abandoned in the middle of the road, all doors open, boot open and with foam mattresses still strapped to the roof. What the hell caused people to abandon a perfectly good car in the middle of nowhere? It hadn't broken down because if it had it would've been stripped of all useful, portable parts. There was something about the truck tracks that circled the car that suggested rapid forwards motion was the safest course of action. Keep moving and don't look back because you might see things you don't want to see . . .'

At midday, Lippold, Pickett and the Blackfella-Whitefella Tour's advance scout, Gary Williams, roll into Docker River and pull up beside the petrol pumps. As they wander towards the store, the white manager steps out.

'We heard you mob were coming,' he says by way of a greeting. 'But we didn't know when. Ya should'a come earlier. Not many people 'ere now. Most of 'em are off at the footy at Areyonga, or in Alice for the Show. It's school holidees, y'know, so a lot of this mob've taken their kids to the out-stations. Yep, should'a come earlier . . . or later.'

Last time the Warumpis played Docker, there were maybe 400 people here . . . and 1,000 dogs. There were kids everywhere, sandy-headed children running naked through the dust, scrambling over cars, skipping through the litter and scaling the fences around the open-air picture theatre. People emerging from humpies in the mulga, from shelters made with car bonnets and tarpaulins and water tanks that had been cut in half and rolled on to their sides, using any materials that could be scrounged to effect a break against the vicious winds that howl through the valley. The air was filled with the shrieks of kids, the scrapping of dogs and the gutteral gurgle of the cars. As the band's crew of Cookie and Ian Anderson Jambajimba and Simon Greene set up the gear, the petrol sniffers looked on, young kids lingering in the cool shadows of dusk, clinging to their cans, inhaling the fumes, the vapour so pungent you didn't dare light a cigarette. Night fell and the women and kids streamed in, packs of dogs skulking between their legs. Cars rumbled out of the darkness and encircled the gig, their passengers sitting on the bonnets to watch the gig through the fence. Cookie sat at the gate collecting grubby 5-dollar notes, marking those who'd paid with a white texta cross on the arm. (Later in the tour, when whites started coming to the shows, he also invested in a blue one.) And when the Warumpis plugged in and Neil said 'Gidday Docker River!' and George shouted 'Hullo Docker River', there were squeals of delight from the kids.

'You know who we are?' asked Neil. 'You do? What's our name?'

'NEIL!' yelled the kids.

'Not my name. What's the band's name? What's the name of this band?'

And one cheeky kid, squatting among all the others in the dirt, cried, 'Ask someone!' At the beginning of every song the kids sprang from the earth, dancing furiously, arms and legs flailing amid clouds of dust, and at the end of the song they'd drop to the ground as one, as if they'd been playing musical chairs.

But this time around, the settlement's deserted. The 'school holidees' have turned it into a ghost town.

At dusk, a light plane comes in low, buzzing the valley, and a freelance film crew from Alice joins the media melee. By show time it seemed that, as at Uluru, there were more media representatives around than members of the local community. Whitefellas with cameras, clicking and rolling and whirring, getting it all down while a couple of dozen blackfellas crowded around fires on the ground waiting for the Warumpis to start.

After the pre-tour disputes, drummer Gordon's non-appearance in Alice and the band's failure to arrive in time for the concert at Mutitjulu, the Oils have had cause for quiet concern about the Warumpis' reliability. The show in Alice had been so shaky, so undeniably rough, that the Oils were wondering if they'd made a mistake, if, in inviting the Warumpis to join them – and they were not ignorant of the band's reputation – they'd perhaps placed the whole tour in jeopardy.

Their fears are dismissed as soon as the Warumpis kick off. With Gordon Butcher back behind the kit they turn in a spirited performance. Gordon's a fantastic drummer, a man who's got the desert in his blood and a great sense of rhythm in his heart. Around him, the whole band comes together.

Their bass player was a big bloke from Haasts Bluff, Hilary Jabaldjari Wirri. He mightn't have been the best of musicians, but he loved the gig and everytlme he heard the band was going away he'd turn up from some place like Halls Creek with a glint of excitement in his sad brown eyes and count himself in for the tour. Sometimes they'd take him; others not.

Their performance is bright and strong, the sort of show that's made them a 'number one' band in the desert. Kids squat in the dirt down the front. Further back, the older folk huddle over fires, politely watching. Throughout the desert, people take a certain pride in the Warumpis' success because they're a settlement band who've made it in the modern world.

A number of their songs are sung in Luritja, the language of the people from the Papunya region: songs like 'Jailanguru Pakarnu' (Out From Jail), 'Kintorelakutu' (Towards Kintore), 'Nyuntu Nyaaltjirriku' (What Are You Going to Do?), 'Wiima Tjuta' (All the Kids), 'Warumpinya' (Papunya) and 'Tjiluru Tjlluru' (Sad and Lonely). To hear Aboriginal languages presented in a modern rock 'n' roll format inspires the confidence that the Warumpis' is 'proper number one music'.

For Midnight Oil, the reception is more subdued. No one seems to know what to make of them, and there's little recognition or applause.

The Oils have been playing together for ten years and this is the smallest and least receptive crowd they've played to since they pulled thirteen people on their first trip to Melbourne in 1978. Their raw, jagged rhythms obviously aren't those of this arid timeless land and, in the face of such a detached response, they try to change the set. But when they try a country and western arrangement of 'The Best Of Both Worlds' it falls apart before the first verse, and any hope of connecting is lost.

For the people of Docker it is, no doubt, like a big ugly slice of the city rising up in the middle of their turf – a place so familiar they know every ridge, tree, gully, stone and wreck – louder and wilder and brighter and much more intense than anything they've ever been confronted with before. The band's equipment has been scaled right back to the most basic system, but still Pat Pickett's pushing 110 decibels which, under the circumstances, is excessively loud.

Unable to get a grip on the gig, the Oils cut through ten songs then Garrett says, 'This is our last song . . .' And with that, before they've even struck the first chord of 'Read About It', everybody gets up and leaves.

'They're so polite,' is the only comment Rob Hirst can later offer.

'That's right,' says Charlie. 'It's good manners. That's what these people think, y'know.'

Later, conducting a post mortem around a campfire in the school grounds, the Oils chat about throwing in a couple of country songs, injecting a flavour that the desert people are familiar with.

'Okay,' says Garrett. 'Let's see what our favourite country songs are.'

Guitarist Martin Rotsey stares into the fire and says, 'Holiday In Cambodia.'

All eyes flash to his lips, but they fail to reveal the faintest trace of a smile. Everyone else cracks up and the discussion is effectively terminated. Sentimentality, as you'd suspect of someone whose sense of humour stretches to thoughts of inflicting one of the Dead Kennedys' more rabid punk efforts on the desert people, is not one of Rotsey's strong points.

He once sold all his records, and claims never to have missed or replaced any of them.

Talking about himself, he says, makes him feel 'like a right Wally', a term that betrays his English upbringing. The son of a metallurgist father and a pharmacist mother, he was brought to Australia when he was 7. At the age of 12, he got his first acoustic guitar. A year later, he got an electric guitar and spent his weekends rehearsing in a garage with schoolfriends in Sydney's southern beachside suburbs. When his parents went to Japan, he was given 'a two-year sentence' as a boarder at Sydney Grammar. There he joined a boarding band called Ganja and met Rob Hirst who was playing with Jim Moginie in Schwampy Moose.

After leaving school, Rotsey lived in Paddington, rehearsed with a band that included Jonathon Coleman, dropped out of an Arts course at Sydney University and went to work at *The Bulletin* as a copy boy before joining the advertising department. Returning to university to do architecture, he met up with Rob Hirst again at the drummer's 21st and joined the fledgling Midnight Oil soon afterwards.

Very early on, Rotsey perfected the classic 'guitarist as machine-gun-toting-guerilla' stance, cigarette smouldering from his lip, shoulders hunched, legs in a crouch as though poised to run a 100 metre dash, trigger hand chopping away at the strings as he surveyed the audience.

Like the band's other guitarist, Jim Moginie, Martin's fought to retain his anonymity within the Oils, studiously avoiding interviews and the pressures of public recognition.

Beside him, Peter Garrett sits on a log in a t-shirt and trousers and warms his toes by the fire. As the others sip mugs of tea, he admits that he's concerned about the band's relationship with the Warumpis who, out of shyness, have chosen to camp in a hall near the store rather than sharing the school grounds site with the Oils and their entourage.

'I can sit down,' says Pete, 'with Coloured Stone or Ilkari Maru, no worries. But Warumpis . . . because of George, because of Neil, Cookie, the Anderson brothers who've just come back in . . . it's difficult . . .'

He's also feeling uncomfortable about the media presence. The gung-ho crew from 'A Big Country' seem to want to work to a script, expecting the band to set up shots for them rather than just letting it flow and picking up on whatever comes about.

The pair from *The Age* are also getting nervous. Janet Hawley's concerned that the story hasn't started developing, that the interaction with the locals isn't happening. Garrett explains that they can't expect anything to start happening, that it'll take four or five days for everyone to settle into the rhythm of the tour, to grow accustomed to what's going on around them. The media might be geared up for thirty-second grabs, neat stories that drop tidily in a prefabricated format, but out here it's obvious that such an approach isn't going to work.

The Oils believe they've come out here in search of the big story, the deep truth, the insight and the experience, and argue that they're at least aware enough to realise that it's not going to be presented on a platter labelled 'Fit For Media Consumption'.

Over billies of tea and their first feed from the big steel tucker boxes that Charlie's put together, the Oils decide to play at Warakurna, a small community just over the border in Western Australia. The Warumpi Band expected to play there and say the people are disappointed that it's not on the itinerary.

This strikes the hitch-hiker as being rather odd. The Warumpis were due to play Warakurna last year, but the gig was cancelled on a couple of hours' notice when Cookie learnt that Hilary had been in a fight with some of the Warakurna mob in Alice. Someone had been stabbed, and it was considered dangerous for the band to even go near the settlement. A year later, they obviously figure it's been forgotten.

'Okay,' says Pete, 'Let's turn up and see what they say. If they want a concert, we'll play.'

Now that's the way to run a desert tour! If the Oils are prepared to fall in with the swing of things like that, to tune in to the whims of the desert, there shouldn't be too many problems.

But first they've got to get some sleep.

It's their first night in the scrub and they've got to come to grips with their swags. Each person has been supplied with a foam mattress and a sheet of canvas 2.5 metres square. Converting them into wind-proof beds proves to be an amusing chore. The idea is to lay the foam in the middle of the canvas, place blankets and sheets or a sleeping bag on the foam, and then fold the canvas, like an envelope, around it. The resulting swag (or 'Matilda' or 'bluey') is essentially wind- and water-proof, warm and surprisingly comfortable. In the morning it can be rolled up and secured with a length of rope. It's a simple enough exercise, but when attempted by a bunch of green city folk the results are very odd indeed. Lippold dashes about, taping people in with gaffa, threatening to lash them in so securely they'll never be able to escape.

The first person to strike trouble is Garrett. He's borrowed a sleeping bag that's not quite long enough for his 193-centimetre frame, and he has difficulty getting settled while his head and shoulders are exposed to the bitter winter chill.

But at least it's the Dry, and the sky is the clearest any of the city mob have seen for ages.

At two in the morning, sheets of rain pelt the canvas and cold wet figures can be seen stumbling for cover. It's a far cry from the comfort of Yulara.

CHAPTER FOUR
WARAKURNA

Out here in the Western Desert, 700 kilometres from the nearest town, the air's so clear, so untainted by lights and smog, you can lie in your swag at night watching satellites drift across the skies. The Milky Way curls like a trail of sugar across the darkness and shooting stars – the spirits of the dead returning home – tumble from dusk 'til . . .

Dawn comes clean and cold and fast, a thin strip of light that lifts the veil of the night and peels it back, revealing camps in the scrub and people stretching, yawning and cursing the cold, rekindling fires, stomping up and down, huddling over blackened billies and greasy pans, frozen hands outstretched towards the flames.

The mulga crackles and the water boils, and as the sun climbs over the barren blue ridges pannikins of sweet black tea are drunk and feeble jokes about the cuisine are made.

Gary Williams doesn't say a word. Just stands off alone, clutching a mug of tea and wishing he'd jumped off the bus.

Tall and stooped with a bushy black beard, he's a 40-year-old Gurri from Nambucca Heads who's deeply troubled, torn between loyalty to his family and his own sense of self. He's been out here for almost a month now, and though no one else in the touring party's noticed it, he's had more than he can bear.

It was 12 June when he left Sydney, climbing aboard the plane with trembling hands and a pounding heart and the bile rising in his guts, such was his fear of flying. His official brief from Gary Morris had been to fly to Alice as an advance scout, liaise with the desert communities, and then head to the Top End to repeat the process, meeting the elders and the councillors to prepare them for the Oils' arrival.

Unofficially, the brief given by Gary Foley was to safeguard the Aboriginal Arts Board's 15,000-dollar investment by making sure the Warumpi Band got it together for the tour. Williams wanted to stay well out of it, but Foley was his cousin and, in the Aboriginal way, if a cousin needed help it could not be denied.

Foley understood the implications of family. 'Aboriginal values and traditional concepts,' he'd once tried to explain to a Melbourne journalist 'are totally different to the white man. We're not into materialism or this competitive society. We're not into individualism. The basic concept of our society is the extended family. At every point, our society is at complete loggerheads with your society.'

So Gary Williams flew to Alice, went to Mutitjulu to meet with the community, and came out to meet with the elders of Docker River. He was expected to go to Kintore, Yuendumu and Papunya as well, but he skipped them, the last because the blood was bad and Cookie had assured him he'd handle that side of the gig. In 1976, Williams had spent almost a year at Papunya, driving trucks and delivering supplies to the out-stations. But his relations with the current council president were sour, and he didn't want to go back.

So he went to Darwin, but instead of visiting the settlements, he hung around until the community representatives came into town for an NLC meeting. Satisfied that he'd done his job, he returned to Alice to await the arrival of the Oils.

For the past three years he's been pursuing a career as an actor and a scriptwriter, but now, when he'd rather be at home behind a typewriter, he's back out here.

At Uluru he confronted Gary Morris and told him he'd had enough. There was no need for him to stay on the tour. He'd done his job and now he just wanted to go home, to get away from the madness of the exercise – from the flashy egos of these whitefellas from the city. (He didn't mention the pay back – the fact that he'd heard rumours in Alice that, if he returned to the desert, he'd be punished for the thumping Neil Murray copped in Sydney at the hands of Foley's minders. A beating? A spear in the leg? He didn't know, and he didn't want to hang around to find out.) 'Look, this is no use,' he told Morris. 'I'm goin' back.'

But instead of letting him go, Morris gave him the role of advance scout, sending him ahead with the roadies to meet people and introduce them to the band.

Williams is beginning to feel he's only here because he's got a darker skin than Gary Morris, as though he's something to look at and focus on. The management side of the operation, he figures, are off in a world of their own. Since Uluru, Gary Morris has become everything to everybody. The only people Williams feels comfortable with are Lippold and Pickett. They, at least, are down to earth; a couple of workers on the road without any of the pretensions he sees in the rest of the party.

He stands by the fire, one hand in the pocket of his baggy khaki work trousers, the other holding a mug of tea. The beanie on his head is pulled down low and the sleeves on his flannelette check shirt have been rolled to the wrists.

He might be here on his cousin's behalf, but now he's getting fed up with the whole idea of the trip, with the presence of the cameras and the demands of the management, and all he wants to do is fade away.

A couple of metres away, Charlie McMahon cooks up a damper in the camp oven – a big black cast-iron pot that sits on the coals – and Garrett stands chatting to Phillip Toyne, the Central Land

Council lawyer who's flown in to meet the band en route to Warakurna.

Toyne, in his mid-thirties, is roughly the same age as Garrett, and almost as tall. In the mid-1970s, when Garrett tossed his law degree in a drawer and started cleaning taxis and squash court toilets while he was waiting for the other band members to finish their courses, Toyne was doing his articles with Clyde Holding. With sympathies that, in many ways, ran parallel to Garrett's, he moved to Alice Springs a couple of years later to represent the Pitjantjatjara, Yankunytjatjara and Ngaanyatjara people whose traditional lands spread across the deserts of the Northern Territory and South and Western Australia.

In 1979, Toyne lodged the historic Uluru land claim on behalf of the Pitjantjatjara Council, which led to the Rock's return to its traditional owners in October 1985. (Toyne has since been appointed Director of the Australian Conservation Foundation.)

'I'm finding it difficult,' Garrett says, 'to grasp the sense of time here. In fact, I'm about a million miles away from it. There's no concept of the future. People blow their money as if there's no point in saving for tomorrow, whereas everyone over our side is preparing for when they hit 55 or something.'

Over breakfast, Toyne offers Garrett and Hardie a lift to Warakurna in his single-engined Piper, allowing them the opportunity to get into the community before the media and the rest of the invading forces arrive on the scene. As they're chatting, the film crew who flew in for last night's performance take off and head back to Alice. Among their number is journalist Erwin Chlanda who's preparing to file the first story to have come out of the tour. Published in the *Centralian Advocate* under the headline 'Oils on show at Docker River; who cares?', the conclusion reached was that 'it was pretty obvious the concert was doing a lot more for the Oils than its audience'.

Toyne, Garrett and Hardie lift off at nine, droning across the litter-strewn valley floor, wings dipping as they sweep over the settlement and climb for the flight along the ranges. As the motor fades, mangy dogs howl in the distance and fat black crows perched in the bloodwoods caw a lonesome echo.

An SSB radio transceiver erupts. Wild staccato bursts of chatter hammer the air. Charlie's rigged it up to his Toyota's battery, its aerial draped across the dust-encrusted bonnet. On air, bites of squelch punctuate riotous gossip sessions in the languages of the desert.

In a region without telephone boxes, television stations, commercial radio networks, newspapers and advertisements, the chatter frequencies provide the news and the entertainment. Anyone can listen in as problems are discussed with the Royal Flying Doctor Service in Alice Springs and telegrams are sent and received.

Standing by the open bonnet, Rob Hirst is in fine spirits, in spite of admissions that, as an asthmatic, he can hardly sing or play or breathe because of the dust.

To *Age* journalist Janet Hawley – a senior features writer whose assignments have taken her to the Philippines, the Middle East, Nepal, the US, the UK and Europe – Hirst is the only member of the band who seems to be approachable. As outgoing and compliant as always, he explains the role of the SSB.

'For instance, if you get bitten by a Western Plains . . .'

'Death adder,' Janet adds hopefully.

'Grandpa Redback, right, and you're lying there dying, I just get on this and *Nine Sierra Hotel Tango calling VJD* and she talks to someone else, so I keep doing that, you're dying there, right . . .'

'Yes,' the journalist nods dubiously.

'And I'm still trying to call. And finally she goes *Nine Sierra Hotel Tango, go ahead, over.* And then I ring up and say *We've got someone dying of a death adder bite, whaddo I do?* And they say *Don't worry, we'll get the doctor on line,* and he instructs us to do a bit of first-aid, right.'

'Yes, yes.'

'*Put the knife in the fire . . .*'

And they both crack up.

The first of the Toyotas pulls out of Docker an hour later. Still glistening from the rain, it's streaked with mud. The red dust swept up by the rain and propelled towards the earth with the splashing brush of a child's painting has set like the rust stains dribbling from an old tanker's bow.

'I didn't expect this country to be so green,' Rotsey remarks to no one in particular. 'I expected it to be a lot more . . . inhospitable.'

As they head west towards the border, Jim Moginie gazes in awe at the Petermanns, the most beautiful hills he could ever want to see, looking as if they've been sand-blasted for millions of years. It's such a different environment from any that he's experienced. It's as though the country they're travelling through isn't a part of the Australia that he's so familiar with. He doesn't recognise any of the landmarks; gets the feeling that he's a visitor, an outsider, an alien who doesn't belong here.

Moginie grew up in Gordon on Sydney's North Shore, the son of 'a businessman who did a few things. He sold the blinds that used to be put in shop windows to protect pairs of shoes or the dresses in the displays. They didn't really take off much. Then he sold used cars, and he ended up making carbon paper, and then he went out of business because of the copying machines. He was bought out.'

Like the rest of the band, Jim's tall and well built, though on stage he gives the impression of being frail and awkward because of his concentration. He's always pale and his eyes stand out like dots on his face, an effect that was even more pronounced when he took to wearing a beard. He's got suspect taste in shirts, favouring loud paisley designs, and to look at him you'd never guess he has one of the weirdest, most fertile musical brains around.

He led 'a pretty sheltered life', and got right into The Beatles ('the first album I ever bought was the *White Album*'), and went to Sydney Church of England Grammar ('it wasn't a particularly great school to go to'). His first guitar was a Westone, and his first amplifier was built from a kit. 'It didn't have a case, it was just this steel thing with valves sticking out the top, and I'd carry it around in a cardboard box.'

As a teenager, he set up a music room in the upstairs part of his parents' house and spent much of his youth cloistered away, playing with guitars and keyboards.

Rob Hirst recalls that Jim 'was very isolated from the rest of the world. He didn't ever seem to leave the upstairs part of that house. You wouldn't have called him a particularly socially adept person. He was always reserved, much less outgoing than he is now.'

Of his teenage years, Jim once said, 'That Upper North Shore environment is not very conducive to anything like this; there's nothing happening at all around you. You've got to go to the railway station if you want to talk to anybody, or go to the milkbar. For a while, there wasn't much else for me, so I thought "oh well I'll just play music and learn something." I guess everyone's got their way. If you're a teenager or whatever, you've got your way of expressing yourself, or your way of doing things, and the way I did things for a while was pretty weird. I wouldn't blame school completely.'

It was this environment that subsequently produced such songs of suburban alienation as 'Nothing Lost, Nothing Gained'.

Like Rob and Martin, Jim went to Sydney University where he did a science degree and post-graduate studies in acoustic engineering. Les Karski, the expatriot Englishman who produced the Oils' second album, *Head Injuries,* and the *Bird Noises* EP, holds the view that Jim is 'about the closest thing I've met to a musical genius'.

One of Sydney's most innovative and meticulous songwriters, out here he's overwhelmed by the space and the conditions, and that feeling of alienation.

Trailing a curtain of dust, the Toyotas cross the border at a point marked only by a yellow arrow on a 2-metre pole. The WA–NT had been hand-painted in blue. Behind it, across a grey spinifex sea, the hills are barren, the red glow of their rocky outcrops betraying the strength of their iron content.

In season, it's a good road for finding bush bananas: small green fruit that are cooked in the coals and chewed like a gum. The skin tastes like peas. The white fibrous material beneath, though good for quenching the thirst, lacks the consistency of chewing gum.

During the summer months, it's also a good road for goanna.

It's March 1985, and as the Warumpi Band head south, their Toyota Coaster jolting down the track to the old Warburton mission, a shout goes up and everyone scrambles for the windows.

Cookie slams on the brakes, the doors jerk open and the rest of the boys pile out, bolting across the desert, scooping up sticks and rocks as they run. They've spotted a goanna ambling across the track and, with the excitement of blokes who've eaten nothing but burgers and baked beans for a week, they chase after it with eager, babbling, laughing glee.

The goanna belts up a beefwood tree and the guys start jumping around, hurling the rocks and the sticks and a tyre lever at it. Every time the tyre lever hits the branches it bounces off with a resonant 'pting' and clatters to the ground.

As rocks and the tyre lever spin through the air around him, George Rurrambu scampers up the gnarled trunk of the tree, chasing the goanna out on to the thinnest limbs. Clinging desperately to the rough, furrowed bark with long sharp claws, its tail flat against the violently shaking branch, the goanna loses its grip, bellyflops to the earth and takes off, scurrying across the sand, darting through a spinifex ring and diving into a hole, its tail whipping about as a lethal shower of stones rains down.

Roadie Ian Anderson Tjampitjinpa lumbers after it, locating the hole and, using the tyre lever as a spade, sends clouds of red dust billowing into the air. A minute or so passes in a frantic flurry of digging and scooping, and then Ian lets out a glorious peal of laughter and drags the scrawny reptile out by its tail.

Sammy Butcher holds the tyre lever horizontally as Ian swings the goanna around and around, dashing its head against the metal with a splat and thud.

After all the excitement, Hilary Wirri has retired to the bus, so the limp goanna is poked through the window and lobbed on to his shoulder. Built like the proverbial brick dunny, Hilary jumps with a scream and the bus rocks drunkenly back and forth on its springs. A few minutes later, as the bus rolls down the road, the goanna regains consciousness and proceeds to crawl around the bus, its head wavering gently and dripping with blood. The tyre lever is retrieved and the creature finished off, but not before more laughs at Hilary's expense.

Just north of Warburton, they pull on to the side of the track to boil a billy at dusk. While the others dig a pit and gather armloads of mulga bleached white by the sun, Neil Murray takes the goanna further into the scrub, cutting a neat incision in its belly and dragging out the slippery blue strings of its guts.

Back at the fire, George Rurrambu flings the carcass on to the flames to stiffen and seal it, and after searing its leathery skin, buries it in the coals and waits. The goanna is barely a metre long, but no one's about to pass up the taste of fresh bush tucker. The meat is lean and white. In texture and taste, it's not unlike chicken.

Out on the Gunbarrel Highway, Warakurna's in the middle of nowhere. To the north lies the Great Sandy Desert. To the west, the Gibson Desert and stories of explorers like Giles and, later, Carnegie who kidnapped Aborigines, tied them to his camels and fed them on salted beef until, in desperation, the hostages led him to water. To the south lies the Great Victoria Desert and the cancerous legacy of the atomic testing program at Maralinga. Conducted in the 1950s, the British nuclear tests spread radio-active fallout far and wide. Aborigines found in the immediate testing area were rounded up, trucked off their homelands, and dumped in settlements so foreign to their traditional way of life that many were killed by the sheer trauma of their dispossession. Others among the nomads escaped detection and they, unable to read the warning signs that had been erected for their benefit, were engulfed in the rolling, choking clouds of oily black smoke. Just how many of them died or were blinded or cut down by radiation sickness can never be ascertained.

The nearest slice of civilisation, 700 kilometres to the south-west, is Laverton, a gold- and nickel-mining town in which you'd need a digital watch to find a good time. To the east, back along the corrugations of the Gunbarrel Highway, lies Uluru and, over 700 Ks away, Alice Springs.

At a point a couple of kilometres east of Warakurna, the Gunbarrel swings north on to the air-strip at Giles, the junction marked only by a sign warning motorists to be alert for aircraft on the road.

Giles, the most remote weather station on the continent, was established in 1956. A couple of years later, its contingent of meteorologists was joined by personnel from the Weapons Research Establishment whose interests lay with the Woomera Rocket Range in South Australia. Within the compound a legacy of that program sits like a twisted old water tank in the gravel. Next to a fence of white pipes skewering 44-gallon drums, it's the remains of a Blue Streak rocket that came down in the desert and was found by wandering Aborigines. They reported it as a crashed plane. An investigative team was sent out, warning the locals that it was important that no one approach the wreckage. The team tried to blow it up, but failed, and eventually it was trucked into Giles where it sits among the antennae and the satellite dishes, the incinerators and the rusting aerials of the modern world. From the refuse of the space age to that of the stone age is a five-minute drive.

Heralded by shredded tyres, overturned cars and the sign that became a catch phrase for the rest of the tour – STRICT RULES – Warakurna sprawls in the dust: a smattering of prefabricated metal shacks, steel power poles, the occasional twisted and gnarled tree, its lower branches stripped for firewood, and great stockades of abandoned cars that threaten to dwarf even the rugged red hills that climb from the plains.

The convoy of Toyotas rolls into the settlement, swinging into formation around the demountable council office. Out hop crews of musicians and roadies and support personnel, who take it all in with dustbitten eyes: the wastelands and the rubbish, the disintegrating cars, the bedraggled people and the mangy, limping dogs.

In front of the metal-clad store, young kids with snot dribbling from their noses and eyes caked with flies push cans attached to lengths of rusty fencing wire across the dirt. Resembling crude toy lawnmowers they rattle and roll through the litter, bouncing and clanging across the hard-baked earth.

Stage manager Michael Lippold pulls out a football and the kids swarm around, shooting stab passes and drop kicks, lobbing torpedoes and drop punts, showing off skills that have long since passed from vogue in the cities. While the film crew and everyone else wander around trying to look inconspicuous, Lippold works with the psychology of integration and acceptance.

With a catch cry of 'Hold it!' that's soon bastardised by every kid in the neighbourhood into a giggling war cry of 'Oldeeet!', he breaks the ice and wins a legion of fans.

Pat Pickett and Garrett and the hitch-hiker join in, slamming the ball through the air and jostling for the mark. But when the hitch-hiker goes the knuckle, getting rough as he goes up against Lippold, Garrett shoots him a look that says 'Strict Rules: behave yourself'. 'Oils vibe' Lippold called it, and no one ever got closer to it than him. It was a little sign that flashed peace, love and understanding, and meant that whatever primordial instincts overtook you, whatever drunken excesses you felt inspired to indulge in, whatever mean and vicious and lusty thoughts you entertained, when you were around the Oils, when you were associated with them as a roadie or a journalist or a fan, you had a responsibility to be on your best behaviour.

As kids run squealing barefoot through the dust and the footy bounces off the metal walls of the council office with a dull clang, the truck rumbles in and the road cases rattle out – a train of black boxes.

The rest of the whitefella party – Stephanie Lewis and Glad Reed, Martin Rotsey, Rob Hirst, Peter Gifford, Jim Moginie and his wife Claire, Martin Hardie, Janet and Ray from *The Age* – wander off in search of a place to have lunch.

Lo and behold, in what Charlie McMahon recalls as one of the most bizarre sights of the tour, they plonk themselves down beneath a wall of abandoned cars, sitting on the only patch of lush green grass between Alice Springs and Kalgoorlie. There they sit, on a tiny island of grass in the middle of the desert, having a picnic.

The hitch-hiker wanders over and he too squats in the grass, shaking his head and trying to work out why he's got a sense of *déjà* vu. And then it hits him: it's Kurnell. Kurnell's the point on Botany Bay at which Captain Cook first landed in 1770. The spot is marked by a plaque, and without it this tour need never have happened.

> The natives resolutely disputed the landing 'although they were but two, and we thirty or forty at least.'
>
> Parleying with these two continued for about quarter of an hour. They remained resolute, so a musket was fired over them, the effect of which was that the youngest of the two dropped a bundle of lances on the rock ... He, however, snatched them up again and both renewed their threats and opposition. A musket loaded with small shot was now fired at the eldest of the two who was about 40 yards from the boat, it struck him on the legs but he minded it very little, so another was immediately fired at him, on this he ran up to the house about 100 yards distant and soon returned with a shield. In the meantime we had landed on the rock.
>
> FROM THE DIARY OF JOSEPH BANKS,
> 28 APRIL 1770

It's a weird place, Kurnell. Captain Cook's Landing Place is a spot favoured on weekends by European migrants who spread their picnic blankets beneath the pinetrees and gaze out over the bay, at the rust-streaked tankers and the container ships and the industrious glow of the refineries, the bulk terminals and the power station. Green grass and industrial waste.

Warakurna hadn't even been on the itinerary a day ago, had only been suggested last night, and yet here they are – Midnight Oil, a band that usually books its gigs three months ahead – hoeing into lunch, staring with disbelieving eyes at the filth and the squalor that surrounds them.

Like the midden heaps of bleached and brittle shells that litter the sand dunes of the coast where, for thousands of years, ceremonial feasts were held, abandoned cars plaster the desert.

When the brute dies push it on to the side of the road and tear its guts out. Conduct an organ transplant and hit the toe again. Registration and road-worthiness certificates don't count for *pantu* out here, 'cos there aren't any coppers within cooee.

The settlements – studded with engine blocks and axles, buckled wheels and rusting diffs, where clumps of spinifex grow through a bent chassis and bald tyres are treasured – are the breeding grounds of the bush mechanics. Blokes like Ian Anderson can take an automatic Fairlane and strip it, converting it to a manual in a couple of days. To hell with mufflers. To hell with starter motors. Never let 'em stop between dawn 'n' dusk, just keep rolling.

The cars are like grandfather's axe, but rather than the replacement of handles and heads, it's the engines and panels and portable parts that are recycled. Abandoned cars on the side of the track have invariably been stripped bare, and their roofs caved in by kids using them as trampolines.

For the nomadic people of the desert, cars have been a godsend.

The increased mobility has allowed them to organise bigger 'business' ceremonies than ever, allowing hundreds of people to gather to carry out their traditional tribal rituals and obligations. If they'd done it on such a large scale in the past, the ground would've perished in a few days. Now they can truck people in from all over the desert, hold their ceremonies, and send hunting parties out in Toyotas to bring back enough food for all.

For the men of the desert, it's nothing to win 2,000 dollars in a game of cards, buy a car and go visiting friends and relatives hundreds of kilometres away. (One rarely sees a woman behind the wheel – some role-playing traditions obviously die hard.) The cars are symbols of temporary status in a society that has so few.

'If it's got four on the floor, mag wheels and a klaxon horn,' says Cookie, 'it'll be big in Papunya. Get three grand for it at least.' And if the car doesn't die on the side of the road, chances are it'll be given away to a relative in need. To buy a Falcon sedan in the morning and swap it for a ute in the afternoon isn't considered to be unstable behaviour. European concepts of ownership and the protection of possessions are so alien out here that the idea of maintaining the 'family car' for more than a couple of weeks would be laughable. Cars are disposable, things to be bought and sold and used and dumped.

Back outside the council office Lippold's getting jumpy. Here he is in Warakurna, some place he's never even heard of, and the difficulties of operating with a two-man crew are becoming painfully apparent. There are dogs soiling the mike leads, the Warumpis' crew seems to be working in another time zone, and Martin Hardie's locked himself away in the council office.

Oblivious to the mounting tension, Hardie sits by the radio telephone, organising aircraft for the Top End. The transponders are howling, phrases are lost in the static, words speeding up and slowing down as if someone's playing with pitch control. 'VJD,' says Hardie, 'this is Six Alpha Mike Sierra again. Is there any possibility of making another call? Over.'

'Six Alpha Mike Sierra, if you can stand by for about a minute and a half when I call the list, I'll put you on top of the next list, over.'

'Okay.'

Outside the window, Pat Pickett kicks the PA into action, the speakers booming with Pete Townshend's *White City*, an album that sounds, in this environment, jarring and violent and unbearably cacophonous. (A more appropriate choice would have been tapes by Slim Dusty or 'The Singin' Bushman' Brian Young: tapes that would give people a familiar thrill instead of shattering their sensibilities.)

With a few minutes to spare before he can bounce his next call through to Darwin, Hardie steps outside.

Lippold's working his butt off. He's covered in dust, the knees have been torn out of his jeans, the furrows on his forehead are deeply etched and the sweat is itchy in his beard. When he sees Hardie, he strikes.

'What the hell do you think you're doing?!' he yells. 'Sittin' on your fat bum all day when we need a hand out here!'

'Oh piss off, I'm busy,' says Hardie.

Lippold jumps, his forehead flicking forward to within a hair's breadth of Hardie's. The tour manager, his bottom lip quivering, steps back. He plunges his hands deep into the pockets of his combat jacket and stalks away. But it's obvious that he's got the message. He retreats to his position by the radio-telephone in the council office and keeps well out of the way.

Outside the community store, people stand in small jabbering groups, watching the road crew trundle their black boxes through the dust. Shy people, they stand back, watching with a mixture of animated bemusement and reserved curiosity.

Between their scarred black legs, mangy dogs limp and scoot away. Scrawny creatures missing great patches of fur, they serve a multitude of purposes: keeping the place clean by eating discarded scraps, acting as guard dogs by giving fair warning of the approach of strangers to the bush camps and out-stations, and by keeping people warm in the bone-chilling depths of winter. Everywhere you look, there are dogs cowering and fighting and rolling in the dust.

And through the early afternoon, when the winter sun is at its zenith in an iridescent blue sky, a young camel plods around munching on apples and cans of Coke and cigarettes and anything else it's offered, while young boys sit behind Rob's kit hammering out rhythms on the snare as Rob stands behind them, racing them, pummelling the skins with another pair of sticks and a grin as bright as the day.

It's still daylight when the Oils go on, playing on the ground-level verandah of the council office. Six kids sit in the dust in front of the fold-back desk, not daring to dance to this strange band. Ten metres away, behind the front-of-house desk, black faces peer through dusty windscreens as groups of men watch the show from the warmth of their cars. Windows are wound up tight to keep out the wind and maybe the noise. Over by the store, bunches of women and children stand and squat by the fence, curious but giving little away, shy of these shameless whitefellas jumping around and making such a racket.

On the other side of the courtyard, whites from Warakurna and Giles sit on the fence and the fenders of Toyotas, welcoming this novel break from their schedules.

The band plays a stack of new songs. There being no recognition factor (Midnight *Who?* . . . Power and the what?) they can afford to work the new songs in. Kicking off with 'Dead Heart' and 'Best Of Both Worlds' the set includes the first live renditions of 'Put Down That Weapon', 'Kokoda', 'Beds Are Burning' and 'Celebrate' mixed in with 'Kosciusko', 'Pictures', 'Helps Me Helps You', 'Jimmy Sharman's Boxers', 'Power and the Passion' and 'Read About It'.

But it's the young camel that steals the show, bucking and kicking like a dancing dervish, chasing people and being chased until its performance during 'Power and the Passion' brings the band to a halt. They're laughing so much they just can't keep it together, and the whole song collapses in a screaming heap as Garrett tries to dodge the camel and Lippold struggles to throw it off stage.

Charlie McMahon gets up to blow some frenetic didgeridoo and before leaving the stage he takes the mike and introduces himself as Marra Hook from Kintore, explaining that the Oils are his friends and therefore 'friends of Aboriginal people'. But when he says 'Thank you' the people by the fence get up and quickly disperse, figuring the whole gig's over and that, in the interests of politeness, it's time to go home.

When the Oils finish, people crowd around the back of the truck buying t-shirts and cassettes. Midnight Oil have three cassettes on sale: *10, 9, 8, 7, 6, 5, 4, 3, 2, 1*, *Red Sails In the Sunset* and *Species*

Deceases. But it's only *Red Sails* that makes an impression. To people who live under open skies in the desert, *Red Sails* is the most attractive with its cover artwork of blue skies and red dirt. By the end of the day the merchandising tally reaches eight copies of the cassette and fifteen t-shirts. (The t-shirts are adorned with the tour logo of two hands – one black, one white – clasped in a handshake. The white hand is obviously limp, the black one strong. The Oils shook a lot of hands in the bush, but there were no comments about the irony of the logo.)

Warumpi Band follow the Oils and turn in a great performance that's marred only by the banter between Rurrambu and Garrett. Under the cultural law that the dead should not be named, the Blackfella-Whitefella entourage has been warned that a man from Warakurna whose name was Peter recently died. Therefore Peters Garrett and Gifford are to be referred to as Kumanjayl, as is George Rurrambu because he shares the Christian name of Sammy and Gordon's father. Such observance of protocol is, however, easy to forget in the heat of the moment, and during the Warumpis' set Rurrambu calls to Garrett from the stage. Waving to the Oils singer, he yells, 'How ya doin, Peter? Orright?'

Garrett, forgetting the situation, makes the same faux pas. 'Fine thanks, George.'

While the Warumpis are playing, Charlie McMahon checks with the locals to ascertain where it's safe to camp, to find out which land isn't *milmilpa* sacred, which land isn't in the domain of the spirits.

He's directed to a creekbed a couple of kilometres from town and, one by one, the Toyotas pull out of Warakurna, bouncing over ridges and sliding in the sand until the spot is reached. As dusk descends, firewood is gathered and blazes light the night.

Three days into the tour and already the whitefellas have split into half-a-dozen camps. The lines have been drawn and the hierarchy established. At the centre of the vortex stand the Oils. On the furthest outskirts, floundering for information, are the working press from the Melbourne *Age*.

Strung out along the creekbed, the separate camps can be pinpointed from a distance by the glow of the fires. To the southwest lies the Oils' camp. The next is their crew's. Further on lies 'A Big Country' HQ. The boys from the ABC are doing it in style with a blinding arc light in the trees, chairs under a canopy and their own private cook. They'd originally wanted Charlie to take the job. He'd been featured in an earlier program and they knew that he had mastered the art of cooking over an open fire. But Charlie was nobody's fool and he certainly wasn't about to sign himself on as chief cook and dishwasher for a bunch of urban cowboys with cameras and recorders and nebulous ideas for a script. So when he ran into a girl named Liz, who was holidaying in Alice, he told her about the gig. She jumped at the chance of hitting the road with her favourite band, and it wasn't until too late that the ABC lads discovered she was a raging Oils fan who'd never cooked more than water in her life.

They were red meat eaters and she was a vegetarian. Her culinary strengths were initially exposed at Mutitjulu when she put chillies in the damper, and then cooked the bush bread in a camp oven over the open flames, rather than burying it in the coals. The results were as black as their collective mood.

The smoke drifting through the spinifex to the east comes from Charlie's camp. And while the ABC mob are using their burnt offerings to hammer out the dings in their Toyota, Charlie's eating like a king, pottering around with an array of dishes laid out on the down-turned sideboard of his truck.

Further out are the white Hi-Ace and blue directors chairs of the pair from *The Age*. There's Ray Kennedy, a balding photographer in a navy blue *Age Locker Room* windcheater, and journalist Janet Hawley, who's forsaken a boating holiday with her husband because of what she considers to be the significance of this tour.

Off another 20 metres or so is the camp of Gary Morris, Stephanie Lewis and Glad Reed.

On the high ground to the west, the biggest fire glow reveals the position of the Warumpis' camp. Away from the sandy bed and the whitefellas who so outnumber them, the Warumpis and their crew – shy desert people who rarely feel comfortable in the overwhelming company of city-bred whites – have fired up a blaze that blisters the air and heats the lining of their swags. (Because this is unfamiliar country – it's another tribe's land, and the implications of that, in terms of the spirits that dwell here, are very strong indeed – they're reluctant to stray from the light of their fire.)

Stews are cooked in camp ovens and, over billies of tea, Garrett and Morris meet with the crews from *The Age* and 'A Big Country' to discuss their approaches to the project. *The Age* want greater access and co-operation from the Oils. Janet Hawley's feeling increasingly frustrated by her isolation from the bands. She's finding great difficulty in getting a story because Midnight Oil appear to be suspicious of her every move. In the process, as she perceives it, they're acting like a bunch of 'colonialist jailors'.

The ABC, on the other hand, seem to want to work to a script, to be given advance warning of when things are going to happen; a situation that's impossible to dictate in a land where the priorities are never geared to the whims of television and deadlines.

The session drags on for hours. A meeting with Ngaatjatjarra elders has been arranged for the morning and *The Age* photographer wants to shoot blackfellas meeting whitefellas.

'No!' cries Garrett 'We're trying to create a story, not kill one.'

Ray Kennedy jumps up, yelling, 'Censorship!'

'Look,' Garrett argues, 'if we're going to get a story, it's going to be done our way or not at all.' Fuming at the problems he's having with the media, Pete then storms out and tramps up the creekbed in the darkness to see if the Warumpis are still awake.

At dawn, swags glisten under a crystalline veneer of ice – the first desert frost Charlie McMahon can remember – and all around them the hardy grey grasses glitter silver in the coldest light of day.

As the sun climbs above the ridges and burns the frost from the spinifex plains, Peter Garrett and Rob Hirst, Gary Williams and Gary Morris, and the crews from the ABC and *The Age* head off for the meeting with the tribal elders. But Gary Williams doesn't want to be a part of it. It's not his country and the whole exercise is only being arranged for the benefit of the Oils and the television cameras.

'We want you there,' argues Gary Morris. 'We need you there.'

'I don't believe this,' thinks Williams. 'I don't believe it and I don't need it. I don't want to sit down in a stream with this mob. I met the man, we're friends, but this acting for the television cameras has got nothing to do with me.'

In the shadow of the desert oaks, they squat by a fire in a creekbed, hearing tales of the region's past. For thousands of years the Ngaatjatjarra and Ngaanyatjarra people have been living here, hunting and gathering food from the desert and upholding the lore and the laws of a complex tribal society. For thousands of years they lived untouched by the outside world. But in the 1930s prospectors swept through from the west in search of Lasseter's mythical reef of gold and the 'sorry times' erupted with the stench of cordite and the gut-wrenching taste of strychnine. Some people were chained to logs and forced to cook for the newcomers. Others were shot or fed slabs of damper laced with poison.

Fifty years later, the tribal elders sit in a creekbed recounting the stories. The creekbed has been the scene of too much violence. Shootings and poisonings and kidnappings that have left an indelible scar on the souls of those who survived: a sense of horror that hangs over the land like the harsh desert sun.

In a blue beanie and matching lumberjacket, Garrett directs the line of conversation, as he will in each subsequent meeting, probing, questioning, seeking answers and tales while the cameras roll and the VU meters jump.

'So, how many people's families here would've been shot and killed in that time? It's not that long ago really, is it . . . Any of your relatives, Thomas?'

Another elder prompts him. 'Your father was poisoned . . . in this creekbed now . . . where we are . . .'

Thomas sits, fiddling with a stick. 'Yeah, this creek . . . They just spread a bit of poison on the piece of bread and give it to them just like a dog. And um . . . my uncle got shot . . . and my father escaped . . . and that old fella, Wally Porter, he was up on that hill there, lookin' down, and he seen my old father crawlin' across here and he came and just carried him up that hill . . .'

CHAPTER FIVE
KINTORE

There's a palpable air of excitement about reaching today's destination. Out there, just inside the Northern Territory border, about 200 Ks nor-nor-east of Warakurna and 500 Ks west of Alice Springs, lies the revolutionary settlement of Kintore. These days, it's home for 500 Pintupi people. Five years ago, it didn't exist.

The Warumpis are keen to get to Kintore because it's familiar country. They have friends and relatives living there; they know the language and have a deep affinity with the people.

And the Oils are looking forward to it because Charlie McMahon, one of the advisors who helped in the setting up of the community, has been telling them about the place for a couple of years now.

The track north to Kintore still isn't marked on most maps. It winds through the desert, skirting the gleaming salt pans of Lake Hopkins and the barren slopes of the Bonython Ranges. Hardie sits in the front vehicle, his glasses coated in a fine film of dust. In his lap there's a clear plastic sack stuffed with Army survey maps. He's been out here a week now, and already he's become a topographic map fiend. While others flick through old magazines or stare vacantly through the mud-smeared glass at the saltbush sweeping past in a blue-grey blanket that stretches to the horizon, Hardie keeps an eye on the charts, noting the ranges, the bores, the changes in the country.

He jabs his finger into a hill and it scrunches into a crater on his thigh. 'Kintorelakutu!'

'Whassat?'

'Towards Kintore!'

An eagle lifts off from the side of the track with slow, graceful flaps, its huge wings languidly, poetically sweeping through the air. Its wings are a couple of metres across, and as it lifts you know that it's in no hurry to get anywhere; the bird knows there's no other creature on the planet that can outclass it.

The dust billows out across the saltbush, over dunes crocheted with spinifex, into the shady groves of the desert oak. Swept up by a howling wind it scuds towards the ranges, rushing through canyons, brushing the ancient paintings of serpents that slither up their walls.

'Whose country's this?'

'Pintupi . . .'

The Pintupi were about the last to come in . . . and the first to go back. Because of their sheer isolation, because of the scorched desolation of the Gibson Desert, the history of their contact with whites is unlike that of any other tribe in the country.

Their land seeps deep into the Gibson Desert in Western Australia and, on the Tropic of Capricorn, it cuts across the border and into the Northern Territory. Not that they're conscious of such boundaries. For them, the borders are those they share in common with the Luritja to the east, the Warlpiri and the Kukatja to the north and the Ngaatjatjarra and Pitjantjatjara to the south.

When Australia's first nuclear reactor was being opened at Lucas Heights, the Pintupi were still sleeping by campfires with dogs. When the Soviets celebrated the launch of the world's first satellite, the Pintupi were still hunting with a woomera and spears.

Tietkins touched on their country in 1880; so too did Carnegie in 1897. In those days, there were lots of possums and heaps of *ninu*, members of the bandicoot family. But in the 1920s, before the Pintupi had ever seen a white man, cats straying from the missions further east moved in and wiped out the traditional tucker. So the Pintupi took to eating the cats.

In the 1930s, a few whites appeared on the scene. Mostly, they were missionaries pushing camels across the desert. Unlike the people further east, the Pintupi weren't greeted with guns but with bags of flour and cast-off clothes. The missionaries tried to lure those they met back to the settlement at Haasts Bluff, hoping to introduce them to God, the King and the European way, the English language and the joys of the Protestant work ethic. A few of them followed, more likely out of curiosity than any desire to redeem their souls. And others followed them, again, from curiosity as well as the traditional desire to maintain contact with relations. Some stayed, but most headed back into the bush. Twenty years later they were still out there . . . still *myall*.

Eight hundred kilometres to the south, the British were exploding nuclear bombs at Maralinga and Emu Field.

As the western world slipped noisily into the '60s, the Western Desert was hit by the biggest drought that had been recorded since the turn of the century. Kangaroos held off in their breeding cycles, which are geared to the seasons. In a good season, the female roo gestates three offspring at a time. One climbs into the pouch as a joey, the other two remain in embryo form until the first has left the pouch or another good season arrives. By 1963, the roos were holding off. All but the most reliable soaks had dried up and food was scarce.

The Pintupi roamed across the desert, searching for soaks in the rocks and the caves and the sand, scouring the earth for food. Word got around that their numbers were falling.

Officers from the Native Affairs Branch were sent out in trucks to effect an evacuation. 'A truck loaded with water and rations,' noted one of the patrol officers, 'is nothing short of bribery to these people who have a life bordering on starvation.'

Some now argue that the Pintupi were in no danger at all, and that the Government simply used the drought as a convenient excuse to bring them in.

The program of assimilation that was being pursued decreed that Aborigines should be brought up to the standards of white society, that they should be prepared for integration into the modern world. But as there was little work for them in the towns, it was decided that they'd be better off assimilating among themselves for a generation or so, and they were herded into government settlements like Papunya.

Those people trucked into Papunya included Luritja, Warlpiri, Anmatjirra, Aranda and Pintupi.

'The idea of Papunya,' says Charlie, 'was that all the Pintupi people would be turned into carpenters or labourers or whatever. But it totally failed. They put people in mess halls for food, they put 'em into khaki clothes, into work gangs, and they'd try to send the kids off to school.'

More trucks were sent into the desert to find the remaining Pintupi. In April 1964, of the seventy-one Pintupi people sighted on the fringes of the Gibson Desert, forty-two were taken into Papunya. It took the number who'd 'come in' since 1963 to seventy-two. By August, thirty-five of them were dead.

For some, the sudden imposition of European food killed them. 'That tucker been kill 'em,' recalled Nosepeg Tjupurrala. 'They spew and spew alla time when they eat that tucker.'

Ten people died from malnutrition, eight from pneumonia, eleven from chest and gastro infections, heart failure, tumours and injuries. A further four died from unknown causes.

They'd been yanked out of the stone age and thrust into houses, into a community with people from foreign tribes. And even among people of their own colour they were considered *myall* – wild blacks who were treated with contempt because they didn't know how to get water from taps or eat with a knife or fork.

'They lived like bloody dogs,' says Neil Murray. 'They were looked down upon because they weren't used to clothes and stuff like that. A lot of people died through grog, killings, disease, car crashes...'

'Half the adult population of the Pintupi,' says Charlie, 'died in the first ten years, and the infant death rate was around about 50 per cent.'

The Pintupi, who'd been spared for so long, had finally had 'the sorry times' thrust upon them. They'd been denied access to their land and, by definition, that meant they'd been denied access to their culture, their religion, and their traditional diet. They'd been thrust into the trappings of a foreign culture that their own history had not prepared them for.

The effects of enforced settlement were devastating for Aborigines throughout the country. Settlement life invariably meant the denial of traditional forms of tucker, the imposition of culturally inappropriate living conditions, the loss of cultural identity, the disintegration of traditional forms of authority, and access to alcohol.

In 1970, in what was then seen as a radical and regressive move, a number of Aborigines who were living in Maningrida, a coastal settlement in Arnhem Land, moved back to their traditional country, establishing camps in the bush and resuming their traditional lifestyles. The bush camps they set up became known as out-stations or homeland centres.

Despite initial white opposition to the move, it's one that's been taken up by communities throughout the Territory, and has led to a rejuvenation of Aboriginal culture.

'Out-stations,' Charlie McMahon explains, 'are small places at least 5 kilometres from a community. They usually have a water supply, probably a small shed, and sometimes a two-way radio set. The out-station is really the basis of one or two or three families, and they live in that area which is also probably the traditional site for an older person in that family And that person, by living in that place, will then pass on the lore and everything to those people who live in that area.'

One of Charlie's jobs in the Western Desert was to help get the out-stations going. 'The first thing all these communities start with,' he explains, 'is a good bore. You need one that can pump about 2 litres of water a second. So you've got to look for country in which it's reasonably easy to dig down a metre with a shovel or crowbar in order to bury the pipes; above-ground pipes give you hot water (especially when summer temperatures get up around 50 degrees Centigrade) and they tend to deteriorate quicker. For instance, in Warakurna they had no back hoe, so the pipes are all above ground, just lying on that quartz pebbly ground.

'If you put a windmill, with a 5-metre diameter and a height of about 9 metres, on the bore you can get a place going. The basic cost for 2 Ks of pipeline and a tank and a windmill is about 50,000 bucks. So it's pretty cheap, I reckon. With that, you can pump 230,000 litres a day, which is enough to supply 150 people.

'The next step for a larger community is the airstrip. That's the next priority because once you're out there you need to have modern communications – airstrip, radio mast, fuel depot so when you get your fuel you don't find the sniffers rolling the drums off down the hill – and a shop. All these things have basically got to happen at once. Medical service and the schools always tend to come last. The Education Department is always slow to move.'

Today, there are 334 out-stations in the Northern Territory, supporting a population of 6,000 people.

Co-author of a report into the homelands movement, Allan Blanchard (former Chairman of the Federal House of Representatives Committee on Aboriginal Affairs), has found that: 'The vast majority [of out-stations] are serious attempts by Aborigines to get away from the problems of enforced settlement, to escape the grog and the violence, to get back to bush tucker and retain a relationship with the land.'

Obviously, it's not a view shared by the Northern Territory's Country Liberal Party Government. In 1987, they brought down a mini budget in which funding for out-stations of less than fifty people was slashed. The decision saved a mere 2.7 million dollars.

Funding for all essential services, except the supply of water, was withdrawn. The decision effectively meant that there would be no further government assistance for health and education, or the provision of air-strips, roads, toilet facilities and power.

Defending his decision, the Northern Territory Treasurer, Barry Coulter, described the Aborigines as 'the richest people in Australia' and said there was a 'holiday camp mentality' on many of the out-stations.

Those inflammatory statements brought the following response from the Northern Territory's Deputy Opposition Leader, Brian Ede: 'Those communities often exist in Third World conditions and the loss of all services would increase our appalling death rate. Territory Aborigines already have an infant mortality rate four times the national average. If Barry Coulter wants to go down as the Treasurer who turned infanticide into a fiscal art form, then he should feel the glare of national attention.'

The productive aspects of the out-stations movement cannot be underestimated. Surveys have shown that people living on them are now eating 80 per cent bush tucker. Many have become family-orientated rehabilitation centres for petrol sniffers, and most are havens in which alcohol is banned. Retreating from the horrors of the assimilation system, the out-stations have given people the opportunity to pursue their own policy of self-determination. People are choosing to move back to their own country, and in the process, their culture has been kept alive.

In 1980, a government geological team sank a bore at the base of the Kintore Ranges, 260 kilometres west of Papunya. Being a government team, they chose to work without the assistance of local Aboriginal knowledge. The spot they picked was a place with little firewood, a location that is, according to Charile, 'the windiest place in the country.'

The site they'd inadvertently chosen was Walangurru, a sacred place on the Dreaming track of the *perentie* (goanna); a legend with its roots in the earth about 1,000 kilometres away to the south-west, on the far side of the Gibson Desert. On the eastern edge of the Pintupis' old country, it was a place that held special significance for the blackfellas who'd been dispossessed of their land and moved to Papunya.

For the first year or so, the spot was simply used as a camp for people who'd take their kids there during school holidays. And then, one night in August 1981, forty Pintupi people chucked all their belongings into the back of a truck, waved goodbye to the sorry memories of Papunya, and took off. They were going back to their grandfathers' country.

And so began the story of the Pintupis' renaissance.

In a sense the move was not unlike that of the pioneers celebrated in the annals of white folklore. The people were defying the bureaucracy and the plans of the Government and heading into the bush. Except that, for them, the bush was home.

Essentially, Kintore started off as an out-station. But it soon lost that status, and quickly became a major settlement that has since become the resources centre for a growing number of smaller satellite communities, out-stations that are spread all over the Pintupis' land, even reaching deep into Western Australia.

The rate of progress was astounding. Within a month the community at Kintore had been incorporated. Within two months Kintore had grown into thirty-two temporary shelters, nineteen of them being mulga or bloodwood humpies reinforced with sheets of tin. A store was operating out of the back of a truck. They had a two-way radio, a portable generator, a health clinic caravan, a tractor and a vehicle.

'The first bore at Kintore,' says Charlie, 'was a hand pump, so the water had to be carted by hand to the camp.'

By November, the population had grown to 118, including forty-seven children.

The move had never been sanctioned by the Government. The people had just grabbed their blankets and their dogs and 'gone home'.

'When the people first came to Kintore,' says Charlie, 'there was an enormous amount of bush tucker. There were a fair few wallabies in the hills, there were quite a few goanna to be got in season, and there was a lot of bush potato, and other *purra* and things like that. *Kalim kalim, pangana* bean, all these things. But once you put these people into a concentrated area in the desert country, all that country gets knocked out pretty quick.

'I think the main nutritional problem that people have out here now is the fact that they haven't got enough fresh bush tucker around the place. The best thing is out-stations. People on out-stations invariably have better diets because they have more access to bush tucker. And the stronger the effort is into out-stations around Kintore and places like this, the more that people will be able to live out bush where the good tucker is.

'When the Pintupi were at Papunya, the infant death rate was around 50 per cent. But if you look at them now, at Kintore, their death rate is down near the national average. During their first three years at at Kintore, there were no deaths – none of the kids, none of the adults.

'Now, nutrition and that hasn't picked up a real lot, but one of the main things that they have got is, first of all, they're living on their own country, close to the places that they consider important to them. And also they have their own independent health services. Their self-management thing is doing very well for them.

'Although you might look at this place now, look at any of these settlements, and you might think these places look destitute, there's rubbish strewn everywhere and it's dusty and kids are running around with snotty noses and there doesn't seem to be much employment going on, much work going on; what do these people do?

'But at least they're not dyin' off. This economic problem, that can be solved in the next couple of generations. At least they're fairly happy now and they're not dyin' off. They're on their own country.'

When Kintore (or Walangurru as it's called in the Pintupi language) was first settled, the wheels of bureaucracy were slow to turn. Predictably, the education department was the last to come in, but by February 1982 Kintore had been given a mobile school that opened four days a week.

'There were heaps of kids out there,' says Charlie. 'In the first couple of years when all the people left Papunya, they had something like twelve teachers at Papunya for about a hundred kids. And at Kintore they had about 160 kids and one teacher and a visiting teacher.'

One of the teachers was the Warumpis' guitarist, Neil Murray. He'd been out at Papunya for a couple of years, working in out-stations.

'The first job I had was driving the store truck around the out-stations, taking tucker out to people, taking their cheques out, getting sheets of iron for humpies, polythene pipe for water reticulation and the bores, bore maintenance work, putting in solar-powered radios and things like that. Interesting work.

'Then I got a teaching job, teaching on out-stations. Had to go out, bilingual education program, y'know, teaching the kids to read and write in their own language first. Then you get 'em on to English. Did that for two years and burnt out. It was real hard. Great kids. I enjoyed a lot of it, but it just got really hard. Frustrating.

'Physically, it was hard at Kintore 'cos there were no facilities there, nothing, just camping out. I was out there for two weeks at a time before I had to go back to Papunya for a week. You get a bit sick of the swag, living in the dust. And when the wind was blowing you'd watch all the teaching aids blow out into the Western Desert, where they belong, and you'd get back to some real schooling . . . like when the camels come and wander through the camp it's just on then, we're all chasing camels. Forget about school, do that tomorrow.'

In 1985, four years after the people had moved back, Kintore was provided with a proper primary school. By that stage, the population had grown to 400.

When the Oils were setting up the Blackfella-Whitefella Tour, they contacted the Central Land Council with a list of the communities they wished to visit. The CLC then contacted each of the community councils, asking them if they'd like the bands to come through and whether they'd have any objections to the presence of a film crew. (In some Top End communities, the ABC crew was banned, presumably because they were late in lodging their permit applications.)

The response from Kintore was forwarded to the Oils' Office via the CLC:

> WILL YOU PLEASE CONVEY THE WARM WELCOME OF THIS COUNCIL AND COMMUNITY TO THE MANAGEMENT AND MEMBERS (OF MIDNIGHT OIL AND WARUMPI BAND) ON THEIR PROPOSED VISIT OF JULY 12TH 1986. WE FEEL HONOURED THAT THEY SHOULD INCLUDE THIS REMOTE COMMUNITY IN THEIR TOUR.
>
> WITH REGARD TO MIDNIGHT OIL DOCUMENTARY, THERE IS AGAIN NO OBJECTION TO THE GROUP TAKING SHOTS OF THE LOCALITY AND THE BANDS PROVIDED THEY LIAISE CLOSELY WITH COMMUNITY MEMBERS, AND THE COUNCIL, AND AT ALL TIMES RESPECT LOCAL CUSTOM.

As the sun slips over the horizon, the fortress walls of Mount Strickland to the north of Kintore and Mount Leisler to the south sink into the darkness.

There's no grass in Kintore. Just red dust and playful kids, a red dirt footy field, a few demountable houses and the obligatory wastage of abandoned cars and old motors in the dust.

Outside the shop, by the sniffer-proof metal cages that house the petrol pumps, people mill around. Friendly kids with bright grins, fiery red hair and wide brown eyes jump into the beams of light. Elders huddle over fires flickering out of 44-gallon drums, their matted hair poking through the twine headbands that denote the status of an initiated man. Women, with babies propped on their hips, stand back in the shadows, melting into the windowless storefront walls. Around them, growling Holdens and Fords churn through the dust.

In his capacity as camp co-ordinator and local guide, Charlie McMahon finds a site on the southern side of Mount Leisler. A flat spot with lots of *waru* or firewood, it's well away from the ceremonial grounds, the sacred sites that women, children and uninitiated people aren't permitted to enter.

'The main thing about a camp site,' Charlie explains, 'is not being in the middle of a community. If you've got an odd mob of visitors you don't really know, you don't want 'em camping in the middle of your place, right? So if we find places a kilometre or two away from the community, it's good for us because we can get into places where there's a bit of firewood. Also, the community and the band can then choose times when they want to get together and have a yarn or something. You know, it's no good being thrust together in one place.'

The hitch-hiker agreed, though his reasons for doing so were somewhat different. From experience he knew what it was like to lie on a swag in the midst of a settlement, gagging on the odours of the ground. Lying awake under a corrugated-iron awning while the petrol sniffers skulked in the shadows and the sniffer patrols rumbled past. Nights broken by the disturbances of mangy dogs burrowing through his gear and people stumbling through the camp. Overcome by the dust and the smells and the rubbish on the ground.

But out here in the scrub, the conditions are idyllic. The ground is clean, there's plenty of wood and the only scents are those from the fires and the trees.

For the trip Charlie's prepared a tucker box for each vehicle, a blue steel box stacked with provisions: cereal, washing soap, washing scourer, self-raising flour, 1kg powdered milk, 2 packets tea, sugar, 1kg butter, bacon, eggs, biscuits, cheese, corned beef, fresh vegetables, fruit, aluminium foil, dried fruit, nuts, rice, canned fish, soups etc, salt & pepper, plus 1 sharp knife, 5 knives, forks and spoons, 1 large & 1 medium billy can, 1 fry pan, 5 enamel plates & mugs, 2 enamel bowls, 1 can opener, 1 egg flip, 1 wash basin.

Jim Moginie's wife, Claire, who's opted to come along for the desert leg of the trip, is burrowing through one of the boxes when the Warumpis and their entourage of friends from Papunya, Kintore and Haasts Bluff roll up. Within minutes there are thirty people standing around, warming themselves by the fire.

'Is everyone staying for dinner?' asks Claire.

'Yua!'

One dinner party for thirty coming up!

Away from the fires, the night is so dark and so clear that its physical presence is almost extrasensory. After dinner, Rob Hirst gets up and walks away from the camp, like everyone does when they need to take a pee.

But Hirst keeps walking, the flames dancing on the back of his black leather jacket, his boots crunching through bone-dry spinifex and shattered stones, trudging away from the fires. He's seeing how far he can walk . . . out into the darkness, the silence, the pitch of the plains, the roll of the starlit skies. He keeps walking until he freaks, until he gets so frightened, so spooked by the space and the darkness, by the sheer mystery of it all that he has to turn on his heel and bolt back to camp.

The hitch-hiker slithers into his swag, scrunches his combat jacket into a pillow, and lies back looking at the stars. They're so incredibly bright out here, providing a vista never seen in the cities.

He recalls leaning out of the doors of the overnight express between Sydney and Melbourne on the night of a full moon, the wind rushing past, his face in the breeze, shaking his head and howling into the night. All that land has been changed and will never be the same again. In a mere 200 years, the country's been raped and gouged, beaten up and left for dead, trampled by sheep and cattle, ringbarked and cleared. All that in 200 years, one two-hundredth of the time the blacks have been here. And it'll never be the same again.

He thinks of the Mundi Mundi Plains out west of Broken Hill. Of nights camped in a river bed, and days tramping across land that had once been fertile and has now, thanks to the sheep and the rabbits, been transformed into a dustbowl punctuated by claypans. There's a rave in Aboriginal culture that when a willy-willy blows up, that's the spirit of a dead person trying to find its special place. And if that is so, then the demise of the Aboriginal people of the Mundi Mundi Plains must indeed have been terrible, for out there, the willy-willies blow up with disturbing frequency.

Even here, in one of the most remote parts of the country, the environment's been changed forever by the feral cats and the dogs and the rabbits.

The dogs in the settlements are scrawny creatures, but the wild ones are big and solid, built like small horses. And the cats are huge and muscular and fast, free from predators; free from everything but a bullet or the bull-bar on the front of a Toyota.

He lies in his swag wondering if there are any places in this country that haven't been affected, that remain untainted, untouched by the invasion.

He remembers barrelling through the Blackstone Ranges in '85. The Warumpis were downing cool cans of West Australian Coke and lobbing the empties through the windows of the bus. And when Neil Murray – a whitefella who couldn't have missed the Keep Australia Beautiful/Do the Right Thing ads – tossed his can into the spinifex, the hitch-hiker demanded to know why. He'd always been convinced that it was better to drive in a garbage dump than through one, and he couldn't understand that sort of behaviour. Why throw litter into country that's virtually untouched and where the metal's not going to corrode for years?

'Country always changes,' Murray replied. 'That's the Aboriginal way. People have always chucked things away, bones 'n' stuff, axeheads, you name it. Western packaging's no different.'

The hitch-hiker finished his can and buried it in his pack.

•

Waking up in the mulga outside Kintore is one of life's more delightful experiences. Black-shouldered kites drift across clean blue skies, flocks of budgerigars sweep across shattered quartzite ridges soaked with red traces of iron, fires crackle and blaze, billies boil and white boys from the city scratch their beards and welcome a brand new day.

Rob Hirst comes trotting in from his daily jogging session, swags are rolled, breakfasts cooked, and as the entourage sit around the fires, Janet Hawley wanders from site to site, looking for a friendly chat. But the communication between print media and band still isn't happening on anything like an enthusiastic scale.

It's not that the Oils and their party are being deliberately unfriendly, it's just that the journalist's approach and her line of questioning are perceived to be naive. Jim Moginie cites an incident that occurred while they were climbing Uluru. The journalist asked him if the experience inspired him to write a song. She duly noted his reply that it inspired only thoughts of having a beer. In that respect, she seems boxed in by notions of musicians, pop stars on the road, discussing influences.

Though they've used it to great effect, the Oils have always been wary of the media, often exercising control over whom they talk to and the subjects broached. They've never taken media personnel on the road to the extent that they're doing on this tour, and while Garrett and Hirst are more relaxed about it than the other members of the band, even they are wary.

As mid-morning approaches, most of the crew abandon camp and head into Kintore to stock up on provisions. It's Saturday morning, that time of week when families all over the country converge on supermarkets. It's a national ritual that hasn't been lost in Kintore.

The stores in Aboriginal communities are generally run by white managers employed by the community councils. Turnover in places like Yuendumu can be as high as 1.5 million dollars per year.

The Kintore store, like most in these situations, is a health fanatic's nightmare. Because of the incredible distances involved, perishables like fruit and vegetables are as rare as milk, which is available only in long-life or powdered form. The nearest railhead is Alice Springs, over 500 Ks to the east, and the only goods that are available are those brought out on a truck once every week or so. The shelves are stocked with a sad array of durables like tins of meat, bags of refined sugar and processed flour, powdered milk, canned vegetables, soft drinks, ice-blocks and sweets.

Attempts have been made to provide bush tucker in the stores. At one stage, cling-wrapped frozen roo meat was introduced to the Papunya store. But no one would eat it because they hadn't killed it themselves, a process that involves certain totemic rituals with strict rules governing the way in which the animal is killed, carved up and its meat distributed. Under traditional law, the meat has to be cut up by the hunter and then specific sections of the animal passed to specific relatives. This process can result in the hunter getting little of the meat himself, so he has to rely on the hunting prowess of other relatives, depending on the nature of their kinship ties, to be assured of a good feed.

The stores also provide the communities' clothing needs: synthetic track-suits, nylon Northern Territory footy shorts, track shoes and beanies and dresses off the rack.

The hardware section includes coils of rope, billies, camp ovens, 200-dollar swags, two brands of rifle ammo, enamel plates and mugs, spark plugs, axes, tomahawks and hunting knives.

In places like Docker River, you can also buy handicrafts made by the local people: little goannas carved from mulga wood and *coolamons* decorated with designs burnt into the wood with fencing wire, which, among other things, are used to carry berries and yams and, in the larger models, babies. Ironically, they're about the only things available that have any real durability.

People mill around the check-out counter, kids roll cans across the concrete floor and old men with milky eyes poke at the shelves with wrinkled hands, coughing, muttering to themselves and peering at the labels on cans of meat, perhaps trying to reconcile the tempting illustrations of the packaging with the squalid conditions under which such items are likely to be consumed.

On the front doors of the Kintore store there are foolscap sheets rustling in the wind. One lists the people who have outstanding fines to pay. Another lists those who are due to appear in Papunya court on Thursday. Beneath them is another note: *If you don't pay the police will get you at Yuendumu Sports and put you in jail.*

The fines and the appearances are the result of drinking infringements and the like. But more traditional offences are still dealt with under tribal law. Where Aboriginal people have drifted away from their traditional tribal areas and gravitated towards the white settlements, law and order have often broken down. Without their traditional forms of discipline, the fringe dwellers have been left to cope with the white man's law.

In the bush communities, though, the tribal law of the elders still survives. Misdemeanours are still punished with a spear in the leg, a symbolic beating, or banishment from the community. And among the Pintupi, because they were some of the last to 'come in', because they've only had to deal with the influence of European culture for the last two decades, the law and the lore are still strong. The Pintupi are back living on their own country, and their ties to the land and the tribal law are so strong that the basis of the culture and the discipline has survived.

At midday, Peter Garrett rolls back into the camp in a vehicle laden with supplies. He strides across to a cooking fire beneath the outstretched branches of the mulga and squats in the dirt, warming his hands over the flames. 'I've just been talking to John Scobie, the council president,' he announces to those members of the entourages relaxing by the fire. 'Now, he's been discussing this with some of the elders and they're going to get together later in the afternoon, around three, and take those of us who wish to go on to one of the sacred sites. It's the sacred men's ground, so the girls'll have to stay here. No cameras. No tape recorders. Now, this is a very important thing, a rare privilege, so if you'd like to go . . .'

'This is a great honour,' Charlie adds. 'They want to show us the strength of their connection with the land and what it means. To be told and shown something about the *tjukurpa* is a rare mark of respect.'

'We're going to meet at the footy field,' says Pete, 'and follow them from there. So those who wish to go, be ready.'

At the appointed time the Oils gather on the edge of the red dirt football field, waiting for the arrival of the elders. Windows are wound up to keep out the cold. Outside, bits of cardboard bounce and tumble across the dirt and young boys boot a ball from end to end.

Gary Morris is getting impatient. He winds down his window and yells out to Garrett, 'You guys wait here. I'll go and see what's going on.' He chucks the Toyota into gear and goes charging back to the store. But there's no joy. Barrelling back to the footy field, he finds it's deserted. In the distance, the other Toyotas are bounding along behind a motley procession of battered Holdens and Fords. Gary sets off in pursuit. 'Sometimes the Oils are so inconsiderate!' he grumbles. 'So bloody selfish.'

The convoy dips through a dry creek bed and pulls up on the edge of the mulga beneath Mount Leisler. In the Dreaming it's known as *Yuuntju*, meaning neck of the *Perentie*.

They wait by the cars, squatting in the dust. A couple of the elders walk ahead, singing, chanting, preparing the spirits of the site for the arrival of the strangers.

Gary Morris squats, raving to Community Advisor John Gordon Kirkby about his perception of the similarities between the tales of the Old Testament and those of the Dreaming. The rest of the party are trying to listen to what's going on ahead of them, to the preparations of the site. Annoyed, Garrett says, 'Gary, some of us are trying to listen.'

Minutes later, they're instructed to walk towards the site, slowly and in single file. But Gary Morris, forever marching to the beat of a different drummer, is out of line, strolling alongside like a company sergeant major.

'Get back in line!' comes the cry from the elders ahead.

The ground itself isn't, to urban eyes, significantly different from the surrounding country; no more spectacular, no more or less awe-inspiring or dull than any of the neighbouring areas. It is neither fenced off nor signposted, and any one of the visitors could've strolled or driven across it without any inkling of its distinction.

The situation is quite extraordinary. The Pintupi elders have invited Peter Garrett and assorted contacts to an area so taboo that for the uninitiated to trespass upon it would generally result in the most dire punishment.

Perhaps it's a mark of their respect for Charlie McMahon that they're prepared to open up to people who lobbed into their territory less than twenty-four hours ago. Perhaps they recognise that, given some indisputable evidence, some understanding of those things that are so intrinsically significant to them, Peter Garrett will serve them well as a propagandist, a useful ally, a powerful advocate of their right to maintain their culture. The honour that they've bestowed upon him – and it cannot be denied that if Garrett had not been present the reception would've been quite different – is so rare, so out of character, that even some of the whitefellas who've worked in the region for years haven't been granted such opportunities.

So what is it about Garrett that's inspired the elders to grant such a privilege? Some observers, watching him in conversation with the elders, have noted 'an ingenuous child-like quality' in the man. Others refer to his sense of responsibility, but how do people as isolated as the Pintupi pick up on that immediately?

The Pintupi elders were obviously aware that they weren't dealing with someone who was just a larrikin rock 'n' roll singer. And yet one cannot overestimate their perception of his chosen path: a path that has little to do with either larrikinism or the excesses of rock 'n' roll, and much to do with a sense of right and wrong, a vision of a future and far better world, a path that would encompass activities that the Pintupi elders, in their supreme isolation, may never get to hear about.

That they chose to share a glimmer of their understanding, a glance at a book that could not be read (for it was in a language that defied immediate translation), speaks volumes about either their perception or their desperation. All for a bottom line that says *what you have seen, you cannot disclose.*

Beyond that point at which Gary Morris was told to get back into line, no one involved is at liberty to discuss what was seen or heard. What was ascertained, however, is that the Pintupi still have their lore, their discipline and their Dreaming, that the processes of law that have been operating for thousands of years are still in train, and that the sense of spiritual strength experienced by the Pintupi people of the Western Desert is one that should never be broken.

That afternoon, while some of the Oils were on the sacred men's ground, Gary Williams heads into Kintore for a shower in the teacher's house, an aluminium demountable with three bedrooms and a comfortable living area decorated with the usual array of books, cassettes and Aboriginal art. It's a sensible place to retreat to; an escape from the wind and the cold.

The Warumpi Band are camping there, well away from the rest of the party, and Williams takes the opportunity to confront Neil Murray. Their contact thus far has been negligible, but now Papunya is getting close and Williams is concerned about how he'll be received in the wake of Gary Foley's fight with Murray.

At an anti-apartheid benefit for the African National Congress in Sydney, Neil had run into Foley, the Director of the Aboriginal Arts Board, in the dressing-room. Foley asked Murray if the Warumpi Band was still in existence, and whether they'd be getting it together for the tour. Murray's response, according to a Radio Redfern interview with Foley, was to call the Director 'an effin' bureaucrat'. Foley says he responded by pinching a scene 'from an old Cagney movie' and pushing an apple into the guitarist's face. Murray blocked the punch, Foley's minders stepped in, and

Murray reeled away with a busted nose. When they caught wind of the episode, the ANC reps freaked, restrained Foley and his entourage from taking to the stage as planned, and had them escorted from the venue.

The incident left Gary Williams with a sense of fear he'd rather not have. For out here, the pay-back system of an eye for an eye and a tooth for a tooth is still a strong deterrent. And in Alice, Williams had heard mutterings that he would be held responsible for Foley's actions.

'You know who I am?' says Williams.

'Yeah,' Murray replies. 'Gary Foley's cousin.'

'Right.'

For Williams, the pressure suddenly lifts. Murray doesn't appear to harbour any animosity, and Williams figures everything will be okay. It's as though nothing more needs to be said.

'Can you pass the towel?'

'Sure, here ya go.'

That night, as fires blaze in the dirt and the Oils stand in front of the community store, shuffling in the cold and preparing to play, John Scobie, Pintupi elder and Kintore president, gives them a warm introduction in which he slips from Pintupi into English: 'You not listen properly . . . can you listen . . . please come up, ladies and gentlemen in the middle, so that everybody can just look and take a pictures . . . so pleased to come up . . . and I welcome . . . Midnight Woil mob, clap hands, long way from home. Thank you.'

'Thank you, John,' says Garrett, 'for all your kind words . . . All you Kintore mob! This is ah, this song, 'Hercules' song, for you, all right.'

'One . . . two . . . one two three!' And on Rob's count the Oils slam into their most relaxed set to date.

They're finally loosening up, settling into the groove of the desert. They throw in a swinging cover version of the Monkees' 'Steppin' Stone' and then they tackle the Stones' 'Dead Flowers', a perennial favourite in the Western Desert. It's an odd one, a junkie's lament that's been in the Warumpi Band's repertoire for a couple of years and which never fails to draw a response. Garrett invites Kumanjayi Rurrambu to sing a couple of verses, and the blackfella sticks to the original lyrics. Garrett, never one to celebrate junkies or the Kentucky Derby, comes up with new lyrics that relate directly to his experiences in the desert. It's a song the band hasn't played for at least ten years, a number in which the members of Farm (as the Oils were originally known) would swap instruments: bass guitarist Andrew 'Bear' James taking over the drums, Rob Hirst playing guitar and Jim Moginie tackling the bass.

Half-way through the set, another of the elders gets up to make an announcement: 'Gonna take a photo. Everybody, can you siddown, please! Midnight Woil band . . . you remember, keep it in your mind, please, can you siddown.' The elders seem to think it's rude that people are actually getting up and shuffling to the beat, dancing in the smoke, raising the dust while the visitors are giving a performance.

'This one,' says a subdued and somewhat mystified Garrett as the old man returns to his place, 'is "Beds Are Burning".' Glad's trombone sweeps in, the drums kick, Giffo's bass rumbles and Garrett, his voice thick with dust, starts singing.

As they shunt out of the song with Glad's trombone blaring and the audience crackling with applause, Garrett steps back to the microphone: 'Thanks everybody. All right, we've got ah a special friend, friend of Midnight Oil tonight, 'cos this is the Midnight Oil/Warumpi Band, Warumpi Band/Midnight Oil Blackfella-Whitefella Tour. But you know this fella I think. You know this fella here 'cos he came out and played with us. It's Charlie McMahon who ah has been a buddy of ours for I dunno it seems like ages really, but it gets better and better . . .'

A howling dog fight erupts by the fires in front of the stage. 'This one's called "Stand In Line", the funky short motor type version . . .'

Charlie's playing is perhaps even wilder than the band's. His didgeridoo is more like a trombone, a pair of PVC pipes that slot into each other, allowing him to change the pitch as he blows by shuffling them in and out. He charges around the dirt floor stage, swinging the instrument this way and that, waving it in the air, getting down and cooking with the savage ferocity of a dog gone troppo.

'Hey, Charlie McMahon!'

'Yo! Thank you Peter, everybody at Kintore. Good to be back, eh? Marra Hook here. Yee ha! This is the band here, Midnight Oil. I been playing with Midnight Oil before, all over the country, but all the time big city, y'know. America, Sydney, Melbourne, Brisbane, Canberra, all over the country. And this time they wanna come here, and they playing for Kintore, Papunya, lot of other places and they playin' because they come here to learn about your country! *Palya?*'

'PALYA!'

'Very good. And they're learning and it's good and they're friends for Aboriginal people I think. So let's hear it for Midnight Oil, hey! Goodah!'

'GOODAH!'

'Thank you.'

It's a performance in the smoke of the fires and the dust kicked up by feet that dance at the front and shuffle down the back, and if Garrett and McMahon fail in their usual articulation then maybe it's because they're out of breath, panting through the dust and the smoke, gasping and gaping and producing the loudest noise these ancient mountains have ever had bounced off 'em.

John Gordon Kirkby, the community advisor, is a civilised man. But the work never stops. Even when he's confined to bed with the flu, barely able to move, people come knocking on the door, requesting his assistance. And he has to get up and stagger out in his pyjamas and dressing-gown. The kids laugh, of course, because in a place like Kintore such items of apparel look absurd. Before he took up the position at Kintore, John Gordon Kirkby was a District Officer in Papua New Guinea. He's as ashamed, he says, of the treatment of Aborigines by successive Australian governments as he is proud of Australia's role in moving Papua New Guinea towards independence.

As Lippold and Pickett roll leads and pack boxes and the Warumpis' crew roll them away, Kirkby hangs around, waiting to lock up the council office. Chatting quietly, he refers to the work in PNG as 'Australia's enlightened colonial policy. In twenty years we got people in PNG through to being doctors and lawyers, people who can hold the responsibility of executive government. Whereas here ... no one's ever come out of Pintupi. And there's no room for women's lib out here.'

The nearest high school, Yirara College, is in Alice Springs, so girls rarely get further than a basic primary school level. Generally, they're married and starting to raise families by the time they're 14 or 15, often as a result of a 'promised' marriage to a man three or four times their age. Their role is one of subservience.

'No high school student would put up with it,' Kirkby says, with an air of dull resignation.

The argument is that if girls of high school age did go off to the big smoke of Alice to further their education, they'd be unlikely to come back. The attractions of the modern world would be too great. And while the community could be advanced through further education of its children, allowing the community to employ its own people as teachers, health workers, secretaries and store managers, the risk of losing a future mother is, at present, too great to contemplate.

As it is, whites fill the roles, taking up positions as community advisors, book-keepers, essential services officers, homelands coordinators, mechanics, electricians, store managers, teachers and health workers.

The hitch-hiker had a dream that night; a strange and haunting dream punctuated by the sound of a bullroarer whirring. He dreamed of long dark planks of hardwood of varying lengths, perhaps 2 or 3 metres, etched with lines and symbols that he failed to recognise. Of dark hands full of sand, trickling over the wood.

Of these planks, 10 centimetres wide and a centimetre thick laid out on a sheet of dusty canvas. Of old dark people stepping around them, singing, chanting, nasal intonations in some language he couldn't comprehend. Of warm dark hands on warm dark wood. Of the bullroarer whirring, the twine snapping, the sound of mulga clattering across the rocks.

The desert does strange things to a person. The light and the space and the intensity of the colours, the infinite depth of the darkness, the extremes of the heat and the cold all serve to burn the mind with bones of ice, crystalline in clarity, chilling in effect.

Mysteries breathe out here where caterpillar hairs blown up the nostrils of a foe can kill without leaving a trace, where the spirits can scare a man half to death, beat him over the head with a shovel or the limb of an ironbark and leave him crouching 'til dawn as cold beads of sweat drip on the rifle cocked in his hands . . .

In the morning Charlie squats beside a fire and pokes his metallic hand into the flames to stir the coals. 'The only drawback with this thing,' he chuckles, 'is if you're muckin' around with the fire it gets real hot. So if you're not thinkin' about it and you scratch your nose . . . jeeze, you soon know about it!'

That arm, with its steel claw and its goanna-skin wrapping, must've really freaked the 'lost tribe'. It was Charlie who was involved in the retrieval of the 'lost tribe' in 1984: a family of half-a-dozen Pintupi people who were found living in the desert west of Kintore. They hadn't seen their own people for two decades, and they'd certainly never come across a whitefella with a mechanical arm.

The first indication that people were still out there, unaware of the modern world, came when a car-load of hunters returned to Kintore, nervous, as if they'd been jumped by ghosts, full of wild claims that they'd seen some 'devils'. With Charlie in tow, a party went out to find them.

Of the people who came in, one – a young man – has since fled back into the bush.

Today, there are stories that another family is still roaming across the country to the north-west. But this time the feeling is that they should be left out there, safe from the media and the troubles of the outside world.

On Sunday night, a group of the elders rides out to the Oils' camp to return the favour of a concert. They include John Scobie and Turkey Tolson. Gary Morris supplies them with clap sticks and boomerangs he's been buying along the way and, sitting around the fire, they do a number of short songs. Very short songs, in fact. Turkey is rather short of breath, the result of too many Winfields and too much tucker.

Charlie joins them with his didge, but when they insist that he sing along, he can't remember the words. 'C'mon Charlie, must know this one!' says John Scobie. 'You heard this song many times . . . you forgot the words? Too much time big city, Charlie.'

Eventually they run out of songs, there being a strict limit to the number of traditional songs that can be sung in the presence of women. So the Oils party takes over, with Hirst, Rotsey and Moginie strumming acoustic guitars and singing, while everyone else taps forks on billies and knives on plates.

It's an extraordinary event. There they are, listening to songs that go back hundreds or thousands of years and the best the Oils can come up with, as Jim Moginie sees it, 'is a couple of old Rolling Stones songs or maybe some Muddy Waters'. It's the band's first acoustic jam in the desert, and one that will eventually set the direction for their sixth album, *Diesel And Dust*.

As the elders prepare to leave, a car roars past in the darkness of the dirt road about 45 metres away. 'That mob been out hunting,' says Turkey. 'They got two kangaroo.'

As the car's tail-lights disappear through the scrub, they look at the clouds in the sky. 'Gonna rain tonight,' says Johnny Scobie. 'Big rain comin' up now.'

'Nah, it won't rain,' says Gary Morris. 'Not tonight.'

'*Wiya*. Rain tonight for sure. No worries.'

'No, it won't,' the Christian argues. 'You've got your spheres of influence: I've got mine. He looks after me. It won't rain.'

The elders leave, shaking their heads at the gall of this young whitefella. Course it's gonna rain. They can sense it.

It doesn't rain.

CHAPTER SIX
PAPUNYA

It's cold; a jarring, numbing, crushing cold that cuts through the canvas like a blade. During these, the coldest hours before sun up, when the chill factor's high, the temperature's low and you can burn your hands in the coals without feeling a thing, the road crew lie shivering in their swags.

Like the homeward-bound Warumpis, Lippold, Pickett and advance scout Gary Williams bailed out of Kintore yesterday afternoon, a good twenty hours before the Oils. Barrelling across the plains to Papunya, 300 Ks to the east, they left early so that Williams could establish contact with the Council. But they arrived too late to do any business, and now they're camped out at the Three Mile, a spot by the boundary fence on the eastern side of town. It appeared to be an ideal place to camp because there's plenty of firewood and it's within waving distance of the main road to Alice.

But soon after dusk, Ian Anderson Tjampitjinpa visited the camp, and the tales he told Lippold and Pickett gave them the creeps.

Now, in these final hours before dawn, their minds are racing and their ears are alert for the call of the sirens – the phantom women of the night who cry out from the scrub, luring gullible men to their deaths. *If you hear them, don't answer the calls . . . don't go looking for the source of the voices, 'cos if you do, you'll never return.*

If there'd been rain tonight, their eyes may also have scanned the ancient ranges to the south for tell-tale signs of the *Pangkalangka* – the hairy man-eating giants who, it is said, can be seen carrying their flaming fire sticks through the scrub in the wake of a downpour.

But Lippold and Pickett are spooked enough as it is. They haven't dared to move more than 2 or 3 metres away from the light of their campfire, not even to take a pee. The hop and thud of a wallaby in the mulga could send either of them into the never-never of their minds.

Gary Williams has other worries. He knows that when dawn breaks over the sites of the Honey Ant Dreaming, he'll have to go into the settlement, without a permit, to confront the council president.

He worked in Papunya in 1976, back in the days when it was a big government settlement of 800 people. But times have changed, and now, because of this tour, he's in trouble. He's been refused a permit to enter Papunya after his meeting with the Warumpi Band in Alice. The council has barred him, and he doesn't really know why. He's been accused of stirring up trouble between the Warumpi Band and Midnight Oil. And he's been identified as a friend of the Central Land Council at a stage when the Papunya Council is fighting the CLC for the right to enter into independent negotiations with the mining companies, and to secure direct royalties for the gas pipeline being laid across their land.

Williams bailed out of Kintore a day earlier than the Oils in an effort to sort it all out. On the way through, he called into an elder's out-station in the Ehrenberg Ranges to explain that he was on his way. If there were going to be any rows he wanted the opportunity to give his side of the story first. But the elder wasn't there, and now he knows he'll have to go in cold.

He doesn't even want to be here, working with a bunch of white boys who, after their experience on the sacred men's ground at Kintore, have suddenly been filled with knowledge without having any yard-stick by which to gauge it. They know it was a privilege, but they don't know how much of a privilege it was. They're drawing conclusions, he feels, that they have no right to draw.

But now, because of them, because of his cousin, he has to go into Papunya to face the council president.

Heading east from Kintore, Charlie McMahon's truck rattles through the dust. On either side of the track, the plains sweep to the horizon. The desert in the Dry; parched and red with spindly trees, bull-bar-bending anthills, shredded tyres and an endless grey sea of grasses that prick the skin and snap off, drawing tiny globules of blood that sting like a childhood taunt.

A sign looms up: KIWIRRKURRA. It's painted on a car bonnet propped against a hunk of wood.

Kiwirrkurra's about three days from nowhere. A Pintupi outstation in the Gibson Desert, it's one of the places Charlie helped to establish. He headed out there in the spring of 1983, sinking seven bores over a 200-kilometre stretch; the idea being that people could move back to their traditional lands and return to the social cohesion of living in small groups. At Kiwirrkurra he sank a bore and installed a hand pump. While he was there, Charlie got to thinking about the design for a store. The local basalt's one and a half billion years old, and Charlie had seen so many tin sheds that he wanted one built of stone.

He headed east that summer, ended up touring America with the Oils. And then, when the worst of the heat had passed, he returned. Just before he left for Alice, he put a call through to 2JJJ to say he wouldn't mind taking a hitch-hiker. The guy who responded was a German tourist, Berndt Kaiser, and just the other side of Katoomba, Charlie found out he was a stonemason.

Berndt started building the store in October. The cement was trucked in from Alice, and the rock was quarried locally. It cost the Aboriginal Development Corporation 70,000 dollars, much of which went on wages for local Aboriginal workers. The job, unlike most others in the region, was local labour intensive.

'That store,' Charlie says proudly, 'is one of the best things that's ever happened to the Western Desert. It'll be there for years. Because it's built of rock, it'll stay up, and it's well-insulated against the summer heat.' He reaches into his pocket for another smoke.

The scrub swishes past in a blur. 'Running trees' the Pintupi called it when they took their first ride into Papunya. Now they're back living in their own country, setting up out-stations and respecting their traditional obligations.

'These people being out here,' Charlie says, pausing to lick the Tally Ho, 'is of great benefit to the country, because they always talk about "looking after country". One of the things I found hard to unlearn is our tendency as whitefellas to put out bushfires. Because out here the burning of the bush is so good for the country. Because once you burn through the country, up comes a great diversity of vegetation. The kangaroo population starts to rise, because the kangaroos live more off the short green shoots than they do off the heavy dry grass. So, by burning off, the Aboriginal people are maintaining the ecology which they set up some thousands and thousands of years ago.

'I think the extinction of a lot of animals in the bush of Australia over recent years has been due to the lack of burning off of the country.

'It took me a long time to learn that, because I used to get horrified when I saw the fires that these people used to light when they went hunting. And I thought "Oh, ya careless buggers!" y'know? "Put that fire out!" But no, no, that's the way you look after country. You burn it.

'The mulga's a perfect example. It's a member of the Acacia family and, traditionally, it was burnt off every five or six years to promote regeneration. The fire cracks the seeds open and the ash from the old trees makes the best fertiliser for the new ones. Out here, round Kintore, you get about 200 millimetres of rain a year. But further east, Papunya, Alice Springs, you get over 300 millimetres a year.'

With such low rainfall to contend with, Charlie's spent much of his time out here sinking bores. The deepest have hit water at 120 metres. The drilling equipment, though, can go to a depth of 2 kilometres. Given the opportunity, he'd introduce smaller, cheaper rigs.

'When you're looking for water,' he says, 'it's a good idea to look for old riverbeds. There, the salt's been washed out of the rocks over millions of years.' When sinking bores, he claims an 80 per cent success rate.

'Most bore drilling and construction teams,' he says, 'are contracted whites who have no interest in working with the local Aboriginal people.'

Charlie always works with local people as guides to determine where the sacred sites are, where the safest places are for a camp, and to pinpoint soaks and places likely to yield reliable supplies of water.

As he rolls past the Ehrenberg Ranges and on towards the jagged old saw teeth of the Macdonnells, he yells over the hum of the motor, 'The mountains around here are among the oldest in the world. When Everest was flat, these mountains were here!'

Further up the track, he talks about the oil wells at Mereenie, a bluff south of Papunya. 'The oil there is so light it simply needs to sit for a while to have the dirt drained out of it. Then you can stick it straight into a diesel motor and drive all the way to Melbourne. No worries, mate, it's been done.'

Standing beside a burnt-out Falcon, further down the road to Papunya, there's a youth from the lost tribe whose hair – a blazing explosion of dusty red fibre – corkscrews out of his head like willy-willies. The effect is so unruly, you'd think he's just plugged his long dark fingers into a three-phase power outlet and given himself a Western Desert perm. It's as if he's been electrified by what he's seen in the past two years, by what he's experienced in the last two days.

The first recorded music he ever heard – drums, guitars, keyboards and foreign words – was a cassette of Midnight Oil's *Red Sails In The Sunset*, which a visiting mate of Charlie McMahon's slipped into the 'gecko' blaster when the lost tribe was brought in in late 1984.

The first rock 'n' roll band he ever saw, just two nights ago, was Midnight Oil. And ever since he's been mooning around.

He's incredibly shy and his command of English is minimal. But when he stands by the side of the track he's got this incredible grin that just won't quit, as if he's just seen the wildest, most exciting thing in the world and he's still high on the memory of it.

He's seen one show and now he wants to experience another. So much so that he and a carload of blokes from Kintore are driving 300 Ks to Papunya to go through the whole trip again.

Gary Morris, keen on getting some photos by the burnt-out wreck, has flagged them down. A billy's been slung on to a fire and enamel cups are being retrieved from Gary's Toyota. The guy from the 'lost tribe' stands by the fire, watching, listening, grinning.

'That Gary Williams fella,' says one of his companions, 'he bin locked up in Papunya.'

'He's been what?' says Gary Morris.

'Locked up. We heard it just then. From the mob what passed before. They comin' from Papunya. They say that fella's in lock-up.'

'Fair dinkum . . . Who locked him up?'

'Council mob, they lock him up. Got no permit.'

Back on the track Gary Morris handles the Toyota with all the sensitivity he reserves for business negotiations – at full bore and locked into four-wheel-drive. He sits on 120 Ks, charging straight through the puddles. 'You know why cars get into trouble?' he yells as he plunges through another brown lake with such power that a jet stream of muddy water showers over the bonnet. 'They aquaplane! People put their brakes on, they've got no traction, so they lose control. But if you put your foot down, you just plough straight through it.'

Thick red mud dribbles down the windscreen, trickles down the back windows of the Toyota across which some wag has dirtied a finger scrawling *Hilton International.*

Morris keeps his foot to the floor. 'Papunya . . . what is it about that place?'

For many years, Papunya had the reputation for being the worst settlement in the Territory. Established in March 1960, it was chosen because it had a good supply of water, while the source at neighbouring Haasts Bluff was running low. Traditionally, Papunya held no great significance for the Luritja people of the region. The only sacred site in the immediate vicinity centres on two trees. When Papunya was established, that was the site chosen for the gaol.

Papunya was a centre of enforced assimilation, a government settlement in which people from the surrounding tribal groups (Luritja, Pintupi, Warlpiri, Anmatjirra and Aranda) were expected to peacefully co-exist and develop to a standard that would allow them to assimilate into white Australian society.

'Most people,' says Neil Murray, 'think it's a real hell hole of a joint. But for a lot of people, it's their home. That's what our song 'Warumpinya' is about. Papunya had a bad reputation; it was always in the papers. There was a bit of an uprising there in 1974, a bit of a riot. Maybe a few stones were thrown at the police station. I dunno what happened, I wasn't here.

'It's not the place but the people who make it good, y'know. 'Cos it's the people you get to know. If you're not used to dry, desert country you'd think, "Oh God, what's this place?" Dusty 'n' that. But beautiful mountain ranges, rock holes. Go out bush and there's plenty of tucker. Big kangaroos, big reds.

'It's been described as like something out of the third world; all those popular clichéd images about being a site like a former concentration camp. People were brought in, brought in from so far out they couldn't walk back to their own country. A lot of people that came in from the bush died, old people coming down with disease and shock and trauma and things like that.'

At one stage, it had a population of over a thousand people. The government sank a lot of money into the project, providing a primary school, diesel-generated power station, a bitumen road, medical facilities, street lights and plumbing. A couple of hundred Kingstrand houses were built – tin sheds with a fireplace and a short verandah plonked down on a concrete slab. Hundreds of houses built in neat rows. By 1977 most of them had been vacated and smashed. (Under Aboriginal culture, once a person has died, people move away from that dwelling or that area so that the dead person's soul will have the space to return to its rightful place.)

After twenty-five years of occupation, the town is a shambles, savaged by a bitter struggle between the old world and the new, with the grog and the petrol sniffing and inappropriate bureaucratic decisions.

In recent years, church and government policy has changed, the will of the people has become stronger and Papunya has been deserted by people returning to out-stations or recent tribal communities in their own country. The current population stands at around 214, and Papunya has settled into the role of a resources centre for the neighbouring out-stations.

When Papunya appears out of the scrub, it's obvious why the third world analogies have been drawn. Amidst the basketball courts and the school buildings, the houses for the European workers and the arts and crafts centres, lie the demolished shacks and the humpies that have been thrown together using sheets of iron and canvas tarps, bits of mulga and overturned water tanks. *Age* journalist Janet Hawley, who's spent time in the Middle East, describes it as 'like Beirut after the bombing'.

When Gary Morris rolls into town, Michael Lippold explains that Gary Williams hasn't been locked up. Instead, he's been shanghaied. Or to put it more precisely, when Gary was being threatened with the lock-up, Michael and Pat drove him out past the perimeter and left him outside town . . . waiting for the cavalry to arrive.

Minutes later, the cavalry hits Papunya Council President Alison Anderson's office with his considerable persuasive powers. 'Is there any way we can solve this?' Morris says, leaning across the desk.

The meeting carries on for half an hour or so, and when it's over a vehicle is dispatched to pick up the exile.

Neil Murray moved out here in the late 1970s, a move that inadvertently heralded the formation of the Warumpi Band.

'I had a guitar and amp with me, right? And I was living in a house with this other boss who was working around the outstations, and most days I'd play the guitar a bit after work, just sit around and play. The guys heard it straight away and came in. 'Oh, take it outside,' they said. 'Sit it outside. Play on the lawn.'

'I think the first sort of gig we had was just my guitar, one amp, and I had a microphone through the other input in the amp. We were outside, singing, and we just had a crowd come around.

'And then there was some equipment the YMCA had that I found out about, some PA gear, so we soon got some more guitars that were lying around, got some drums together and started jamming. They could all play, played country 'n' western, most of 'em.

'I can remember the first trip to another community I did with the band. It was in 1980, about the middle of the year sometime, and I was shovelling gravel off a truck in Papunya and an HD Holden pulled up, guitars sticking out of the windows and things. Sammy got out and a few others and they said, "Oh we're goin' to Hermannsburg". It was a Friday afternoon, about 2.30, just after lunch. We'd just started work again and they said "C'mon, we want you, we need you". The boss said "Yeah" so I just dropped me shovel and jumped in and away we went, broadsidin' down the road, pullin' up for goannas here and there. Played at Hermannsburg and Jay Creek that weekend and then came back on the Sunday. Got our takings stolen at Jay Creek.'

Six years later, the finances aren't looking much better.

The Warumpis are on their home turf and they want some money for their families. They're under the impression that they're to be paid 300 dollars per week for the tour. Not so, says Gary Morris. This is a benefit tour for Aboriginal people and all services are being donated. Only the road crews, black and white, are being paid.

Cookie argues that he brought the matter up weeks go in a telephone conversation with Martin Hardie. Hardie recalls advising Cooke to take the matter up with Morris. By late afternoon, even the people in the arts and crafts store have been told that the Oils aren't paying the Warumpis.

Despite the rumour-mongering, Papunya provides the most appreciative audience thus far. The people here are more familiar with the rock 'n' roll idiom, and they've been joined by others who've travelled from as far as Kintore, Docker River and Yuendumu for the show.

Late in the evening the Oils retire to a series of camps in the scrub on the eastern side of town. Everybody's exhausted. The pressure's been building and the day's had its share of crises. The hassles over Gary Williams' permit are something the tour could've done without. So too is the confusion over the Warumpis' financial position.

Ten days into the tour and most of the party are looking forward to the comforts of Alice – simple things like a bed and a shower and maybe even a beer . . . or a shave.

Gary Morris, stubble bristling through a tan that's turning darker by the day, drifts off to sleep with visions of snakes on his mind.

Since his encounter with the snake on the road to Uluru, he's been having serpentine dreams every night. In the scrub outside Papunya, his movies of the mind flash to the end of the world. Great rivers flow from beneath Uluru, spreading out, meandering across the desert. The *Kuniya* call. The snakes turn into rivers; the rivers turn into snakes. Slithering across the desert, their scales the waves, the ripples on the water, glistening in the light.

There's not much time off, not when in the space of twenty-four hours you're collecting firewood, cooking breakfast, packing up, driving 200–300 kilometres, cooking lunch on the side of the road, meeting people, setting up the gear and doing a gig, striking a camp in the scrub, sleeping, eating, meeting with the elders, barrelling out of town.

Not much time to get to know each other, let alone those you contact so briefly.

All stops have been pulled; this is an Oils tour, the advance contact has been made, communities are doing their best to cooperate, to meet with the band and discuss their problems, their solutions. The Oils are being shown, perhaps, the best sides of the communities.

There are such extraordinary differences between this tour and the Warumpis' last. The Warumpis were just a band passing through; the Oils are a political caravan with a crew of twenty-two that's being fed scraps of information.

It's a route that's been travelled before, by white politicians, bureaucrats, public servants and anthropologists rolling through with notebooks and tape recorders and questions that betray their lack of a full understanding of the people and their aspirations, their links with the land; people bouncing from settlement to settlement, tribe to tribe, seeking a truth when their senses aren't attuned, and they cannot, therefore, gain an appreciation of the bottom line. And without a sensual appreciation – stop, look, listen, taste, smell, learn – there's no telling what sort of impression they'll come away with.

Dawn strips the skies of stars and the roadies' camp emerges from the darkness. It's surrounded by little clots of toilet paper, at least half-a-dozen of them, none of which is further than 2 or 3 metres away from the swags. Such is their fear of the sirens.

A couple of kilometres away, some women, armed with digging sticks and *coolamons*, are down on their knees in the scrub, coaxing long, fat white grubs from the trunks and roots of trees.

Before breakfast, Peter Garrett drives into Papunya for a preliminary meeting with Alison Anderson. An hour or so later he returns to the camp with a french fries bucket brimming with live witchetty grubs that some of the women have collected and presented in appreciation of the concert. Charlie wraps the grubs in foil and cooks them on the coals. They taste like a cross between Kraft cheddar slices and an over-fried egg.

Your senses are not our senses. Our senses are not yours. Listen. Touch. See. Smell this. Rub this between your hands and feel the grease, your hands are red, red dust and human hair. Feel this wind, there's a change. What's that? That sound? Hear it? There . . . check your boots in the morning, make sure nothing's crawled in overnight . . . so many falling stars, the spirits of the dead lunging home, trailing across the sky. See that? Hey *Kumanjayi! Palya?* Taste this. Him shot last night. Slabs of sweet red roo meat fresh from the coals, dripping . . . Up in those mountains there's an old carving in the quartz. Rainbow Serpent dreaming that one. Rainbow Serpents all over this country . . . These grubs are good for you. Proper number one tucker, that one.

Back in the days of creation, the witchetty grubs (or *maku*) emerged from Kunatjarri, a cave out near Central Mount Wedge, about 50 Ks north of Papunya. When they appeared, two of the grubs turned into snakes and did battle with each other. The rest of the story? Well, I guess that's a secret. You wouldn't want that sort of information to get into the wrong hands, would you?

There's a women's Witchetty Grub Dreaming ceremony (women being the gatherers) that's been held at that cave since time began. It's been passed down from mother to daughter through the ages, told by word of mouth and song, illustrated with ochre body paintings, and drawn in the dust and blown away.

A couple of years ago, the Department of Aboriginal Affairs bought a painting by Paddy Carroll Tjungurrayi, a man of the

Anmatyerre and Warlpiri tribes, which shows the ground design used in those ceremonies. It's a dot painting done in acrylics on canvas, using a series of short blunt sticks as brushes.

Imagine a Union Jack: at its centre is a series of concentric circles that represent the ceremonial site. The St George's Cross is a series of straight lines indicating the roots of the witchetty tree, home of the nutritious grub. The arms of the St Andrew's Cross are wavy, representing the tracks of the snakes. 'U' shapes facing the shorter arms of the St George's Cross are the women participating in the ceremony. At the end closest to the site are oblong shapes, the *coolamons* used to collect the grubs. Surrounding them are clusters of S-shaped grubs. Like many of the paintings for the region, it's painstakingly symmetrical and three-dimensional in its design.

Until recently, the art of the Western Desert was completely overlooked by white anthropologists because of the transitory nature of the surfaces on which it was done. For thousands of years, people dabbed ochre on their bodies in preparation for ceremonial activities. Dreamtime legends and tales of heroic journeys by the ancestral beings were illustrated with drawings in the sand – a circle here, dots there, that fella kangaroo, him come up thissaway. The drawings in the sand were topographic maps that were executed with a finger or a stick . . . and whisked away by the wind. Today's dot paintings – acrylics on canvas – are in a form that's only developed in the past decade.

In 1971, at a time when the strength of the elders – and the willingness of the children to learn – was being usurped by European influence and the temptations of Western society, a teacher at Papunya encouraged the older people of the settlement to transfer their stories and their art to more durable surfaces. He bought cans of paint and brushes, and the first of the dot paintings appeared on a wall at the school. From such beginnings, one of the strongest art movements of recent times has emerged.

The Western Desert paintings differ radically from the art of the Top End, which portrays essentially one-dimensional aspects – x-ray paintings of crocodiles and kangaroos and spirits that are instantly recognisable as a certain creature associated with the artist's Dreaming.

The desert work defies interpretation to all but the practised eye, prompting the Director of the Australian National Gallery, James Mollison, to describe the paintings as 'simply the finest abstract paintings that have been produced in Australia to date'.

The paintings are generally associated with a person's Dreaming, representing a ceremony held at a specific place, relating to a person's totem (though it's not always the artist's, their perception being, perhaps, too powerful, too knowledgeable, to dare even attempt it).

Internationally acclaimed, the paintings are essentially charts; topographic maps that represent a person's Dreaming, showing journeys undertaken in the Dreamtime, pinpointing the sources of food and water, telling of hunts for game and reliving the stories that are so crucial to the survival of the culture of the Western Desert.

To see the conditions under which the paintings are done is an extraordinary experience. The canvases, secured to the dusty red earth with rocks and billies and old wheels, are painted with the aid of short blunt sticks.

Some paintings are small, no larger than a paperback, and others are so big they can only be hung on something approaching the size of a squash court wall.

The dot paintings are now being produced in Papunya, Kintore and Yuendumu and their neighbouring out-stations. The style of the paintings varies from community to community. In Papunya, the birthplace of the movement, the colours used are restricted to the traditional colours of the desert: pinks and mauves, greys and browns. Further north, around the Warlpiri country of Yuendumu, bright greens are used, adding to the psychedelic nature of the work.

Out around Kintore, the complexity of the paintings is astounding.

It's a movement that's produced a number of artists whose popularity is growing fast: artists like Clifford Possum Tjapaltjarri, Maxie Tjampitjinta, Pinta Pinta Tjapanangka, Pansy Napangardi, Paddy Tjapaltjarri, Frank Nelson and Larry Tjangurayi.

Arts and crafts advisors hired by the communities supply such materials as canvases and paints and take responsibility for the marketing of the paintings.

In the process, the recent upsurge in painting is keeping the culture alive and generating income that owes nothing to social security cheques and government hand-outs.

On the side of the Papunya store, a low building with roller doors and heavy metal security grills, there's a strip of graffiti: *Papunya Honey Ants – No Worries!*

Inside, women queue at the social club counter for their child endowment cheques. Various members of the band stroll through, searching the shelves for supplies to supplement those in Charlie's tucker boxes.

Outside the jabbering mayhem of the establishment, all that can be heard are the barking crows and the howling dogs, the rattle of a soft drink can rolling down the tar, the swish of the wind in the desert oaks and the throaty roar of passing muffler-less cars.

Beside the nearby arts and crafts store, a filmed meeting is arranged with Alison Anderson and some of the older people of the community. Alison Anderson, a commissioner with the Aboriginal Development Commission, is the most articulate community representative the Oils have come across.

In Papunya, she explains, kids start off with a bilingual education, learning Luritja first and then the English translations. On Wednesdays, the schoolchildren are given cultural lessons by the old people.

'We want to keep our culture and not sell it out for the quick dollar,' she says. 'We don't want mining companies and tourists.'

Outside Papunya, she explains, a 'museum' containing sacred objects was destroyed and the items stolen by whitefellas.

The desert blacks, she says, don't want to be involved with or tainted by the 'radical city blacks'.

'Long time ago, when we was kids, DAA ran the settlements. People were trucked in from all over. People just couldn't relate to each other ... DAA said we had to live in all these houses ... all these houses in a line ...

'Soon as a person died we'd evacuate that house. It's sad they didn't negotiate with us. They built houses in straight lines. They didn't teach us to use push-button toilets and use taps.

'We had to learn for ourselves. That's why plumbing was blocked. But they didn't want to waste money teaching people how to live in European houses.'

Today, under the guidelines set down by the community-run Papunya Housing Association, people are moved into a European house for a three-month probation period.

'If they demolish that house, we don't give them a second chance. They have to prove they can use shower and toilet and stoves, that they can keep house clean and plant trees and lawn. Strict rules!

'People now, they want to live in traditional family groups in humpies on out-stations away from hospitals and schools and big mob houses. They want to be left alone.'

Within twenty minutes of the meeting breaking up, a dust storm rips through the settlement, shrouding the buildings and the distant ranges in clouds of red dust and litter that drift along the fencing lines, chasing dogs with broken legs so misshapen that they poke back under their ribs like twisted landing gear, crippled beasts foraging for scraps in the wind. The skies are grey and banked with clouds.

'There's rain coming,' says Giffo. 'I can feel it in m'bones.'

If it does rain, the road to Yuendumu could be closed.

Charlie finishes packing his truck and wanders across. 'Big rain up that way,' he says, pointing to the north-east. 'Georgina's done its banks.'

'It's not gonna rain,' says Gary Morris.

'Okay God.'

'I'm His mate; I'm not Him. You've gotta show some respect, Charlie.'

CHAPTER SEVEN
YUENDUMU

The hitch-hiker stands on the side of the road. He looks down the track at the crows perched in the branches of dead trees. He looks into the sky; heavy dark clouds out this way. Out here, the sky begins at eye level and, like a good joke, rolls over your head and lodges in the back of your brain. The horizontal plane. The hitch-hiker recalls being told once that Aborigines should never be placed in jail cells, because in a cell the predominant planes are vertical, whereas the only plane the blackman's psyche has ever had to deal with is horizontal.

He stands on the side of the road. The air's so dry he considers giving up smoking, just taking deeper breaths, scorching the throat, burning the lungs and singeing the supercilious cilia.

Every August, thousands of people from settlements and outstations all over the country squeeze into cars and fishtail all the way to the Tanami Road, a dirt track laced with huge puddles that swiftly turn to deep quicksand bogs. Fired up with sports fever, they converge on Yuendumu for the annual sports carnival.

Overnight the settlement's population grows to 5,000 as people from about thirty communities in Queensland, South Australia,

Western Australia and the Northern Territory pile in, setting up hundreds of camps in the surrounding scrub and getting ready for the weekend's activities.

It's a major event on the Aboriginal calendar, an opportunity to see old friends and relations, settle old scores, and engage in a weekend's sport. All weekend Yuendumu runs amok with football matches, basketball games, fire-lighting and spearthrowing competitions, displays of dancing and singing, and a raging battle of the bands, a full-tilt gig with up to thirty bands and gospel groups thrashing their way through a borrowed and often distorted PA for the honour of winning.

People arrive from settlements and out-stations all over the country. Decked out in tracksuits, footy jumpers and basketball dresses proudly bearing the name of their place, they hit the fields one after another. A football team reaching the grand final might have played four knockout games over the weekend. Bare feet in the dust; fantastic Aussie Rules players who pound across the earth, some in jeans, the rest in shorts, going in hard and fast. It was because of their 'football commitments' that the Warumpis had been given six months off – six months to get ready in the green and gold jumpers of the Papunya Warriors and forge a path through to the grand final.

For the rest of the year, Yuendumu's police contingent consists of a sergeant, two constables and a pair of Aboriginal police aides. During the sports carnival, however, the numbers double. All the way through the tour the bands have come across the notices on the community office walls: *Pay your fines or the police will get you at Yuendumu sports and put you in jail.* It's the perfect approach because nobody wants to miss out on the sports. It's the event of the year.

The sports carnival is three weeks away when the Blackfella--Whitefella entourage arrives, so the settlement's population is steady at 1,000 Warlpiri and sixty whites.

Established as a Baptist mission in 1946, it's now run by Yuendumu Community Inc. The local primary school has a bilingual education program using the Warlpiri language, and offers a wide range of adult education programs as well as Aboriginal teacher education programs.

One of the educational aids is a photocopied Phantom comic translated into Warlpiri. *Phantom Kurlu Puku Warlpiri Rla*, published in 1985, sees the Ghost Who Walks freeing shiploads of slaves and punishing the evil slave traders. The Phantom has made such an impact on Warlpiri culture that as far north as Lajamanu, 450 Ks across the Tanami Desert, there are Phantom Club stickers proclaiming 'We Serve Against Evil' in the Warlpiri Hypermart.

Evil, of course, is in the eyes of the beholder. It's a concept that we're familiarised with in accordance with the pressures of our culture. Out here, because of devastating cross-cultural influences, there's no shortage of evil.

Traditional Aboriginal culture presented the Warlpiri people with a concept of evil, one that they understood and accepted. Dreamtime stories told of wrong-doers being turned into birds and animals and inanimate objects, which would serve as a constant reminder or deterrent to people contemplating a similar path.

Then along came the whitefellas who told the Aborigines that their whole culture was evil, and proceeded to dump them with concepts like God, Satan and Hell.

Firstly, it was the pastoralists who moved in and broadened the scope of the blackfellas' concept of evil by sending out police parties to shoot them. The pastoralists were followed by the Baptist missionaries who, in turn, instituted their concepts of good and evil. And now they're under seige from Pentecostal evangelists whose concept of evil is even more far-reaching.

So what has resulted is a conflict between the teachings of the Dreaming and those of various Christian sects. The most basic concepts of Christianity, and particularly the Protestant religions, are anathema to Aboriginal beliefs because of the emphasis placed on individualism, a trait that goes against the kinship laws of traditional culture.

Today, the Baptists, armed with five-page computer printouts listing the Pentecostals' short-comings, are intent on casting the evangelists out of Yuendumu.

Such battles are raging in many parts of the desert where different fundamentalist groups are trying to win the hearts and minds of a people who, until the intrusion of the missionaries, had their relationship with the universe sorted out quite nicely. At night, in places as far apart as Warburton and Yuendumu, the silence of the desert is shattered as groups like the Baptists and the Pentecostals rail against each other in an effort to prove the strength of the conviction that theirs is the greater God. The whites – even those who initially headed out there as missionaries and have since renounced their faith – stand back and shake their heads in bewilderment. And the young blacks, torn between the laws of the Dreaming and the abject fear of God that's been drummed into them, are left straddling a religious chasm that's beyond their comprehension. Taught the stories of the Dreaming by their elders, they're told by fanatical fire and brimstone preachers of their own race that such tales are the work of the Devil. And torn between the religious foundations of two cultures, they're left with nowhere to turn.

To make matters worse, an appalling education system has left them so vulnerable to brain-washing that they seem to have been denied the capacity to question what they're having rammed down their throats.

To witness an evangelists' meeting in the desert is a strange and unnerving experience. You might find a black preacher sharing the stage with half-a-dozen guitarists and a tatty PA system. Amid screeching feedback, wild testimonials, warnings of hellfire, damnation and the showering sparks of brimstone, the preacher – a man possessed – screams at his flock and motions to the converts at the front: 'They're gonna talk to Jesus! They're gonna hear the word tonight 'cos He's a powerful God... We're gonna ask the Lord for His word... Jesus is the way for the people! Jesus is the way that people can find peace and joy! You gonna come here on stage and we gonna pray a little! We bin pray already, but we gonna pray that He speak to us! Jesus! Jesus! In my father's name, in the people that receive Him . . .'

Then the band will drift into 'In the Name of Jesus' or 'Jesus Is Lord', all squealing feedback and mournful, woeful singing and garbled confessions.

'Praise the Lord. Y'know, when we got something we gotta share it. You can run out to the people who got nothin', see? But they got nothin'! Jesus Christ, Lord, that He can kill us! With His power! Of the Holy Spirit! When you got somethin'! You don't have to run nowhere! When you got Jesus, you can share it! That's our responsibility. In the name of Jesus! Hallelujah!'

Such matters are not to be taken lightly. As Neil Murray has said, 'People are in the process of embracing Christianity out here (for better or worse) and they are very sensitive to criticism of this. The quickest way to be kicked off a settlement is to declare that one doesn't believe in God.'

These are indeed strange times . . . when the combined and conflicting influences of the Red Ochre Men, the white missionaries, the black evangelists, the purple Phantom and the khaki coppers all serve to warp the minds of the young with fear and ignorance and fantastic threats of retribution.

Within the touring party, we have at least two committed Christians. Gary Morris is the most assertive, calling on Biblical quotes whenever he feels the need to offer guidance. His own impression is that he refers to Biblical quotations only when counsel is required. To those unaccustomed to such references, he seems to spin into the raves at the drop of a clutch. He found the Lord in late 1979 (though his own assessment is that it was Jesus who found him), made a radical departure from the Oils, leaving them in limbo on the eve of the release of their second album, *Head Injuries*, and spent the next two years 'following the Lord's path'. When he returned he was full of vivid tales of the horsemen of the apocalypse, relating the path of world events to Biblical prophesies, and those who endured his raves – as vigorous and passionate and visionary as anything he'd ever said about the Oils when he first took them on – figured he'd finally wigged out. Since then, he's toned the sermons down and generally satisfies himself with using the Bible as a guide for life and business, a reference book from which he can assess the value of the desires and motivations of both himself and those he's dealing with.

The other Christian is Peter Garrett, though his approach is far more low key, so low key in fact that it's a subject that's seldom broached by the media. A journalist from the *Sunday Mail* who did broach the matter elicited the following response: 'I'm a Christian, but not a branded, labelled, waving it as a flag one. The problem is many people draw from it selectively to suit their own ends, and I find that enormously distressing. The gospel is very straightforward; it's difficult to misinterpret it. We need a place we can draw the fabric of values from. It gives us a purpose, a hope, the ability to go on.'

Perhaps it's one of Garrett's strong points that he draws from the gospels and influences others by the weight of his actions, rather than trying to convert anyone through preaching. In short, he doesn't wear his Christianity like a badge, and therefore has the opportunity of making a greater impact without being written off as a convert to the God squad.

In Yuendumu, for the first time on the tour, Midnight Oil have been given a house to rest in. It has a shower and a bit of sparse furniture, a kitchen and a couple of bare beds.

Among the members of the group and their management personnel are a number of news junkies – voracious consumers of daily papers and hourly news bulletins. And in a week they've heard nothing of the outside world. All connections with AAP and Reuters and Tass have been severed by the remoteness. Anything could've happened in the outside world and the Oils, for the first time in their lives, would've been totally ignorant.

In the front room of the house at Yuendumu there's a formica table, and on it a copy of *The Australian*. And as each of the whitefellas spots it he swoops, pouncing on it and sweeping it off the table in a flutter of broadsheet leaves. But expressions of anticipation quickly dissolve into disappointment, for the paper is three months old.

Out here, in a land devoid of newspapers and television bulletins, where the radio-telephone serves as the only immediate means of communication, there's been a certain imbalance in the influence of the Western media. In recent years, however, Yuendumu has developed its own video production unit, which specialises in making local programs. They make education programs, film sporting events and concerts. In Yuendumu, you can also pick up 8 KIN FM, the Alice Springs based CAAMA station.

The most exciting development in the Australian media in recent years, CAAMA (Central Australian Aboriginal Media Association) was established in 1980. Today, the Aboriginal-controlled organisation is the largest public broadcaster in the country, with a Central Australian network of FM stations covering an area the size of New South Wales. CAAMA's 8 KIN FM is beamed out of Alice Springs, Santa Teresa, All Curung and Hermannsburg for fourteen and a half hours every day, broadcasting in five of the local Aboriginal dialects (Pitjantjatjara, Warlpiri, Kaytej, Anmatyerre and Aranda) as well as English.

In conjunction with the ABC, CAAMA also puts out almost ten hours of programming every day on the short-wave band that reaches from Alice into the desert regions of South and Western Australia. They reach a potential audience of 46,000, 53 per cent of whom are Aboriginal. (The other 47 per cent are the Europeans who live predominantly in Alice.)

Yet another of CAAMA's projects has been the instigation of the country's first Aboriginal recording company, Imparja. With mobile 16-track recording facilities and an extensive distribution network, Imparja has released cassettes by Coloured Stone, Warumpi Band, Isaac Yama, Ilkari Maru, Bob Randall, Herbie Laughton and compilations like *Rebel Voices From Black Australia* and *Aboriginal Choirs From Central Australia*.

As a vital community service, CAAMA has also been the prime moving force behind the crucial Beat the Grog campaign.

CAAMA has also established a video production unit that sends monthly programs to about forty of the Aboriginal communities in the desert. Having won a television licence, CAAMA is now, with the assistance of AUSSAT, in the process of setting up a Territory-wide TV network that will feature mainstream commercial material as well as programs aimed specifically at the Aboriginal communities. Called Imparja TV, it's a commercial network catering for black and white tastes, which gives Aboriginal communities the opportunity to insert their own locally made programs. Communities that already have a local television broadcasting infrastructure include Yuendumu, Ernabella, Ngukurr, Galiwin'ku and Maningrida. (While Imparja will carry ads for alcohol, provision has been made for 'dry' communities to black out the ads.)

Imparja TV will broadcast in eight languages in an effort to strengthen or at least maintain the strongest Aboriginal dialects. (Even this presents problems, in that some English words like 'legislation' defy translation.)

The emergence of Imparja TV came as a result of fears that, with the advent of the satellite system, Aboriginal communities throughout the Territory would be corrupted by sudden access to television programs. Imagine, for instance, the effect a show like 'Dallas' would have in communities in which people are living in overturned water tanks and canvas humpies. Such visions of Western decadence in the midst of such squalor would do little for the self-esteem of a people whose standard of living is among the lowest in the world.

Videos have already been banned in communities like Warburton because of the adverse effect they were having on the behavioural patterns of the people, the violence of the programs being reflected by an upswing in the level of violence in the community.

Wander through a place like Kintore and you'll see a young guy wearing a t-shirt with the slogan *M-16: Peace Through Superior Firepower*. Wander through any community and you'll see kids wearing Rambo t-shirts (though they haven't a clue where Vietnam is) and blokes handling their cars as if they've just had such a heavy dose of *Mad Max*, *Duel* and *Deathrace 2000* that they've got to mangle some metal.

Such activities have given the community elders a fundamental understanding of the power of the media, hence the recent push to have at least some control over what's broadcast by setting up an Aboriginal-run radio and television network. Through this they are able to balance the amount of rubbish coming in with local content that's culturally appropriate and all the more enticing to the young because it's dressed in a Western form.

Another indication of the influence of the Western media is provided by the walls of the Yuendumu hall in which the Oils and Warumpis are to play. For the first time on the tour the bands are doing a show indoors. And for the first time since Docker River, the Oils are headlining over the Warumpis.

The hall that is now the Yuendumu Youth Centre started out as the settlement's welfare kitchen and dining-room, a long brick building with heavy steel-mesh grills in place of windows. But with the advent of the community store (which is operated by the Yuendumu Social Club Inc. with an annual turnover of 1.5 million dollars), the building was abandoned. Boredom led to vandalism, and the building was on the brink of being condemned when the resident youth, sport and recreation field advisors and locally employed workers stepped in to clean it up, turning it into a place for activities that would draw kids away from petrol sniffing.

The walls are plastered with psychedelic graffiti proclaiming the glories of AC/DC, INXS, 'Bruce Springfield', Iron Maiden, Cold Chisel, Hip Hop, the Rock Steady Crew, Michael Jackson and Midnight Oil. It's ablaze with colour and vitality, a recognition, a day-glo celebration of homogenised rebellion. And the only name on the walls that these kids will ever see in the flesh is Midnight Oil.

Most of the names are of acts that roll up to gigs in stretched limos and refuse to perform if, in accordance with the contract rider, all the brown Smarties haven't been separated from the red and green and yellow ones. Acts who've never heard of Yuendumu and wouldn't want to unless such recognition translated into 'units' and 'product' and another couple of grams of cocaine.

But here come the Oils, walking down the street, saying 'Gidday' to kids hanging out in the front yards while the cooking smells of dinner waft through the chilly evening air.

There's a traffic jam at the door to the hall, a congested build-up of people shuffling in and out, some shy of the light, others waiting for friends.

As the crowd files in, the kids take up their positions down the front and the older people settle at the back, away in the shadows, leaving an enormous gulf in between.

When the Warumpi Band swings into 'My Island Home', Oils guitarist Jim Moginie joins them on keyboards. Glad Reed, looking as nervous as ever, steps up to blow the trombone on 'Breadline'.

The Warumpis are firing tonight. Rurrambu, in a yellow Land Rights t-shirt, is going for it, turning in a powerful and convincing performance.

It was here in Yuendumu that Neil Murray first saw George on stage. It was the winter of 1980 and Neil and the boys in the band had travelled up for the sports carnival. Naturally, they went along to the battle of the bands to check out the competition.

'George was singing a Little Richard number with Yurrampi (the Warlpiri name for honey ant). Everyone was telling us to get up and play, but we didn't. But the following year we did play and George sang with that Yuendumu mob again. We did 'Roll Over Beethoven' and an original thing, an instrumental we don't play anymore. It was in the battle of the bands and we went over well, but Ted Egan, who was a judge, didn't like us 'cos we were swapping around guitarists. He wasn't sure of the line-up. So he commended us but he didn't give us a place. He gave it to a Milingimbi gospel group instead; not that we're too worried about what he thought of us. About the same time George came to Papunya and joined up with us.'

For the Warumpis, this is almost home territory. But despite the fact that it's a free concert, the steel-mesh grills around the hall are hooked with the clinging hands of those who are too shy to come in. They stand outside, hanging off the grills, looking in.

The hall's a shimmering kaleidoscope of colour as dozens of fat-cheeked Warlpiri kids run wild, chattering and giggling, rolling and tumbling, throwing balls, swishing each other with plastic bags, brawling and laughing and ducking and diving and dodging, while the rock 'n' roll rides through from the stage.

The Oils, too, are having a fine time, debuting Rob Hirst's 'Runaway Bay' and another new song with a chorus of *I can show you something*, which recalls the delights of The Who and The Monkees.

They're tired but enthusiastic. And, in the interests of 'continuity', they're looking pretty ragged around the edges: Jim Moginie, unshaven and in a subdued paisley shirt; Giffo, unshaven in a chequered workshirt of blue and brown; Hirst, unshaven in an aqua-blue singlet and swimming in rivers of sweat; Garrett, clean-shaven as always, in a red and blue tartan shirt, a silver bangle on his left wrist and a wedding ring on his right hand.

For 'Dead Heart' the whole joint's rocking. Everyone's on their feet, adults and kids, blacks and whites, dancing all over the shop. It's the last show in the desert and, for the Oils, a definite high point of the tour. For here people have heard about them, and the initial reserved curiosity has given way to cheerful appreciation.

'They're an outgoing mob, these Warlpiri, eh?' Neil yells as another kid slides into his legs.

'Tall too, eh!' adds Charlie.

How, then, do we deal with the Aboriginal dead? White Australians frequently say 'all that' should be forgotten, But it will not be. And forgetfulness is a strange prescription coming

> from a community which has revered the fallen warrior and emblazoned the phrase 'Lest We Forget' on monuments throughout the land ...
>
> If we are to continue to celebrate the sacrifice of men and women who died for their country, can we deny admission to fallen tribesmen? If they did not die for Australia as such, they fell defending their homelands, their sacred sites, their way of life.
>
> PROFESSOR HENRY REYNOLDS,
AS REPORTED IN *THE AUSTRALIAN*, 5/6 SEPTEMBER 1987

It's been said that if Captain Cook had arrived a hundred years later, he would've come up against the brave desert warriors of the Warlpiri nation. Regarded as the great imperialists of the Western Desert, their lands stretch 500 Ks from Lajamanu in the north to Yarripilangu in the south, and 700 Ks from Balgo in the west to Ali Curung in the east, encompassing much of the dreaded Tanami Desert. Feared by their neighbours, the history of their contact was written in the blood of the 'killing times'.

In the hills around Yuendumu, away from the dust bowl conditions of the settlement, springs of cool, clear water trickle through the quartzite ridges. Quartzite, the rock of bone and blood, its jagged edges never eroding, just cracking and shattering in the sun.

From the cracks and the crevices emerge the tiniest of rock ferns, the *Cheilanthes*, dark green furry plants only a couple of centimetres high. There are plants here with leaves like sandpaper, so dry they snap, so coarse they'll scrape the duco from a Toyota's fender.

There are choughs uttering their four-note calls from the bloodwood trees overhanging the gullies. Black kites and eagles soar across the sky, their wings so finely tuned, their sense of balance so acute they can ride a thermal to heaven and turn on a pin, dropping like a stone with the twitch of a wing tip.

In the mulga scrub you can see the wrens, the females dowdy dun brown to grey, the males dark brown and light brown with cheeks the colour of an iridescent sky.

Anthills burst out of the plains, craggy mountains of mud, weird skyscrapers that poke from the earth like icebergs adrift in a sea of clay floating on the dust, awash in the waves of spinifex, waiting to sink the modern ships of the desert – Toyotas bashing through the scrub in search of game or piles of *waru*.

It's Warlpiri country, country from which they were dispossessed by the invading pastoralists, country in which at least thirty-two of their people were shot dead in 1928. In August of that year, at the height of the drought that crippled the surrounding cattle properties, an old dingo trapper named Fred Brooks was killed when he failed to meet his obligations to Warlpiri camped at a soak on Coniston Station. He'd secured the services of a Warlpiri woman for the night, and when he failed to provide her husband with the promised payment of tucker, he was hacked to death and stuffed into a rabbit hole.

Led by a Chief Protector of Aborigines, Mounted Constable William George Murray, a party of white settlers set out to find Brooks' murderers. In the ensuing battles at least seventeen Warlpiri were shot dead. A month later, at least another fourteen Warlpiri were killed when another of Murray's parties rode out to find the attackers of Nugget Morton, a cattleman from Broadmeadow Station.

'We shot to kill,' Murray told a subsequent enquiry. 'What use is a wounded blackfella a hundred miles from civilisation?'

The Board of Enquiry into the Coniston massacres found the killings justified.

There's something comforting about belting through the scrub at night. Foot flat to the floor, windows up, heaters on, eyeballs locked into the tunnel of light, corrugations coming in so fast ... Jammed into a cocoon of warmth, unable to see anything but what's being pulled into the beam of the headlights. When you're driving at night there is no past, for that simply falls away into the cloak of darkness. There is only what's up ahead, and that, as soon as you see it, is passed.

Dead trees become 'road kills', chucked in the back like the others: the goannas and the roos. You don't need an axe when you've got a Toyota. Bleached white mulga crushed beneath the tyres.

Bouncing headlights zap skeletal trees, bare branches arching for the sky, so dry you can just push them over, their trunks eroded by termites, their guts eaten out, rotten, decaying, their meagre life forces chewed up and spat out. There's no shortage of firewood out here, and on a night as cold as this, *waru* is what you need.

A few Ks out of Yuendumu, the Oils pull over and prepare to set up a camp. The *Age* crew, who've followed them out of town, follow suit, moving in close and lighting a fire. Minutes later, after discussions about the site, the Oils move further on. The *Age* team, still hunting for a story during their last night on the tour, extinguish their fire, pack up their belongings, and shadow the band.

It's spooky out here. You can lie in your swag at night, listening to the almighty silence, and out of the silence will come a hum, a low rumbling hum that builds into a roar. You lie there, tense, waiting for something to happen. It's getting louder, like a train howling down the tracks. Suddenly it HITS! A wind that explodes through the scrub, whipping up sand and dust and rubbish, a wailing storm from the depths of hell. And then it passes, just blows through and disappears, and nothing moves. There's just the silence.

While the Oils lie in their swags, Gary Morris pulls out of Yuendumu and hits the frog 'n' toad to Alice Springs. His passengers include Glad Reed and Stephanie Lewis. His other regular passenger, tour manager Martin Hardie, has been shunted into the road crew's vehicle.

Along the way, Morris drifts past the Warumpis. Neil Murray's behind the wheel of the truck. The truck's battery isn't charging and neither the headlamps nor the tail-lights are working. Blazing through the dust, the truck is flanked by Cookie in a Toyota and Ian Anderson in a battered yellow HQ.

It's not often that people connected with the Warumpis have the pleasure of driving a Toyota. 'Toyotas,' as Neil Murray will tell you, 'are for when we really make it. When you've got heaps of dough, that's when you get the Toyota. That's the pot of gold. In the meantime, you have to be realistic and think of HQs and Kingswoods, Fords 'n' things.'

Three hours later, Morris gets stuck into coffee and a pile of raisin toast in the restaurant of the Shell Todd, a legendary roadhouse in the heart of Alice Springs. He checks into the Oasis Motel ('Welcome To Outback Australia') at four in the morning, arranges for *Ice Pirates* to be played over the in-house video system and crashes a couple of hours later.

After ten days in the desert, enveloped by that almighty silence, the noises of Alice are somehow familiar, comforting.

At seven in the morning the phone starts screaming. A courier's just delivered a parcel. It's a video Gary had made of a potential new venue in Sydney, and he spends his first morning back in civilisation sitting in front of the telly.

Glad and Stephanie spend the morning op shopping, returning with armloads of synthetic clothing that Gary proceeds to ridicule, demonstrating the way in which nylon fibres sap your strength, drain your energy and generally have a poor bearing on the wearer's constitution.

Meanwhile, a couple of hundred Ks to the west, the Oils are getting well and truly lost. Following Charlie McMahon, who's unfamiliar with this part of the country, they've headed too far west. Charlie suggests they try correcting the problem by taking a 'short cut' through the scrub.

The journey becomes an exercise in scrub bashing and sandhill climbing – up and down, ships in the desert, climbing the waves, peaking, and tumbling down the other side, following Charlie who's trying to find his way with only a Reader's Digest atlas to guide him, hopelessly out of kilter, trailing sand and dust and broken trees, dropping over the dunes, ploughing down through the spinifex, fishtailing across the desert, trying to find the way back to Alice.

Further west, Lippold, Pickett and Hardie are having similar problems: Heading out of Yuendumu, Lippold's vehicle turns right and heads west for 200 Ks before the mistake is realised. They realise, with a plummeting feeling, that they're 200 Ks further away from Alice, and that the taste of a cold beer is another bunch of dry, dusty hours away.

They return to Yuendumu to get more fuel. But Hardie's broke; he's got no float money and Lippold's got to pay for the gas with his last 50 bucks. On top of a 400-K goose chase it doesn't make him happy.

On the way back to Alice, just out of Glen Helen, Lippold takes one hand off the wheel and reaches into the back seat, taking Hardie by the throat and gently letting him know that if there's one more foul up . . .

Charlie and the band finally lob into the motel bar late in the afternoon and order their first beers for a week.

'Trashed the cars,' says Giffo, with a wink and a grin.

'Mine took most of it though,' Charlie says defensively.

'Yeah, well you *were* goin' first.'

An hour or so later Lippold, Pickett, and Hardie stalk in. Lippold confides that he's on the verge of quitting. He wants to live out here in the Northern Territory, he wants to support and encourage Ian Anderson as a roadie and custodian of the Warumpis' gear in Alice or Papunya. He wants to get away . . .

It's not an entirely inappropriate way in which to finish up the first leg of what is turning out to be the most memorable tour the Oils have ever embarked on. For there they were, roaming around the desert and heading in the wrong direction, a bunch of young whitefellas who can't even tell east from west.

What was it? Twelve days ago? There was a sense of adventure, standing at the airport in Sydney, down by the flight desk at dawn, the hitch-hiker whistling 'Summer Holiday' in the depths of winter, half-expecting his mother to walk up and enquire whether he'd packed a change of undies, like the crowds at the bus-station on the dawn of a holiday camp, a new bunch of friends, a new swag of experiences, thick as thieves and twice as cunning, getting to know each other so well in the space of a few days.

And now this.

Roving across the plains, squatting beneath the desert oaks . . . out there where the strict rules apply; where alcohol is banned and the elders are fighting to retain the only law they can trust; one mob, one law, one land; out there where the population, for perhaps the first time in 40,000 years or more, is increasing; where people are returning to a diet of bush tucker and finding ways of dealing with the problems they've encountered over the last fifty years or so; where a people on the verge of extinction are fighting back, determined to preserve their culture, their languages, their lives, their beliefs, their traditions and their Dreaming; out there, where the people have emerged, against all odds, as pioneers whose strength and resilience can never be doubted. Land is life, they argue, and the proof of that claim is in their survival.

It's less than twenty years since they were accepted as Australian citizens and given the rights that privilege entails. It's just ten years since they were given the opportunity to resume ownership of their land. It's just five years since the Pintupi moved back into their traditional country and set about rebuilding their people and their culture.

Flit through this country and you'll see little but the down side – the wastage, the car wrecks and the rubbish, the torment of conflicting religious values, the carnage induced by petrol sniffing and grog and bad food and a whole host of other destructive elements that have been foisted upon the Aboriginal people by the policies of a society they were never prepared to deal with, an invading force that stepped in and destroyed many of their tribes.

Out there, between Kintore and Papunya, there's a place no one ever talks about. Diseases wiped out a whole tribe. The language was lost, it died in the dust, and with it the secrets . . . the secrets. (Such a strange looking word, secrets, as if it holds them all and we'll never know.)

Squat in the dust, learn to breathe the air, catch the smells, examine the tracks, listen carefully; there are people out there who hold the key, who can answer questions we never even knew existed. We're slowly coming to realise that our country contains a wealth of information we've never had cause to think about, information to which the traditional owners – those still deeply in touch with the spirit of the land – hold the key.

Western society has been through so many radical changes – changes in moral values, attitudes, technologies, forms of authority, forms of management – in the last few hundred years, and still we haven't got it right.

And yet, out there in the Western Desert are a people whose society has been so finely tuned that it's survived for 40,000 years or more.

Western technology has advanced because of our constant desire to find more effective methods of killing each other, and yet what more remarkable weapon could you find than the boomerang, a piece of wood thrown by a man which travels 50 metres and returns to his hand. The utter simplicity of it; a piece of wood carved from the mulga with chunks of stone. And yet it displays an incredible grasp of aerodynamics. It would be foolish to think that we can go backwards, or to think that the people of the Western Desert can go backwards, can resume their nomadic life, return absolutely to the culture and the conditions in which they survived before we found them and insisted on introducing them to civilisation.

What can happen, though, is that we can encourage them to follow their own path, give them the freedom of choice that's been denied in recent years, and allow them to make decisions about how they're going to deal with the new set of circumstances with which we've presented them – a constantly changing set of circumstances that they have accepted with extraordinary grace.

For now, the fortunate ones of their race are back living in their ancestors' country and adapting to the modern world.

CHAPTER EIGHT
FUNNEL WEBS IN THE BEDROOM

About 12 Ks south-east of Alice, down by the putrid, murky waters of Emily Gap, I killed the hitch-hiker off, knocked him over the head with a *nulla nulla* I'd picked up in an arts and crafts store on Todd Street and left him sprawling on the rocks.

Like a typewriter or an undeveloped sense of the absurd, the *nulla nulla's* a blunt instrument that's designed to be used in a heavy-handed manner. Weighing around 2.5 kilograms, it's a metre long and as thick as a fluorescent tube. The ends roll out to a point, which is useful for the occasional tactical jab, and with a good swing it can do untold damage. It's primitive, but under the right conditions that piece of mulga is a useful instrument.

The job done, I pulled on his boots and stopped off at the Territorian Bar in the terminal of the Alice Springs airport. It has an effective air-conditioning system, and that was needed, because like telegraph lines and tempers, the truth gets stretched in the heat.

The bar was crowded, and Gary Williams was taking up most of the room. He'd been going since early in the morning, sinking green cans by the dozen, preparing himself for the terrifying prospect of climbing into a tiny aeroplane and enduring a long and heartburning flight. Every time another plane touched down, engines whining, wings whistling and wheels squealing, he got a little more squeamish and turned a little greyer, no mean feat for a blackfella with skin as dark as his.

You hear some strange stories in the bars of Alice, stories like the one about the weather station.

About 250 metres below the war memorial on Anzac Hill, down on Schwartz Crescent, lies the Alice Springs RSL Club. And opposite that, backing on to the invariably dry junction of the Todd and Charles rivers, sit a couple of low buildings and a bristling rack of antennae.

When they appeared in 1955, inquisitive locals were told it was a weather station. Eighteen years later, Defence Minister Barnard revealed that the Joint Geological and Geophysical Research Station was principally being used to monitor underground nuclear tests.

Staffed and operated by US Air Force personnel, the installation was established under a secret agreement between Australia and the US in the days of the Menzies Government. Under the code name of Project Oak Tree, it was the first permanent American installation on Australian soil.

Rather than contributing to 'the achievement and monitoring of nuclear disarmament' as Barnard told the Parliament in February 1973, defence analyst Desmond Ball argues that Oak Tree contributes to the development of America's nuclear arsenal by providing intelligence about the characteristics of Soviet, Chinese and French nuclear weapons.

> With our so-called 200th birthday coming up, are we going to be a little puppet with the Paul Hogan grin and the slightly glazed eyes of Rupert Murdoch's latest television acquisition, allowing ourselves to be a giant aircraft carrier, to be a platform for the transmission of information to satellites and ships and submarines that carry nuclear weapons and that might be used in a nuclear war, and mining uranium which ends up as those bombs, and not knowing anything about

the bases, and having a base of another country's spy system on our own soil?

Or are we going to decide what we want to do for ourselves ...

Are we going to grow up at last? Are we going to be truly, independent? A sovereign state? Our sovereignty, as far as I'm concerned, is at risk.

I realise that this is a view that Aboriginal Australians will find a little bit uppity, and I'm saying it with that in mind, that our sovereignty is predetermined by their sovereignty, but as far as I'm concerned Land Rights and the nuclear issue have got a linkage anyway – it's pretty obvious what it is.

If we accede to becoming part of the war machine of one of the great dinosaurs of the end of the 20th century, then we've failed in our responsibility completely as citizens of the world, and as citizens of Australia as well.

PETER GARRETT, 19 NOVEMBER 1985

Pine Gap's like having a funnel web spider in the bedroom, but it'd be political suicide for any government to shut it down.

CHARLIE MCMAHON

It's difficult to mull over such things in the Territorian Bar; the place is too noisy. Alice is a busy airport, a strip of tar that's forever being overrun by 727s disgorging gaudily clad tourists. They stagger into the heat, buckling under the weight of designer suitcases and cameras, ill-prepared for the impending realisation that their motel doesn't match the pictures in the brochures by backing on to Ayers Rock at sunset.

Once a week or so, the airport terminal is dwarfed by huge US Air Force transport planes: C-5A Galaxies and C-141 Starlifters unloading semi-trailers full of equipment for the Joint Defence Space Research Facility, an American intelligence base at Pine Gap. An acknowledged prime nuclear target, the spy base nestles in a valley in the Macdonnell Ranges, just 19 kilometres to the south-west of Alice.

There's a story that an Aboriginal man once penetrated its perimeter, slipping through the fences and the sensors and the roving patrols, a challenge that no mortal being has yet accomplished. It's said that when the guards found him he was sitting cross-legged on the ground. At gun point they demanded to know who he was and what the hell he thought he was doing there. And when finally he snapped out of his reverie and looked up with the burnt, milky eyes of a man who has travelled far, all he said was 'I think you mob doing bad things here'.

Getting into Pine Gap is not an easy task. Indeed, getting within cooee of the joint is likely to be an indictable offence. Aircraft aren't permitted to fly within 3 kilometres of it, and the nearest accessible vantage point is a good 10 Ks away. Certainly, the number of peace activists who've managed to broach its outer perimeter can be counted on a couple of hands, or, more accurately, on the charge sheets in the Alice Springs courthouse. But on Sunday 6 July 1986, Peter Garrett became the first anti-nuclear activist to be permitted through the spy base's front gates.

His entry was brief, a matter of mere seconds, and he was only escorted 30 metres up the road to the checkpoint ... but for Pine Gap that's not a bad tenure. On the way he was photographed by feds from both sides of the Pacific: the CIA, the National Reconnaissance Office, the National Security Agency, and the Australian Security Intelligence Organisation. They had a telephoto lensman sitting on the roof of the checkpoint, and others lingered in the crowd, photographing the protestors.

The candid camera stuff was comically blatant, considering what was at their disposal – like Big Bird, a series of low-orbit satellites that can photograph and film objects as small as 20 centimetres in diameter from an altitude of 150 Ks. The pictures from Big Bird are transmitted to Pine Gap for analysis.

Essentially, the base operates as a reception and analysis centre for signals intelligence from the numerous American military satellites orbiting the earth. To intercept radio and telephone communications, they're linked to Rhyolite, a 'giant electronic vacuum cleaner' in a geostationary orbit over Borneo. The communications are intercepted and beamed down to Pine Gap for sorting and transmission back to CIA headquarters in Langley, Virginia. To pick up secret messages from operatives 'behind enemy lines', the Pyramider program has been deployed. For early warning of the launch of nuclear missiles, they rely on Project 647 – three satellites in a geostationary orbit that feed information back to Pine Gap.

In April 1985, Australia's Defence Minister, Kim Beazley, conceded that Pine Gap was likely to be targeted by the Soviet Union in the event of nuclear war. According to an AAP report, 'Mr Beazley said he did not anticipate that an attack on those facilities would have a substantial effect on any major Australian population centre'.

For the 23,000 residents of Alice Springs, a mere 19 kilometres to the north-east, it wasn't the most comforting news. As Australian governments see it, Pine Gap is a clause in an insurance policy called ANZUS (and the residents of Alice are, therefore, lumped in with the collateral).

ANZUS is a defence treaty between Australia, New Zealand and the United States that was signed in 1951. (New Zealand is now a silent partner, having been evicted when the Lange Government banned nuclear-armed warships from its ports.)

The signing of the ANZUS treaty saw Australia swapping her allegiance from the British Empire to the United States. As a result, 'The parties will consult together whenever in the opinion of any of them their territorial integrity, political independence or security is threatened.'

Since the treaty was signed, Australian governments have demonstrated their support for the Americans by committing troops to Korea and Vietnam; standing by while the Indonesians invaded East Timor; allowing the Americans to install a Very Low Frequency transmitter at North West Cape (facilitating communication with submerged nuclear-armed submarines); allowing the Americans to build the facility at Nurrungar which is also associated with Project 647, and to build the installation at Pine Gap (which has been described as the most important US base outside the United States). As further concessions, nuclear-powered and nuclear-armed vessels of the US Navy are permitted to dock in Australian ports, and Air Force B-52 bombers (their cargo unchallenged) have been granted landing rights in Darwin. In return, the Americans – according to the ANZUS treaty – will come to our aid if we're attacked.

The official argument in favour of retaining the facilities at Pine Gap and Nurrungar is that they play an important role in arms verification by providing information on the number of missiles the Soviets have, and the number of nuclear warheads in each missile.

The more sinister aspect of the programs, however, is that they give the Americans a first-strike capability by providing intelligence about where Soviet missiles are stored, thereby enabling the Americans to hit them before they can be launched.

So if the satellites are the eyes and ears of the US intelligence network, and Pine Gap and Nurrungar are the central nervous system, it's reasonable to assume that, in order to blind and deafen the Americans in a period of mounting hostility, the Soviets would knock out those bases. Without the bases, argue the peace activists, we wouldn't need America's protection in the first place.

Set up under an agreement signed by Australia and the United States in December 1966, Pine Gap became operational in 1969. Now, in 1986, a ten-year lease was coming up for renewal, and the campaign to close the base was gathering momentum.

When Brian Doolan of the Alice Springs Peace Group heard the Oils were coming to town, he invited Garrett to launch the campaign. It was a strange morning – kids playing in the gravel, hippies tinkling bells, public servants and teachers and parents standing in the sun, gum-chewing coppers, bull wagons and bull horns, and lots of cameras.

Within twenty-four hours, the scene had been splashed across news outlets throughout the country: Peaceniks Lay Down the Law/Garrett Leads Bid to Close Pine Gap/Arrest Warning From

Garrett/Protestors Call For Pine Gap Closure/Notice Given to Close Base/Midnight Oil to Burn in Peace Campaign . . .

Ironically, Garrett was unaware of the extent of the media impact. By the time the printers ink had dried, he was deep in the desert, where newspapers are as scarce as water.

Peter Garrett – rock star / newspaper columnist / constitutional commissioner / husband / father / Christian / surfer / environmental and anti-nuclear activist – wears many hats. That day it was a broadbrimmed Akubra, a squatter's hat that shaded his pate from the desert sun. His initial platform was the back of a flat-top truck parked on the side of the Stuart Highway. At his feet stood about 300 people. Across the road, marked by a NO THROUGH ROAD sign, was the cul-de-sac that may well become the dead-end of Australia.

Cars and trucks and bikes were parked in the dust, and in their midst stood a mock-up of a street sign that read PINE GAP 12 KMS.

As a small convoy of police cars and paddy wagons cruised past and took the turn-off to the gates of the base, press photographers scurried about. The principal object of their attention was Garrett.

A man without a party, he's on his way to becoming a popular figure on the political scene. He's a lawyer who's never practised at the bar, a political campaigner who's never won an election, a singer who some critics are keen to point out cannot sing. Yet in the coming months, he would be approached to join the Australian Democrats, the National Party, the Unite Australia Party and various other political organisations.

And with disarming bluntness, he would reject each offer in favour of maintaining his independence, his political effectiveness.

Pine Gap was Garrett's third media engagement for the week. On the previous Sunday afternoon, in Sydney's Centennial Park, he'd lined up with former Arbitration Commissioner Sir John Moore and author Thomas Keneally to launch an issues paper for the Constitutional Commission's Committee Examining

Individual and Democratic Rights under a constitution that was framed eighty-five years earlier.

The day before the Pine Gap rally, he addressed the Blackfella-Whitefella press conference in Alice Springs, explaining why Midnight Oil were visiting Aboriginal communities and what they hoped to achieve.

During the week, he wrote a column for the Hobart *Mercury*, questioning the validity of the ANZUS agreement. In his spare time, he also worked on a submission for the Senate Committee Enquiry Into Safety Procedures Relating to Nuclear Powered or Armed Vessels in Australian Waters.

Garrett wasn't always such a political animal.

He started university in the year of the Springboks demonstrations, anti-apartheid rallies that erupted on campuses and city streets throughout Australia in 1971. They were heady times on campus: the sexual revolution was in full swing, Australian troops were being withdrawn from Vietnam, women's liberation was coming to the fore and Gough Whitlam's Labor party was on the ascent.

But according to university friends, while he was involved in things such as the Springboks demonstrations, Garrett wasn't politically inclined. His extra-curricular pursuits at the time were more hedonistic: surfing, womanising, drinking, and singing rock 'n' roll. In the mid-'70s, Rob Hirst saw him as 'a Leftist student surfing hippy, like a lot of people at that time. Those early lyrics like 'Koala Sprint' about him going up the coast in a beaten-up old Peugeot, the best place for burgers and where the best swell was . . . just really simple pleasures of life, enjoying what Australia is, I think, basically was him.'

A decade later, those early traits would be unrecognisable.

Garrett's involvement in the anti-nuclear debate can be traced back to 1978 when the Oils did their first benefits for Greenpeace and the Movement Against Uranium Mining. The concerts were events such as the Before the Bomb Ball at Sydney Town Hall, a gig at which the Oils headlined over Mi-Sex, Wasted Daze, The

Kamikaze Kids and Mental As Anything. That gig was held the night before the release of the band's first album, a record that kicked off with their first anti-nuclear song, 'Powderworks'.

At that stage, the Oils were an unknown quantity. Garrett had collected his law degree, stuffed it in a cupboard, and thrown his lot in with a rock 'n' roll band whose uncompromising nature suggested that they'd be doomed from the start. But against all odds, the Oils started to make a serious impression. By 1983 they had a number one album and they'd become one of the most popular acts in the country. They used that popularity to draw attention to the nuclear issue by staging a massive Stop The Drop concert at the Myer Music Bowl in Melbourne. All proceeds were donated to PND (People for Nuclear Disarmament). Three months later, they staged a concert in London for the CND (Campaign for Nuclear Disarmament), sharing the stage with activist E.P. Thompson.

In 1984 the band recorded an album, *Red Sails In The Sunset*, in Japan. Garrett spent much of his time in Hiroshima, meeting with the *Hibakusha*, the surviving victims of the first atomic bomb dropped in 1945. It was an experience that galvanised his commitment to the anti-nuclear issue. Upon his return to Australia, Garrett accepted the nomination of the newly formed Nuclear Disarmament Party to stand as a candidate for the Senate. He campaigned vigorously, getting the issue up to the point where even Prime Minister Hawke had to focus on it, and attracted some 300,000 votes in the process. He missed out on winning a seat after the distribution of preferences, and has since argued that he only took on the campaign to focus attention on the issue. In that respect, he succeeded. The three fundamental planks in the NDP's platform were the removal of the American bases on Australian soil, the banning of nuclear-armed and nuclear-powered vessels in Australian waters, and the cessation of the mining and export of Australian uranium: three matters that weren't at issue until Garrett hit the boards.

Since then, he's been inextricably linked with the anti-nuclear movement, despite his resignation from the NDP in April 1985. As an anti-nuclear campaigner, he's conducted a lecture tour of New Zealand, attended disarmament conferences in Japan and Europe, been involved in anti-nuclear rallies in the United States, and continued to use every means at his disposal to draw further attention to the issue. Eventually, that campaigning led him to the perimeter of Pine Gap.

That morning, as he stood on the back of a flat-top truck by the Pine Gap turn-off, he was introduced by Brian Doolan from the Alice Springs Peace Group. Doolan's closing words set the tone for the day's activities: 'This will be a non-violent campaign all the way through. Thank you.'

'When we're talking about closing Pine Gap,' said Garrett, at the beginning of his address, 'we're really talking about doing something else altogether. Now I think what we're talking about involves two fundamental assumptions; assumptions that aren't shared by the people who are running this country at the moment; assumptions that aren't shared by the people who own the newspapers; assumptions that probably aren't shared by the people who own most of the productive resources of this country.

'The first of these assumptions is that if we are serious about contemplating our futures, we have to contemplate them in a different way, with different affirmations from those we've had up until now. You see, these two systems that operate to dominate the globe both seem to result in more and more nuclear weapons being built. We recognise this as a simple fact, and yet somehow it goes on and on and on, day in and day out. And it doesn't matter how much they talk about doing something about it, there's no change to it whatsoever.

'The second assumption is the assumption about our own sovereignty – what Australia's role and Australia's purpose is in the world. And our leaders think Australia's role and Australia's purpose is to be part of one of those two systems – the free system, thankfully – but the free system which goes on about its business of actually diverting resources (which could be better used on people who suffer continually) and making the research and military establishments of the United States – the gun makers, the arms manufacturers, the washing-machine manufacturers, the plane manufacturers, all those other people – wealthy beyond their wildest dreams and beyond your and my imagination. And Mr Hawke and Mr Hayden and Mr Howard and the procession of compliant souls that have dominated and lived in Canberra for many years accept that that's the way the world is. They accept those two assumptions, and I'm afraid we don't. And that's the very great difference.

'The other very great difference is that as time goes on, as years go on, as our children grow up they won't accept those assumptions either . . . until eventually there will be so many people who don't accept the assumptions, don't accept the lunacy, don't accept the wrong, that we will see change take place. Today is part of that process. Today is part of saying *No, I'm sorry, it's not acceptable any longer. Not for Australians. Not for Australians who believe in a future. Not for Australians who believe in equity.*

'I know that there are a heap of people around this country who believe passionately that Australia should be nuclear free. I know that there are a heap of people around this country who are prepared and ready to get involved in campaigns. I know that there are a heap of people around this country who believe in the necessities of change, who believe in the necessity of doing something like closing Pine Gap. Closing that base is not going to be easy, but making a decision not to allow it to stay open forever is the first step.

'Ah, the only other thing that I can say about this is that we're going down to the gates a little later on and it would be really good for this campaign, as today is its starting day, it would be really good with all the cameras and newspapers here if we didn't get dragged across the road and thrown in the back of a [police] truck. Otherwise, those people who are sitting in their lounge chairs in other cities around Australia will think, "Well, am I going to get involved in this or aren't I . . . Whoops, no, I think I'll wait another six months." It's time for them to get involved now. Today is an important day.'

Climbing down from the tray of the truck, he stepped across to the PINE GAP 12 KMS sign, around which was tied a piece of ribbon. With scissors in hand, he looked up with a smile and said, 'It's a little bit like launching a ship, except that this one will not sink, I can guarantee it. I declare this campaign open and I declare this base closed.'

As he cut the ribbon a stencilled CLOSED sign swung down to a round of solid applause.

Such symbolic gestures are the stuff of which peace campaigns are made. Just how effective they are is another matter.

A quote from former US President Eisenhower comes to mind: 'I like to believe that people in the long run are going to do more to promote peace than are governments. Indeed, I think that people want peace so much that one of these days governments had better get out of their way and let them have it.'

Whether that's going to be achieved through the manifestation of New Age philosophies or direct action in the form of physical or political sabotage is the big question. Peter Garrett, from all accounts, would prefer to opt for the former.

Twelve kilometres away, the gates to Pine Gap were blocked by a phalanx of thirty Northern Territory police. They stared blankfaced at the colourful array of demonstrators piling out of the arriving cars. The police stood still with their hands clasped over their crotches as latter-day hippies sang and chanted and rattled cowbells a couple of metres in front of them.

Behind them is an over-sized cattle grid that, no doubt, has tank-stopping capabilities. Above that are the gates, cyclone-wire mesh and tubular steel about four lanes wide and plastered with a couple of STOP signs. (Two nights earlier, demonstrators had secured the gates with a kryptonite lock that took Commonwealth Police three hours to cut through with an oxy-acetylene torch.) About 30 metres beyond the gates is the security checkpoint which, at that stage, was graced by the presence of a man on the roof hunkering down over a tripod supporting a massive telephoto lens.

Further on, and out of sight, lie the huge white perspex radomes that house the antennae; the computer rooms; the 30-metre tower; the high-frequency antenna for direct communications with Clark Field, the US Air Force base in the Philippines; the bores, the dams and the diesel-powered generators; and the motel-style accommodation, kitchens and other recreational facilities.

As the skies cleared, Garrett and ten members of the Alice Springs Peace Group read out their Notice Of Intention to Terminate an Agreement – a twelve-part document explaining how and why the people of Australia wanted the base to be removed. Upon completion of the public reading, Peter Garrett had a word to the police and – to the astonishment of all – was escorted through the gates and on to the base.

'Come back Peter!'

With his head dipped to talk to the Commonwealth police escorting him, he walked up the road to the checkpoint. There he was met by a high-ranking Australian officer – one of the few Australians on the base who isn't a cook or a gardener – and handed over the Notice.

Within thirty seconds or so, he was on his way out again, having thought better of the impulse to question the integrity of the receiving officer. At the gate he raised his hat with a smile and rejoined his friends in the outside world. The cameras rolled, supporters clapped and cheered.

The impression it left was of a show devoid of hooks, a whitefella ritual that ran smoothly enough, won good reviews and threw the critics by eschewing the cliches of gratuitous violence and ill-matched chases.

I was thinking about the implications of that gig as I strolled across the tarmac at Alice a fortnight later.

Staggering along behind me, half of the crew were suffering from the effects of a night on the booze. After eight days of abstinence, the bar at the Oasis had done a good trade. Pat Pickett had the dregs of a beer in his hand. 'I'm not on the wagon,' he gulped, 'I'm just running beside it for a while . . .'

Our pilot was a young bloke from Sydney who'd been flying for about eight years. He said he liked the gig because 'it pulls birds, and you get to see a lot of the country'. He'd flown half-a-dozen of us from Sydney, via Bourke and the Birdsville pub, a fortnight earlier. Now he was back in Alice to take us into the Top End.

As I stepped up to the plane, a twin-engined Aero Commander, he trotted up. 'Are you going to use that machine on the flight?' he asked.

I was carrying the WP 600, a battery-operated word processor that weighs less than 3 kilos, is as high as a cigarette packet is wide, and is as large as the average coffee table book. He'd shown an interest in it on our first flight, and I figured he wanted to explore it further.

'Yeah, sure, if you like.'

'Well, can you tell me when you're going to turn it on and off? That's why we got lost over Thargominda. It jammed the navigation system.'

After a moment of confusion, it made sense. A few days earlier, in Warakurna, I'd discovered that if I switched the word processor on within the vicinity of a radio transceiver, it was capable of jamming the medical calls for the Royal Flying Doctor Service.

The pilot seemed to be an easy-going bloke, but there was a darkness behind his shades that suggested he'd spent sleepless nights trying to sort out why his million-dollar aeroplane couldn't get a fix on a beacon in the desert. I'd seen the same grim look on that first flight from Sydney, when he started getting edgy about 300 Ks north-west of Bourke. Suddenly he was seeing too much of the country, and all it was yielding were channels that slithered like snakes to the horizon, stock tracks that converged on slimy green bores, skeletons that lay bleached in the sand and gunbarrel-straight seismic lines that ran on forever.

'We've lost Thargominda!' he yelled. We were about a thousand feet over the flood plains of western Queensland, and what the sun and his instincts were telling him, the compass was refusing to confirm. He reached for a map and tried to place himself, but all he got when he peered through the plexiglass was the blinding flash of lakes that lay across the landscape like sequins on a dress.

West of Birdsville, the sandhills of the Simpson Desert run almost to the Macdonnell Ranges. There are hundreds of kilometres of these glowing red ridges. Like the ripples in a sheet of roughly corrugated cardboard, they run to the north-west and disappear into the smokey blue horizon.

'You know,' he yelled, 'there are places down there where no white man's ever set foot . . .

'From Birdsville, you talk to traffic control in Charleville. But out here in the Simpson . . . well, no one's likely to pick up a call . . .'

Especially when your communications are being sabotaged by the slim black box in a passenger's lap.

As the aircraft took off from Alice, swinging back over the Macdonnell Ranges, we were treated to a view of the radomes of Pine Gap. They stand out like a bunch of golfballs waiting to be hit, waiting to be blown clean off the face of the planet.

The Aero Commander's a noisy little beast, a twin-engined ten-seater that emits a constant rumbling hum, an effect that could only be reproduced by plugging the ears with damp cotton wool and plunging the head into the howling vortex of a reliable Hoover.

So what with the noise and the cabin pressure and these inexplicable drops in altitude, it's no way to travel with a hangover. At least there's no chance of getting lost. Out here, on a flight to Darwin, you can always circle around and find the Stuart Highway.

That highway, all 1,533 Ks of it, was bulldozed and sealed in 1942. Working day and night, the construction crews moved through. Any trucks that broke down were simply pushed on to the side of the track. With the Japanese on the doorstep, the road crews couldn't afford to wait around.

Our pilot wears aviator shades and bars on his shoulders. His head-set system's slung over his left ear. The gold pen in his breast pocket glints, its reflection bouncing off the circular dials that jiggle and spin on the panel. He switches to automatic pilot and plasters the windscreen with maps to obliterate the glare.

Between Alice and the fuel depot outside Katherine you've got to fly over 1,000 Ks of semi-arid scrub, pastoral leases, and endless sandhills. It can be a long and painful trip.

I've done it in an eight-seater with Lippold and Pickett, a pack of cards and a carton of Melbourne beer. We were flying south, and about an hour out of Alice I started succumbing to the sensation of an excruciating pain. There's no toilet on those planes, no relief at all in a tubular tin can with wings. You can't even stand up and jump around, hopping from foot to foot, swaying from side to side to alleviate the pressure on the bladder. All you can do is sit tight, scrunched up in your seat. Lippold and Pickett might be roadies, but they were perceptive enough to suss that they could compound the problem if they talked about dripping taps, rivers in flood and waterfalls they've seen in their travels. The pilot wasn't much help either: 'Piss in my plane, and you can lick it up.'

This time around, the flight was painless. After about four hours in the air, we landed at Tindal to refuel. It's a strip about 30 Ks south of Katherine which is being developed into a major RAAF base. Three hundred Ks from Darwin, and south of the Katherine River, it's the most strategically viable position in the Territory. Blow the bridge over the river and you'd strand any land-borne invader in the Top End. Tindall is being developed as the home strip for a squadron of frontline F-18 jet fighters. Nearby, the Army plans to station a cavalry battalion that can strike north into Arnhem Land, east into the Gulf of Carpentaria, or west into the Joseph Bonaparte Gulf and the Kimberleys.

At present though, the Tindal terminal is a low building that houses a soft-drink vending machine, toilets, an old tourist map of the Territory, a couple of rows of plastic bucket seats and unattended counters for Budget, Tillair and various charter companies.

While the planes are refuelled, the crew stands around playing silly buggers behind the charter counters, stretching their legs and wishing there was a car available for a quick beer 'n' burgers run into town.

We were still standing there when the Warumpis' Queen Air taxied down the strip to take off, and white smoke started oozing from its starboard engine. It had blown a pot, and while everyone else flew on to Darwin, the Warumpis were forced to spend six hours on the ground, waiting for another plane.

Darwin's a frontier town.

I remember my first trip up here, a long hitch in the winter of 1978, a teenage adventurer with a sheet of plastic and a duffel bag full of greasy clothes and battered paperbacks. I was fresh from Sydney, and Darwin was a point on the map, a wild and unruly joint on the edge of the tropics, an ill-bred town where beer was served for breakfast.

All the way up the Queensland coast – wild rides with bible-bashing hippies and beer-swilling petrol heads – I'd been told about Raintree Park: stay there for a while and you'll meet everybody you've ever met. Like Trafalgar Square.

So I lobbed into Raintree Park with a can of Coke and a copy of Capote's *In Cold Blood*, and lay on the lawn and buried myself in the book, not wanting to think about where I was going to sleep.

I met my first Aborigine that day. A guy of 17 sauntered over and squatted down.

'G'day.'

'Gidday,' he replied.

'Hot, innit?'

'Hot's not the word . . . Bin 'ere long?'

'Just got here.'

'You got place to stay?'

'Nah, not yet.'

'You can come with me. We got camp on beach.'

I shouldered my bag and followed the blackfella down Knuckey Street, passing blocks that were vacant but for a buckled letterbox and a weed-infested concrete slab, all that remained of houses torn from the ground during the devastation of Cyclone Tracy. My principal thought, the foolhardy paranoia of a young whitefella from the city, was, 'Okay, I'm likely to get my watch ripped off, but I'm up here now, at the end of the line, so why not? More experiences to write home about . . .'

But even the worst scripts can be rejected. The blacks were from down Adelaide way, seeking refuge from the cold. We camped for a week on the red stony beach below the steep tropical jungles of Lameroo, sharing cigarettes and cartons of milk and cans of pineapple juice, sleeping on towels in shorts and t-shirts, waking up sweating at two in the morning and plunging in for a swim – flat water in a sheltered bay – unaware of tales of a huge croc and his mate in the mangroves on the point. And each morning, the ranger would come down, wake us up, and recommend that we move on.

I took my clothes to a laundromat one afternoon, and got talking to the bloke who ran the place. After the cyclone, Darwin had been evacuated. He'd stayed on.

'Good slow life up 'ere . . .'

'Changed much since Tracy?' I asked.

'Oh yeah! She used to be real nice. But since the cyclone, it's got a lot faster, the whole place.

'Used to be real slow . . . Yeah, reckon you'd notice the difference if you're from South . . . Y'know, I went t'Perth few months back. Bloody hell! Rush, rush, rush. Cars 'n' buses all over the joint. Bloke could get run over in a place like that. Too bloody fast . . . Where ya from?'

'Sydney.'

A strange glaze comes over people when you say that. Every big city cop show they've ever seen flashes through their minds, and they undergo a physical change, steeling up, wary, as if they've picked up a lunatic. I've seen it on faces in Tasmania and in the backblocks of Western Australia. Tell them you're from Sydney and they recoil.

The bloke in the laundromat didn't say a word after that, just walked back to his table and polished a dryer or three, always watching, one eye on the cloth and one on the foreigner.

We live in a country where there are no language barriers, no international borders to cross, no radical variations in political, artistic, or religious culture, and yet the size of the land itself is alienating to a lot of people. A xenophobia exists in our suspicion of people from the bush, from other cities, from other parts of the country.

In Darwin, thankfully, it's been over-run by the post-cyclone invasion of Southerners.

Today, it's a small city, a slow one, a relaxed one, a city that can be done in thongs. Mention you're from Sydney these days and the locals are likely to buy you a beer and offer commiserations.

It's become the end of the line, the dust bag of a vacuum cleaner that sucks young refugees from the south and tumbles them around amid the heat and the sweat and the beer until they either settle and find their niche or get spewed back out to the chaos of the cities, or someplace that's even quieter, looser . . . Like Broome.

Darwin – a city with a population of around 55,000, average age 25. A city in which, in the depths of winter, you can sit on the beach at sunset, watching an iridescent orange ball of light sinking into the blue waters of Fannie Bay. And not feel cold. Where you can stretch beneath palm trees watching wedge tails, kites and hawks drift on the breeze, soaring high on the strength of an unseen thermal with the mere twitch of a wingtip. Where, on a winter's evening, you can wander down to the Botanic Gardens in shorts and a singlet with an armful of beer and join people sitting around hitting bits of bamboo against each other and singing 'Ghost Riders in the Sky' and 'Folsom Prison Blues'.

Billowing palls of heavy brown smoke linger around the city at this time of year, as the surrounding desiccated golden speargrass is burnt off.

It's such a delightfully relaxed town in the Dry, and yet you can never get away from the feeling that you're on the frontier. Timor, after all, is just a few hundred kilometres away to the north-west.

Jet fighters, ditched in the swamps around Bagot, ooze black clouds of oily smoke. Burnt-out Doves on the edge of the airstrip are set alight with gasoline every week for fire drills.

You can be standing on the footpath having a beer and a chat when the sky explodes; an enormous earth-shattering, nerve-zapping explosion. It comes, BANG!, and scares the hell out of you. And when you look up, the twin after-burners of an F-111 are disappearing into the blue, climbing straight up, screaming so high that the aircraft disappears from sight, so high you can't even hear it anymore. And then it reappears, dropping from 40,000 feet, straight down . . .

And that's just our boys. When the Americans roll in, you really hear about it.

They thunder across the city in huge dark-green B-52s, Boeing Stratofortresses that are about 35 years old, so old that they plastered Viet Nam with thousands of tonnes of TNT and napalm. So old and yet so effective.

I remember when I was a kid finding one in a Corn Flakes packet. It had four double jet pods hanging beneath its swept back wings and it was coffee-brown in colour. A single piece of mildly flexible plastic, it was a fine example of modern technology. I took it to school to play 'wars' at lunchtime, and in the end I chewed its tail so badly that the fuselage was blistered with tooth marks and the tail was transformed into little twists of brown plastic, as if it'd been hit by a couple of heat-seeking surface to air missiles.

Designed as a nuclear bomber, the first Boeing Stratofortress took to the air in 1952. The last to come off the production line ten years later had a bomb bay capacity of 24.5 tonnes of conventional explosives and a maximum cruising speed in excess of 1,000 kilometres an hour. Their wings are wider than an olympic pool is long, and their length only marginally shorter. And with the aid of refuellers they can stay airborne indefinitely.

There are B-52s in the air twenty-four hours a day, cruising at about 50,000 feet, watching, waiting. There's a story about the black eye-patch brigade, B-52 pilots based in an idyllic tropical paradise like Hawaii or even Guam who clamber into their aircraft and in preparation for take-off, flip black patches over one of their eyes. In the event of them getting too close to the end of the world – too close to the blinding flash, so close that it burns the retina and scorches the pupil, so close that the orange light is the last they'll ever see – they can lift the patch and still have one good eye to complete the mission.

In February 1980, two months after the Soviet invasion of Afghanistan, US Air Force B-52s began low-level training flights over North Queensland. They'd take off from Guam, over 3,000 kilometres to the north, come screaming over Queensland, and then cruise back to Guam in time for Budweisers in the officers' mess.

Thirteen months later, Tony Street, Minister for Foreign Affairs in the Fraser Government, exchanged Notes with the US Embassy which paved the way for the use of Darwin as a staging post for the flights. According to a statement presented to the parliament by Prime Minister Fraser on 11 March 1981: 'After completing the low level training exercises, the aircraft will land at Darwin and refuel. After appropriate crew rest, the aircraft will undertake sea surveillance and navigation training operations over the Indian Ocean – an area of great security interest to both Australia and the United States. The flights will then return via Darwin to Guam.'

The agreement allowed for 'periodic deployments through Darwin of up to three B-52 and six KC-135 aircraft, supported by about 100 USAF personnel' who 'would remain under US command'.

Despite Prime Minister Fraser's assurances to the contrary, at no point in the agreement is there a specific reference to whether or not the bombers are barred from carrying either conventional or nuclear weapons over and on to Australian soil. On the day the agreement was signed in March 1981, Fraser told the parliament 'the flights landing at Darwin will be unarmed and will carry no bombs'.

Four years later, in March 1985, Senator Gareth Evans said simply that, 'The United States is not prepared to disclose which of its aircraft are nuclear-armed and which are armed with conventional weapons. Its policy in this respect is identical to that which prevails in relation to ships.'

In the first six and a half years that followed the signing of the agreement, according to Senator Evans, there were '141 B-52 aircraft landings' in Darwin.

A major headache for the Americans is security (or lack thereof) on the ground in Darwin. It is the only airport in the country in which a civilian passenger terminal ('Gateway to Australia's North') is stuck in the middle of an RAAF base. Across the strip, like darts on the tar, sit the Mirages of 75 Squadron, antiquated fighter bombers that proudly wear the insignia of the Collingwood Football Club's magpie. They've been in service for over twenty years and every so often something goes wrong; the pilot hits eject, a canopy blooms, and a couple of million bucks worth of hardware slews into the swamps around Bagot.

In the interests of security, the American bombers and their refuellers (Boeing 707s modified into KC-135 Stratotankers that can pump close to 3,000 kilos of jet fuel a minute in mid-air) are kept well away from the rest of the facilities. Surrounded by sensors and manned around the clock, the planes are so vulnerable that the Yanks have dreamed up scenarios in which terrorists hijack civilian airliners and get close enough to the bombers to do some damage. But even the anti-terrorist exercises, conducted by the police and the elite SAS, have been fumbled so badly that journalists have been able to infiltrate the security cordons with apparent ease.

Security was obviously tight when we arrived. On the way to the light aircraft terminal, we had to pass through an RAAF checkpoint, giving assurances we wouldn't venture near the USAF aircraft on the strip. No more than 500 metres away, two B-52s and a pair of grey KC-135 Stratotankers basked in the sun.

With Midnight Oil and a film crew on the tarmac, the RAAF guards were edgy. When ABC cameraman Laurie McManus unclipped his case and reached for a camera to film the bands loading their planes, lights flashed, radios crackled, and tyres hummed across the tar. A female driver in a police car with RAAF registration plates parked among the light aircraft and ordered that the camera be put away. No one's allowed to film the bombers or their refuellers.

Peter Garrett stood off by himself, squinting at the bombers and shaking his head. It was quiet out there, just the breeze in the grass and the clunk of black boxes bumping white metal. He took a dozen steps towards the bombers, thought better of it, and turned back towards the band.

Those planes, designed before Elvis cut his first record for his mother, were sitting on Australian soil. But to photograph or go near them was a Federal offence. And at that stage of his career, Garrett couldn't afford to get busted.

CHAPTER NINE
MANINGRIDA

I'm sitting on my swag beneath the wing of a Cherokee Six, taking advantage of the only slab of shade for 100 metres.

It's muggy here in the tropics, and the skies are unseasonally cloudy. The air is warm and sweet, like the mangoes on the trees. They've bloomed early this year, and the locals are muttering about another bad Wet. Conditions, they say, haven't been like this since the Dry before Cyclone Tracy, and already people are planning to spend the summer in the south.

It's said that by the time Tracy blew in across the Beagle Gulf on Christmas Eve in '74, reared up in the darkness and flattened Darwin, all the Aborigines living around the city had bailed out, grabbing their blankets, jumping into cars and light planes and fleeing into the bush.

Some of them fled out here, to Maningrida, a community on the mouth of the Mann River. It's 370 Ks east of Darwin, and for five months of the year it's inaccessible by road. There are no telephones out here, and the most regular contact with the outside world is through the fortnightly barge service that chugs in with supplies. If you want to get out of town during the Wet, you've got to hike down to the airstrip and wait for a plane.

Fast and low, the planes drift over the mouth of the Mann, a wide muddy river that slithers through the mangroves like a King Brown, scaly like the snake and just as deadly. Bordered by patchy scrub and savannah grasslands that run rife in the Wet and wither in the Dry, the Mann and its tributaries – the Liverpool, the Tomkinson and Marrgalidban Creek – spew milky, silted water into Boucat Bay. As the planes approach, ruffling the pandanus fronds and flattening the spear grass at the end of the strip, orange-tailed black cockatoos explode from the minneatas squawking and shrieking and dispersing like smoke. The planes pull through the trees, bounding down the tarmac and rolling to a halt near the passenger terminal.

The logistics of getting this expedition into the air were insane.

The initial plan was to swing round the Top End in a Caribou, but the Air Force wouldn't wear that one. So a DC-3, an ancient Gooney Bird, was chartered from Air North. That blew a motor about three weeks out and Hardie had to track down replacements. Somehow he had to find enough aircraft to carry about twenty people, 2,110 kilos of equipment and a stack of swags and personal baggage.

In the end, he rounded up the Aero Commander, a Navajo and a Queen Air from Budget Air in Sydney, a King Air from Lloyds in Darwin and a pair of single-engine Cherokee Sixes from another Darwin mob called Gammon Aire. A 402 has been commandeered from Tillair in Katherine to replace the grounded Queen Air, and the ABC crew have chartered a Shrike from Darwin.

A winged circus! A squadron of light aircraft drifting in with a growl and a splutter . . . disgorging black boxes and pop stars and film crew and support teams, leaving them in the sun, waiting for the Toyotas and the trucks to arrive.

The passenger terminal at Maningrida Airport is a small Bessabrick building with a corrugated-iron roof. Painted in shades of blue, it's decorated with paintings of such local totems as a bird, a fish, a mud crab and a stingray.

There's also a sign:

LIQUOR ACT
WARNING
RESTRICTED AREA

THE POSSESSION OR CONSUMPTION OF *LIQUOR* BEYOND
THIS POINT WITHOUT A PERMIT IS A SERIOUS OFFENCE.
VEHICLES CARRYING LIQUOR MAY BE SEIZED & FORFEITED
& THE FOLLOWING PENALTIES MAY ALSO APPLY

FIRST OFFENCE	UP TO $1000 FINE OR 6 MONTHS GAOL
SECOND OR SUBSEQUENT OFFENCE	UP TO $2000 FINE OR 12 MONTHS GAOL

Kumanjayi Rurrambu didn't see the sign.

Riding into Maningrida high as a whistling kite, he was carrying a cask full of wine and a skinful of beer. The conquering rock star returning with Midnight Oil ... getting closer to his island home. He was back in his own country, the surroundings were familiar, the languages and the people were his, and he was as wild as they come.

Until this point in the tour, the Warumpis have been firing on all six. Throughout the desert leg they delivered consistently good shows. Neil Murray and Cookie have revived the band for the tour, covering the weak spots, camouflaging the lack of discipline, holding it all together. But after a night in Darwin, the seams are coming apart ...

Bassist Hilary Jabaldjari Wirri is still in Darwin. Clutching a brand new pair of R.M. Williams boots, he was last seen popping into a pub for 'just one more, boss'. Take out the tour log and mark in 'Hilary Jabaldjari Wirri: AWOL'.

It's not the first time Hilary's found some friends and forgotten a tour – what is a tour, after all, but an opportunity to go away and meet people? And Hilary is of that ilk, a soft man with a real fondness for friends and times and places all over the country. He can weep when he thinks of good times in Fitzroy Crossing; he can bandage a wrist in Broome to attract attention when others are hogging the lime-light with their violent behaviour; he can sing and dance when he's had a few beers in Darwin; he can stop off in a pub and step off a tour. In a week or so he'll think about finding his friends again. So Hilary's departure is not a problem: that's his way.

But Rurrambu *is* a problem. A one-can screamer at the best of times, he's carried his Darwin binge into Maningrida and is now laying waste to the settlement's beer supplies.

And while the Warumpis are expressing concern, his countrymen figure it's okay. Reinforcements are on the way. For there, steaming into the mouth of the river, about twelve hours ahead of schedule, is Maningrida's most reliable contact with the outside world: the fortnightly barge, laden with supplies for the store – and beer.

Maningrida isn't strictly dry. Every couple of weeks, the locals fill out an order for their quota of liquor – a flagon, or a case of beer, perhaps.

Those with some knowledge of behavioural patterns figure that barge night is not the one on which to stage a rock 'n' roll concert. Barge nights, they reason, tend to get a little out of hand.

With this on his mind, Gary Morris sets about trying to postpone the barge's unloading until after the show. But in a community like Maningrida, the barge's visits have been a major source of amusement since the settlement was set up as a government 'trading post' in the early '50s. The trading posts and missions of the time tended to draw people from all over the region.

In *The Destruction of Aboriginal Society*, C.D. Rowley refers to the attraction in almost cargo cultish terms:

> As the subsequent history of the Maningrida government post in northern Arnhem Land showed, the nomads would be attracted to the headquarters established for patrolling, as a source of processed food and trade goods. The gatherings of people waiting for the ships to come illustrated the irresistible

> pressures away from nomadic existence which had marked all this history; it was not only the absence of positive policies which led to the institutional situations.

The curiosity value of the European settlements was high, a trend that echoed the experiences of the desert. But there the similarities end. For this is a different land, and the culture's a thousand generations removed from that of the desert.

It's a matter of environment. Harsh and foreboding, the desert has bred a strong, disciplined people who are accustomed to making hard, tough decisions, strict rules and an iron-clad lore.

But the Top End's a rich land where food and shelter are abundant and the climate is idyllic. It's a land of warm nights and open beaches, dense forests, palm tree groves, the wafting cooking smells of turtles boiling in the pot, clean breezy villages overlooking sandy bays and the pervading sense of a relaxed lifestyle.

It's a land brimming with mineral resources and communities thriving on mining royalties.

A land in which there's no shortage of fresh tucker: fish and turtle, wallaby and goanna, lobsters and oysters, sweet yams and mangrove worms and eggs of every shape and size.

You're unlikely to die of thirst up here; there are far more exotic killers in this part of the world: crocodiles, sharks, stingers, king browns and mosquitoes that carry malaria, Australian encephalitis, dengue fever, dengue haemorrhagic fever and epidemic polyarthritis.

To the Top Enders, the desert is a wild, tough place that breeds wild, tough people. The tribesmen of Arnhem Land have a certain fear of the men from the desert, a grudging respect for warriors. 'They're wild, that desert mob, eh?' they say with a degree of awe that's never reciprocated. 'Fierce eh?'

To the desert people, the Top Enders are merely 'fish eaters', an inherently different, softer mob whose sense of discipline is comparatively lax.

Traditionally, there was little contact between the two. Top Enders rarely ventured into the harsh emptiness of the desert. Why should they, when their own environment was so idyllic? The occasional desert person, a songman or someone fleeing the consequences of a tribal crime, might have ventured into the Top End, but the migration was essentially one way.

Traditionally, the Top Enders are more accustomed to change and outside influences than their desert-dwelling counterparts. They have a history of trading with the Macassans of the Celebes, which dates back to the 1600s. For hundreds of years the coasts of Arnhem Land were visited every Wet season by Macassans in search of trepang or beche-de-mer. As a result, they're a far less timid people than their desert-dwelling brothers. They're friendlier, more outgoing and less intimidating. And they've had the advantage of long-term tenure of their land. Unlike the desert people who, so often, were dispossessed, few of the Top Enders have ever been shifted off their traditional lands en masse.

The artwork of the Top End people, their languages and religious ceremonies, reflect the influences that drifted in from abroad. In coastal communities like Nguiu and Milingimbi, there are huge tamarind trees planted by the Macassans as a source of fruit for their annual camps.

Interestingly, while some Top Enders refer to themselves as *Yolgnu* people (as opposed to the *Anangu* of the desert), their word for whites or Europeans is *balanda*, a Malay word derived from 'Hollander' introduced by the Macassans.

Anthropologist Donald Thomson, who worked in the Arnhem Land region during the '30s and '40s, noted that, unlike the reception inspired by the Europeans, that afforded the Macassans 'was one of respect, amounting almost to hero worship, which the Europeans have never been able to achieve. This respect was based on the pattern of behaviour which included recognition by the Macassans of the territorial and other rights of the Aborigines and respect for the integrity of their women.'

The artwork of the Top End is strikingly different from that of the desert, featuring x-ray bark paintings of animals and spirits. The bark is cut from the trees early in the Wet season, and when he sets to work, the artist will recount the tales of his Dreaming. The process of painting involves the singing of the songs associated with that particular tribal story, listening to the didgeridoo (or *yidaki*) pieces associated with it, and recounting the tales. The work, done with a sharp stick dipped in ochres with human hair brushes, is intricate and detailed: lines and wiggles and whorls indicating parts of a journey or totemic influences. Now, because of the recent upsurge of interest in the dot art of the Western Desert, Top End bark painting – once relegated by whites to the realms of table mats and tea towels – is enjoying a resurgence of keen interest from collectors. (The really weird stuff comes from the Kimberleys, further west, primitive space cadet spirit paintings that Von Daniken would've had a field day with.) It's the land of the didgeridoo, an extraordinary woodwind instrument fashioned from treetrunks that have been hollowed out by termites, a log that howls and roars and sings and calls the spirits from the depths of your soul. The men smoke long-stemmed softwood pipes that were introduced by the Macassans, and everywhere you go there's a relaxed, colourful lifestyle.

Top End people have been a lot more open than desert people in their acceptance of religions. One conclusion is that they're so sophisticated that they only see whites as temporary traders, another bunch of visitors who've come to enrich Top End culture and swap ideas. Whites have been establishing outposts in their country for fifty or sixty years and they've no reason to suppose this will change. So they'll take the education and mining royalties, welfare cheques and Toyotas and outboards, and they'll cut up ditched bombers for spearheads and use sparkplugs as sinkers when they're fishing.

Their ready acceptance of the Fijian ceremonial beverage *kava* is a recent (and increasingly controversial) example of their adaptability. Introduced to the Yirrkala community in 1982 by a Uniting

Church worker from Fiji, its use and abuse has become endemic in some communities. Originally presented as a substitute for alcohol, it's now gone the way of grog and been banned in some communities.

I was involved in a couple of *kava* sessions on Elcho Island in 1985 and, for weeks afterwards, I thought the stuff was called 'garba'. It has an effect not unlike a dentist's local anaesthetic – a numbing of the tongue and the nasal passages and a temporary paralysis of the jaw that causes people to speak of 'garba' rather than 'kava', which requires a little more effort.

Cold muddy *kava*. Set the stars dancing across the sky. Leave the ashes glowing in the fire. Pull up a blanket or a patch of grass, join the circle, clap your hands, twice! And some bloke with a sweet grin and yellowy eyes, unkempt hair and a sagging chest, dips the coconut shell into the bowl and scoops out the juice. You take it in both hands and pour it down your throat, ignoring the earthy taste, fighting back the clenching of the gut, draining the shell. 'Cella Vella. Ah Mama mama mama . . .'

It's made from the crushed roots of the *Piper methysticum forst*, a huge shrub that grows throughout Melanesia, Micronesia and Polynesia. It's prepared by taking a bag of the crushed roots and wrapping it in muslin and soaking and squeezing it in a big bowl of water until it turns a murky brown.

Among the Fijians and Samoans its use is limited to ceremonial activities and, more recently, sociable drinking in the clubs of Suva. But in Arnhem Land, where there aren't any traditional restrictions on its use – there are no stories of how it evolved – its abuse has become a major problem in some places.

It's a mild intoxicant that, if anything, has a sedative effect. Aboriginal people love to sit around and talk, to have long meetings, and *kava* is conducive to that. The only activity it encourages is to sit cross-legged on the ground and rave for hours. So, whereas in Fiji its limited use has meant it's an effective meeting ground, a problem solver, in Arnhem Land its use is so rife that some people just become vegetables, never moving from the bowl, lost in a world of their own, unable to communicate and failing to share the responsibilities of the community or the family.

'The problem,' as one observer sees it, 'is that your big *kava* head, the non-stop marathon man of the *kava* bowl, will sit down and discuss problems twenty-four hours a day. And not do anything. They'll have all the solutions. It's like dope in the '70s; you'd sort of sit around dissecting the planet, but you'd never actually go out and do anything about it.'

Maningrida went through 108 kilos of the stuff in seven weeks between March and May 1985.

When Martin Hardie was planning the Blackfella-Whitefella Tour, he selected Maningrida as an example of a well-established Top End community. Shaded by palm trees and surrounded by lawns, it's got bitumen roads, streetlights, footpaths and modern buildings like the tastefully designed council chambers. It's clean and open and forever brushed by the breezes from the sea.

It's the home of around 700 people – Gunavidji mostly, with a few from the Burada, Gunwinggu, Rembarrnga and other clans. A further 700 people live on neighbouring out-stations or homeland centres, the first of which were established in 1970, early in the out-station movement's history. There's a large school (at which actor David Gulpilil learned and later taught) with two bilingual programs and a series of adult education programs.

For most of the pilots, this is the first night away from the Big Smoke. For Chuck Mango and Captain Coop from Gammon Aire, it's something else.

They're a couple of cowboys from Darwin who've rolled in with an illicit bottle of rum and heads smoking with the colourful dreams of a pair of locals intent on making an impression. And while the rest of the pilots have opted for the comfort of a demountable shack on the beach, these jocks are happy to roll their swags out by a fire and get down to some serious partying. Mango, as one of the southern pilots sees it, is 'all prick and ribs like a drover's dog'. And his mate's a tall rangy bloke whose speech is slow and thoughtful and tumbles from a mouth devoid of teeth. But despite their obvious predilection for high times, partying is not the order of the evening.

The show's being staged on an area of freshly mown grass, and for those of us who haven't seen such vegetation for a couple of weeks there's an urge to roll across the ground and soak it up.

But Rurrambu is so drunk that the Warumpis' show is appalling. He loses all control of his voice and the resulting mess is so painful to listen to that there's a general feeling he's let the side down.

The Oils' set isn't much better. Despite a great stage sound, out front it's a top-heavy mess, bouncing off buildings and echoing all over the place, so loud it's unbearable. During the set, fruit bats bring relief by crashing into the wiring on the electrical board, an act that blows the power for the entire community.

Meanwhile, Rurrambu's getting the third degree as the remaining Warumpis take him to task for his drinking. They've got him cornered by the council chambers, and by the end of the session he's in a sorry state.

The Oils aren't feeling much better. Half of their swags have been left in the Queen Air or somewhere between Yuendumu and Maningrida – no one's quite sure. Not even Martin Hardie, the man responsible for such things.

While Hardie cops a grilling, various city-bred whitefellas bemoan the loss of their gear. Which is ironic, 'cos this, after all, is the Top End. In the Dry Season. The closest place to heaven on earth.

Because the primary mode of transportation has switched from four-wheel-drive Toyotas to fixed-wing aircraft, the touring party is now at the mercy of the communities. No longer do the Oils have the mobility to head into the scrub in search of a decent campsite with lots of *waru*. But Top End communities tend to be a lot cleaner and more visually pleasing than their desert counterparts. It costs 1,000 dollars or more to bring a car in on the barge, so the communities aren't inundated with rusting wrecks. Also, many of them have been established for longer and, because of their strategic value, more effort has been put into their development.

So who could possibly complain about a base of operations as well serviced as the Maningrida Council Chambers? There's a fridge, a kitchen, big glass doors that open on to a view of the lawns and the sea, a beautifully polished boardroom table, overhead fans and an orchestra pit full of geckos.

Outside, by the Gammon Aire campfire, Rurrambu's running blind. 'I'm gonna leave, y'know. Finish it. End it all. Go back to my out-station, y'know. Mata Mata, my place. Go back there. End it all. Tomorra! Sick of those bastards. Hate me. I'm gonna finish up. Tomorra!'

When Gary Morris strolls over, he listens to the Mata Mata mutter for a couple of minutes and says, 'If you still feel the same way tomorrow, not tonight, tomorrow, then you come to me and we'll talk about it, okay?' As Morris heads back inside, Rurrambu stumbles off into the darkness.

Strolling towards his swag, Garrett stops and gazes at the night sky, at the stars you can see only in the bush, at the glorious patterns of the galaxy, at the millions of lights that prick the heavens like flecks of glitter spilled carelessly across a carpet. He stands there for a minute or so, totally blown away by the spectacle. If that is the inside of God's mind . . . where's His head at?

It's morning, and out on the edge of town there's a brace of swags scattered across the tarmac. Blue and green sheets of canvas with foam mattresses and bedding, all rolled into tight bundles and stacked beside the planes.

The ones that stand out are those belonging to the managers of the two bands. David Cooke's is a toy swag thrown together with sheets of poly tarp and blankets and odd lengths of rope. Gary Morris's is a jungle-green button-down number with twin leather straps and reinforced stitching. He could've paid 170 dollars in Yuendumu or 120 dollars in Alice, but he forked out 200 for it in Kintore. It's part of his trip, having the best swag that a dollar can buy. In six months it'll be rotting in the Oils' Office back garden, its straps chewed by the Rottweilers, the canvas fraying in the rain.

But for the moment it's a flash of one-up-manship from the man who arranged the finance for everybody else's swags.

Next to the swags are bags labelled with Midnight Oil baggage tags, heavy-duty carry-alls with reinforced webbing and international airline stickers. There are mike stands and fold-back wedges and an orange multicore lead that's been rolled beneath the wing of the Navajo.

Fifty metres away, the Warumpis are unloading a stack of black boxes from a Dyna truck. They're pulling them down – drum cases, EV boxes, the mixing-desk, more fold-back wedges, stage amps, PA bins and all the rest – squeezing them into the Cherokee Sixes of Gammon Aire.

The pilots crouch beneath the wings, taking samples of the fuel with little bottles, checking for water. Everybody's assembled; everybody except Gary Williams. He is so scared of flying, so tired of this whole gig, that he's disappeared. Hiding out somewhere in Maningrida, he's chosen to hop off the tour and stick around, enjoying the pleasures of a Top End Dry season.

CHAPTER TEN
GALIWIN'KU

Their letters came, carved up by the RAAF censors, marked 'On Active Service', dateline 'Somewhere In The North'. In another age they would've been down the front of an Oils gig, raising the sweat and the beer, chasing girls and stumbling drunkenly through the night. But instead they were hiding out in horseshoe bunkers beneath strips of camo-netting and fraying canvas, amid the timber crates and the ammo boxes, the fuel drums and the anti-aircraft guns, eaten alive by sandflies and huge mosquitoes, dealing with malaria tablets and tinea powder, scrawling letters home, their hands so wet with sweat the pen keeps slipping from its grip . . . blobs across the page . . . letters home by the dancing light of a hurricane lamp.

> The trip up was interesting in parts but I wouldn't care to do it too often. At one stage of the journey we had to travel overland in trucks for a few days and it's not the best. One thing I do like and that's the warm weather. Even though it's still winter we run round in shorts all day.
>
> (13570 ACI HORKINGS M.W, DARWIN 12/7/42)

I've seen three hostile planes in daylight. We are more cautious these days with the planes and wonder whether they are our own or theirs.

(VX.24576 SPR. S. SAVAGE)

By April 1943, the Territory was playing host to a wing of RAF Spitfires, two squadrons of RAAF Hudsons, a squadron of Beaufighters, an American Liberator squadron and a Dutch B-25 squadron.

From the bush strips of the Northern Territory, RAAF Beauforts were able to hit targets in New Britain, and the Liberators, Hudsons, Beaufighters and Mitchells had sufficient range to tackle enemy positions in New Guinea.

During the war, airstrips were plastered across the Top End like bandaids on the bare rump of Australia. And all during the course of that war, the skies droned with all manner of hastily assembled aircraft. Overnight, places like Milingimbi were transformed into fighter bases.

Swing in low over the strait, hit the island's coast and sweep over the mangroves and the mudflats, both engines howling, the whole plane shaking, swinging from side to side in the turbulence. Swoop low over the remains of the old red mud-brick operations stations, their mortar dribbling out over bricks fashioned from the crushed dust of anthills. Tear down the strip, just above the treeline, just high enough to make out the horseshoe bunkers bulldozed from the earth to protect the fighters from the bombs and the spread of gasoline fires. Straight on down, rushing over the speargrass, the tamarind trees planted by the Macassans looming up through the plexiglass, over the fuselage of an abandoned Beaufighter, its alumina body as free from rust and decay as on the day it was made. Down over the settlement, over the houses that rest beneath towering palms, and out over the beach, over the rusty landing barges that lie half-submerged in the mud.

Milingimbi: a mission established in 1921 by the Methodists. Under the Whitlam Government they relinquished control in 1973, the social security cheques flooded in, the mission system broke down, the white advisors talked of self-determination and people chartered planes full of booze from Darwin. In 1978 alcohol was banned and the town quitened down. In 1982 *kava* was introduced. By 1985 Milingimbi was really quiet, getting through 100 kilos of the stuff every week.

The Warumpis played with a fantastic band there that year – Black Wizard Rock Band, a heavy metal outfit doing chunks of Slade and Quo, AC/DC and The Angels. They were a nine-piece – eight huge towering blacks and a midget singer about a metre tall who had all the moves down pat, strutting like Rod Stewart and Noddy Holder and Robert Plant. They did the Box Tops' 'The Letter' and 'another song from Cold Chisel, 'Knocking On Heaven's Door'.'

They were wild and wonderful, a bizarre flash in the tropics. They'd been together for a year but no one had ever seen them. And then on the morning the Warumpis arrived they started rehearsing like mad, belting through songs all day. That night, just as the Warumpis were about to start playing on the basketball court, they came up and demanded a gig.

Plucking out points on a map while turtles float by on an emerald-green sea and the pilot struggles with the controls, fighting the winds coming off the waves, buffeting the craft 'til your finger slides across the map and ends up on Cape Hawke.

A punitive expedition sailed these waters in 1923, searching for Aborigines who'd attacked a Japanese diving operation, stealing weapons and boats while the divers were below, scouring the reefs for pearls and beche-de-mere.

Screaming across Castlereagh Bay, skimming the waves, hurtling across the water towards Elcho Island.

Two decades later the Japanese returned, forsaking their nets for shrapnel, their luggers for airborne fighters and bombers.

In January 1943 a naval supply vessel, the *Patricia Cam*, was crossing the strait between Elcho and the mainland. On board were five Aborigines, two officers, several seamen and the Reverend

Leonard Kentish, head of the North Australian Department for the Methodist Overseas Missions.

A Japanese seaplane swept in low, sinking the boat and strafing the survivors. The seaplane landed beside the wreckage and Kentish was taken aboard, the first Australian to be taken prisoner on sovereign territory.

Little more than three months later he was beheaded on the (now Indonesian) island of Dobo. (In August 1948 the former commander of Dobo, Sub-lieutenant Sagejima Mangan was hanged in Hong Kong after being found guilty of the Kentish execution by an Australian military court.)

George Rurrambu's grandmother recalls the tale of a Japanese pilot who ditched on to Elcho. The Aborigines found him, and for a time, because they'd had contact with Japanese fishermen and divers for decades, they looked after him. But when they heard that Australia was at war with the Japanese they took him out turtle hunting and sent him overboard to wrestle the beast into the boat. When he surfaced, so her story goes, they clobbered him over the head with an oar.

Swinging in low over the mangroves on its final approach to Elcho international airport, a Cherokee 6 banks around the northern end of the red dirt strip.

On the strip, an Air Force ground crew hauls the last crates into a Caribou. Cargo nets hanging limp in the hold begin to quiver and twitch, shaking violently as the propellors start turning and the whole ship starts vibrating, rattling like a cattle truck, hot and dusty, windy and noisy. Time to strap up and strap in.

On the far side of the strip, the blacks sit on fuel drums in the shade or around the scales and the tyres and the crates in the cool darkness of the MAF workshop. The walls are lined with rolls of wire and sheets of tin and a dusty rack of tools. The office windows haven't been washed in twenty years and the door won't budge. I look around for the obligatory nude pin-ups, but in their place there is just a chunk of graffiti: 'JUS TINK, SIX MUNTS AGO I COUDENT EVEN SPEL MAF PIOLET. NOW I ARE ONE'.

MAF. Crazy buggers on eight grand a year and a Christian commitment. The pilots of the Missionary Aviation Fellowship (or the Missionary Air Force as it's known among the resident wags), run the local charter service with eight light aircraft in eastern Arnhem Land and branches all over the world; little shacks like this one in such hospitable places as Papua New Guinea, Indonesia. Borneo, Irian Jaya, Brazil and Zaire.

It's quiet in here. Just the flies and the distant drone of the Caribou, the whine of the Cherokee, and the cawing of the crows. No one stirs.

Whispers of red dust erupt from the strip as the wheels of the Cherokee bite and bounce and spin towards the trees. The other planes follow through, one after the other, swinging over the mangroves, standing on their port-side wings, buffeted by cross winds, bouncing down the dirt ... passengers clambering out, stretching, standing in the sun, watching the tree line, looking for some sign of life.

There's not even a sign to say *You are now in Galiwin'ku: Welcome to Heaven.* Just the dust and the heat and the trees.

Elcho Island is delightful; a chunk of paradise adrift in the Arafura Sea. In Galiwin'ku, the old mission station, palm trees fringe the clear cool waters of the bay and people wander the dusty streets, not shy like those in the desert, but bold and friendly, waving to visitors and yelling hello. In front of shacks above the beach, women and children sit with bowls of water and bags of seeds, soaking the seeds and threading fishing-line through with a needle to make intricate strings of beads.

Step into a house and you'll find a deep-freeze packed with barramundi and crabs. There are two TVs and a video machine in the front room and a turtle cooking in the kitchen, bubbling away in a pot below the microwave. Bring on the mining royalties!

Abuzz with the excitement of the big city visitors, people want to know what time the show gets underway. 'Seven o'clock!' comes the reply.

But the boys from Gammon Aire have got other ideas. The other pilots, soft city slickers from the south, have all flown on to the motel at Gove, so the jockeys from Gammon Aire figure it's high time they introduced themselves and established their credentials.

As puffy grey clouds shimmer with silver against a pale pink sunset, a Cherokee 6 climbs to 3,000 feet, levels out and comes in over the village. It's almost directly overhead when the parachute blooms.

The Oils are thrashing away, doing a soundcheck in the open-sided 'opera house' – a big open hall like a grain silo with half sides and a deep sandy floor. They're flailing away through a tiny PA that's stacked on a couple of 44-gallon drums in the sand, when suddenly – over the top of Hirst's booming snare and Rotsey's squealing guitar – they hear a screaming, like a million cockatoos exploding from a tree. They look outside and there are kids running everywhere – boys in jeans and t-shirts, but mostly shorts, and girls in shapeless floral dresses – all running and shrieking and pointing into the sky.

The parachute blossoms, all shiny fire-engine red in the dying light, and as it descends it starts spiralling, jerking about, hanging on gusts of wind and swinging from side to side, changing direction, jack-knifing across the sky, edging through the starstruck gums and finally slipping into a red dirt carpark right next to the hall.

Chuck Mango hits the ground and is instantly surrounded by hundreds of excited children, all jabbering and yelling and running along behind him as he picks up his chute and strides back towards the hostel. They're chasing him, giggling and yelling, when the Cherokee swings silently across the bay, winds in out of the sunset, banks over the tree tops and slides over the settlement at about a hundred wing-wobbling hair-brushing feet.

The Oils, who've got to follow the whole shebang, gape at each other open-mouthed and chalk up one for Gammon Aire.

The first group to play in the hall is a local seven-piece outfit, Dharrawa Band, who do Dragon's 'April Sun In Cuba' and AC/DC's 'It's A Long Way to the Top (If You Wanna Rock 'n' Roll)', screaming out its 'hotel/motel' lyric in a place that has none. They play Steppenwolf's 'Born to Be Wild' and the kids go crazy, rap dancing, doing headspins and backflips in the sand until a haze of dust hangs in front of the stage and their big brown eyes sting red with grit.

The breakdancing's an odd one, another example of the way in which contrived American televised youth culture has permeated even the most remote communities in the country. A year ago, the kids here were doing Michael Jackson and Bruce Springsteen impersonations, but this year they've hit the flipping urgency and ghetto style of the New York subways and tenement blocks.

This being George Rurrambu's homecoming, the Warumpis go down a storm. The Oils, on the other hand, are a wild noisy flash from the city, and no one quite knows how to react.

During the show a grey-haired woman named May walks up to the stage between songs and presents Peter Garrett with handfuls of beads. She was a star in the series 'Women Of the Sun', and she and her family have spent the afternoon making the beads in the shade outside their home above the beach. But that's the only sign of recognition.

Gary Morris strolls around in a pair of King Gee work shorts. Bare-chested, he plays with the kids and photographs the band. But when he sits with the kids – squatting down with a whole bunch of them – they, almost respectfully, get up and relocate, moving away, keeping their distance as if to acknowledge that any adult, black or white, who sits with kids has to be quite mad.

It takes no more than half-a-dozen Oils songs for the bulk of the audience to lose interest in the band. It's past their bedtime, or something, and the Oils finish to an almost empty venue, the crowd having dropped from a thousand to no more than a couple of hundred. The Oils, thoroughly disappointed with their performance, stalk back to the hostel to brood about it. But the Elcho mob are a friendly bunch. The traditional owners are the Warramirri, who share the island with Gupapuyngu and Ganalpwingu people among others. The next morning some of the men take most of the cast and crew fishing.

The Oils' bass player, Peter Gifford, is in his element. He's a practical man who likes working with his hands. He comes from a family of tradesmen, and his house and shed in a patch of secluded bush in Sydney are testament to his skills. Bass players are generally the most reserved members of any band, and the least committed. They adopt a workmanlike approach to their gig, standing back in the shadows and holding down the beat. Perhaps it's because they have to work with prima donna guitarists and drummers who insist they can keep time and get a primeval joy out of hitting things. When you get right down to it, happy bass players are as rare as metronomic drummers. Giffo's copped a lot over the years because he's not locked into the rigidly conformist lifestyle of his colleagues. He's a hawk-browed man who enjoys the simple things in life, like doing odd jobs around the house and making breadboards for his friends. He admires improvisation and, as a practical man, he's impressed when the fishermen of Elcho use a huge rock as an anchor, and that when they run out of sinkers they simply switch to sparkplugs.

Fish are caught and cooked in a fire on the beach. Leaves are used as plates to keep the sand off the food. Giffo returns inspired: 'When you can use spark plugs and rocks and leaves, the only thing you need up here is matches for the *waru!*'

The people and the dogs are much healthier here. You can sit on the hostel verandah watching them wander past against a backdrop of a shimmering blue sea and the gently waving gums hanging with great clumps of leaves, while young women in brightly patterned sun dresses walk on by with babies propped on their hips.

Glad Reed and Stephanie Lewis have become star attractions. Everywhere they go, they're tailed by a bunch of happy girls holding their hands and hanging on to Steph's waist-length hair. The kids want to know what sort of work she does, what sort of house she lives in, and how she gets to work. The kids are enchanted and so is she.

Among the guys, camouflaged army shirts are all the rage. It's down to the peer group status of Rambo t-shirts and jungle greens, and among the girls references to Rambo and Rocky abound. As in the desert communities, Rob Hirst is hailed as 'Rocky' ('because he's got strong legs'), and Gary Morris fits visions of Rambo. Not that he does a lot to avoid the comparisons. In Darwin he bought himself a blade, a huge and heavy knife that's at least half a metre long and solid enough to fell a decent sapling.

Rambo's appeal, as a Top End teacher explains it, 'is the gut-busting maleness, the road warrior, the real man, tough, violent . . . same appeal as it's got down south. Only without the chauvinism. No Aboriginal people, or very few of them, would be aware of the jingoistic side of Rambo. The fact that he's shooting Russians or some unidentified Asians doesn't really matter. They could be anybody. He's just shooting at them. He's tough . . . Cowboys and Indians were a really big genre in the Northern Territory for many years on movies. And even in really isolated places, they've always had movies, so they're used to the idea of moving images and people talking. I remember going to see Kung Fu movies in the hall at Numbulwar, and some of the kids would get so excited by what was going on on the screen, on the sheet, that they'd jump up out of the audience and go up to the screen and punch the villain in the film. They'd go up and give him a big kick in the groin or something.'

The influence of Western media, particularly television, has been extraordinary. There's a thesis waiting to be written on the effects of prepackaged Western youth culture on remote communities.

'When I first came up here,' says a teacher from a neighbouring settlement, 'the teenage kids were really interested in pop music. And there was this business of claiming pop stars and taking on the identity of a pop star.

'They actually took on the identity of a star, and that was their person. Nobody else could have it. The boys in my class in '82, for example, were all big AC/DC fans. I had a group of five boys and each boy was a 'member of AC/DC'. I didn't call them Reggie and Hank and Gregory; I called them Malcolm and Phil and Bon. I had to call them by their AC/DC names because that was who they were.

'I remember giving one of the kids a picture of Dallas from Rose Tattoo. This guy was really into the Tatts, and I found a picture in a newspaper where Dallas had been given a motorbike by Harley Davidson – it was a publicity thing – and it had the caption underneath the picture *A Harley for the drummer*. And he thought that this guy's name was Harley Davidson, so I had to call him Harley. He used to write in his books *Harley Davidson, Drummer from Rose Tattoo*. Every page of his exercise book would have this.'

Look around any of the Top End communities and you'll find Heavy Metal graffiti all over the place. Judas Priest appear to be particularly big. And so are the bad stereotypes from Hollywood.

At night, Galiwin'ku is wild with kids shouting and giggling and chattering in the streets, and, as the night slips into morning, girls stand around in the shadows near the hostel's verandah, trying to attract our attention: 'Hey, you boys, you want some company?'

All the while, the boys lurk further back in the shadows, playing pimp. There's one guy in particular who's seen too many bad American videos, and he's convinced that he's an African American hustler in New York. He's got the Panama hat and the cane and the swagger and the shades: a 'bad dude' whose coordination has been shot to pieces by petrol fumes. He struts over for a light and makes a great display of igniting his cigarette, eyeballing Garrett with the meanest, blankest peepers you ever saw.

The petrol sniffing, apparently, was introduced up here by American bomber crews during the Second World War. Today it's a severe problem among kids who haven't yet reached the drinking age. It's created enormous problems throughout the Top End and right down into the desert.

A few years ago, when petrol sniffing was getting really serious, the Council at Galiwin'ku introduced an additive to the fuel, making it unpalatable to sniff. It was a bold experiment with obvious merits, and it worked . . . for a few days . . .'til the sniffers discovered that if they left the contaminated fuel in an open bowl in the sun for a couple of days, the additive would evaporate and they could get on with the hideous business of sweetly frying their brains.

Today, Top End Aborigines are trying to deal with the problem by setting up rehabilitation centres on out-stations like Birany Birany. There, well away from the main settlements, the sniffers are introduced to a clean lifestyle of hunting and gathering. They're taught the ancient lore and all efforts are made to develop their strength and their self-esteem.

In the desert, the problem is also being tackled from the level of the community, by exerting family pressure on the wayward individuals.

When I discussed it with Charlie McMahon, he said, 'There's an effective program which goes on now, where there's some very intensive consultation between a local bloke from Alice Springs and another woman from there. They picked up a fellow they knew from Yuendumu and they tried out a test program, going into great detail and depth over the sniffer's family contacts: most kids don't sniff because they're restrained.

'But sniffing is a problem that Aboriginal people have got to deal with themselves. There's a lot of problems that they're facing that no government scheme is going to help.

'There was a big problem years ago, when petrol sniffing first got going in the desert in a big way, and all the communities got together at Ayers Rock to have a meeting. All the central desert communities thought 'We'll have a meeting at Ayers Rock and we'll decide something to do about petrol sniffing'. And the result of that meeting was to have a meeting in Canberra!

'It's a home problem, it's a humpy problem, and I think the best way that the Government can combat it is to support intensive work in the communities by people who get in contact with the sniffer and the sniffer's families and the people that sniffer's associated with, and find out what the problem is and what they can do about it. And they have effectively begun to control sniffing at Yuendumu and Kintore by that process.'

The final solution, it seems, is to banish the sniffer from the community. During the course of the tour a Kintore sniffer, Anthony Jabarula Butler, was jailed for fifteen months in Alice Springs after breaking a twelve-month good behaviour bond.

Said Magistrate Timothy Hinchcliffe, 'The Senate Select Committee into substance abuse recommended that petrol sniffers be returned to their communities. But heroin addicts aren't sent back to their communities to overcome their problems. There is a dilemma in Central Australia with no facility for rehabilitation of sniffers. If it was a crack or cocaine addict before the court there would be a facility to send them to.

'The committee recommended that petrol sniffing should not be made illegal.'

In the dunes on the shores of the Arafura Sea, there's a solar-powered radio up against a tree. The tree, standing alone against an armada of clouds, is a gnarled old casuarina. Winds blowing up out of Indonesia tear through its branches, and sheets of rain lash the camp below. Huge raindrops hit the nylon lean-tos with full-bodied splats. A pool forms on top of the fuel drum. Droplets gather and tumble down the sides of jerry cans full of water. The smouldering ashes of a cooking fire sizzle and spit.

'This place,' calls George Rurrambu, 'we call it Fourth Creek. This is Peter's out-station, my brother.'

It's on the north coast of Elcho, about 4 metres above sea level on a dune between the creek and the beach. There's an aluminium dinghy moored in the creek and up the beach a way are half-a-dozen big turtle shells curing on the sand.

The radio crackles with the fast gabbling chatter of Yolngu matha: *crunch*, short bursts of static, *crunch*, staccato chatter, high-pitched and urgent.

Jabbed into the sand nearby stands a brace of spears.

This is Peter Rurrambu's country, the place he's responsible for. His family camps here. Sometimes two people, other times fifteen.

Their days start at dawn when they emerge from their canvas humpies and lean-to shelters to boil the billy and prepare damper and mussels and crabs for breakfast. At low tide the beach is hundreds of metres wide. Naked kids play in the sand, a huge sea eagle soars above the water, puppies try to sip enamel mugs of tea and are hurled yelping across the sand.

During the day, the women will stay behind to look after the camp and the kids and to scout around the scrub for sweet bush potatoes. The men will head out in the boat after breakfast and plough through the wash to a point a couple of kilometres up the beach. There, they'll pull in and scrape oysters from the rocks, grabbing buckets full of soldier crabs and other bits of bait. A couple of hundred metres offshore, just in this place, not 10 metres either way, they'll toss handfuls of bait into the water and drop their lines overboard, pulling in twenty parrot fish in thirty minutes, enough to give everyone a good feed.

Or they might head further up the coast on a turtle hunt, circling over the reefs, poised on the bow with the long turtle spear. It's about 4.5 metres long and capped at each end with metal to stop it from splitting. Into the business end of the spear is inserted a barbed metal harpoon that's about 8 centimetres long. The barb is tied to 6 metres of nylon rope and a Koolite buoy. The theory is that the barb hooks into the turtle's shell, the spear disconnects and bobs to the surface and the turtle swims off, trailing the rope and the buoy behind it. Then you simply follow the turtle around until it gets tired and, at the appropriate moment, plunge in and drag it out.

Peter Rurrambu stands, taut as a guitar string, on the bow. The spear is hooked into a 1-metre woomera in his hand. George has his hand on the outboard throttle and, in Gumatj, Peter directs him – over this way, now that – until he's right above his prey. The spear slips into the water with barely a splash, wobbles for a moment, and pops back out of the water. The rope and the buoy bounce overboard, dragging against the swell as the turtle swims for the beach. George eases back on the throttle and follows.

Checking for sharks ('You swim underwater so you can see the shark,' says George. 'If he comes for you, you grab him and cover his gills for five minutes 'til he dies.'), Peter dives overboard, plunging down towards the reef, wrestling the turtle to the surface. It takes three people to haul it over the side.

To these city eyes, it's big and heavy, a harmless seaweed eater that's spent maybe fifty years on the planet without hurting a soul.

'That one female,' yells George. 'Too small. If we find bigger one we throw her back.'

Neil Murray pulls George's jacket out from under the turtle's head. I splash handfuls of water over the head and flippers, worrying about the way they're drying out in the midday sun.

The head is hacked off on the beach and the entrails dragged out, great piles of long blue intestines, and then the meat is scraped out and boiled in a billy, like long white strips of rubbery bacon.

The men scout along the beach, looking for the flipper marks of the female turtles. At the point where the flipper trails turn above the high water mark, they start digging, scooping the sand out, down a metre or so to the caches of eggs. The eggs are like soft, leathery ping pong balls and in each nest there are upwards of 120 of them. Hundreds of eggs are piled into buckets and old sawn-off kerosene tins and loaded aboard the boat.

On the homeward journey, as the sun goes down and the wind comes up, Spanish mackerel leap from the water, diving through the wake.

At sunset the sea turns to mercury, glistening shades of pink and blue, mauve and purple, opalescent in their intensity. Another tank of fuel is exhausted, the outboard splutters to a halt and the only sound to be heard is the water lapping against the hull. There's no safety gear aboard: no lights or flares or life-jackets. The tank is refilled by hand and we're on our way again.

Along the coast the hunters pull into other out-stations on the beaches to warm themselves by the fires, to trade turtle eggs for cigarettes and fish cooked and wrapped in vine leaves.

We plough through the night, guided only by schools of phosphorescent green fish that 'tell you where it's deep and where it's shallow' until the fires of Fourth Creek come into view. And then the feast is on – billies of tea and chunks of damper, turtle eggs boiled, punctured and sucked out, sickly sweet bush yams and fish cooked in the coals.

Later, George and Peter will go out with spears and torches, hunting for crayfish. They'll come back with a bucketful and toss them into a kerosene tin on the fire to boil, the creatures screaming in the heat.

While they're out, others will sit around the fire, drinking *kava*, telling stories, strumming a guitar and singing gospel songs in Gumatj and English, gazing at the ashes and the stars.

To spend a few days on an out-station on the coast is an incredible experience. When Neil Murray and I stayed at Fourth Creek in 1985, the sense of hospitality was unlike that I experienced anywhere else in the country. There, it was important to people that we visitors ate, that we got enough food, that we too had cigarettes or damper or tea or *kava*. There was a family concern for our wellbeing, and everything was shared. George deferred to his elder brother, and when their father came to the camp it was our shelter that he took over because he was the elder and ours was the most comfortable lean-to – an affair I'd modelled on the sails of Yulara, a wonderful polytarp dwelling with lots of ropes and poles in the ground, a true prince among bush camps.

'From my experience,' said Neil a few nights later, 'the bottom line remains that if you're on the breadline, if you're down and out, Aboriginal people will take you in every time. And that's the important thing to remember. Not all of us are well off. There might come a time when you need those skills to live off the land; who knows? But if there's places in Australia where you know you could go and possibly be welcome . . .

'After spending this much time around Aboriginal people, I go back down south and maybe go into some country areas and something seems strangely amiss or absent when there aren't Aboriginal people around on the scene. I have a distinct feeling of loss, of an absence.

'You saw the way George was. That's the first time I've seen George in his own environment and he was just at ease with everything. He had an incredible nonchalant ease with everything – fish, catching this, catching that, anything.

'It was really refreshing to see that because seeing him in the desert he looks so awkward with the other guys lots of the times. Seeing him at Fourth Creek and realising how important it is for Aboriginal people to have a part of a place where they're really at home with the environment and in tune with it.

'When you've got Aboriginal people in a place you tend to feel more secure. Well, I do, because you know you can go and ask somebody about something and they know it intimately. They embody all the secrets of the place and they make it feel more like home. That's the feeling I get.'

CHAPTER ELEVEN
YIRRKALA

Cookie stands in the shade on the edge of the strip, tapping out a cigarette on the rusty rim of a fuel drum. Tiny tiles of sunlight slip through the trees, glancing off the frames of his aviator shades. Ahead of him, Morris and Hardie trudge through the dust with the Gammon Aire twins.

'They're mad,' he says, affecting a frown.

'Who? Cosmo and big foot?'

'Yeah, them too.'

Three days into their tour of duty, the Gammon Aire pilots are a certifiable hit. Since signing on, Captain Coop and his mate Judge Chuck Mango have been working hard at winning creds. They've swagged it out on the ground with the bands, jumped out of aeroplanes and buzzed a village, coming in so low the slipstream ruffled the leaves in the trees and the nerves in the elders' hearts. Being labelled as 'mad' by someone as close to the edge as Cookie has added to their tally of brownie points.

Neither of them brought maps along for the trip, so they've been relying solely on visuals to find their destinations. (Soon after lifting off from Darwin, as if to justify the absence of maps, both realised their compasses had been thrown out by about

10 degrees, affected by the magnets in the PA stacks wedged behind their seats.)

The planes, a pair of ageing Cherokee 6s, are the slowest aircraft in the squadron. Slug-like single-engined jobs, they can't go much faster than 130 knots. But these bug-splattered workhorses are stable, and they can carry a decent load, and that's all that counts at this stage.

As Martin Hardie was fond of saying before the tour, 'time can be measured only by the intensity at which it is lived', and flying with Gammon Aire makes for a memorable one.

Captain Coop, for instance, has a neat diversion from the boredom of being a glorified taxi driver. At about 3,000 feet he likes playing with the clouds, flying not through them or under them but around them, barrelling down frothy white canyons, swinging around towering cliffs of bubbling snow and twisting and rolling down the massive fluffy tunnels, never knowing what's around the corner. Flying blind becomes a spine-tingling game, punctuated by tight turns around the cloud banks as he throws a couple of tonnes of metal around the sky and soars along the sheer white walls . . .

He's so game he'll even allow someone like Hardie, who doesn't hold a driver's licence, to take over the controls and fly the bird along the coast. There's not much to do in that situation, except maintain height and balance and direction. In all, it's a pretty dull gig, and you soon understand why Coop seeks out the clouds for a bit of excitement. The alternative is to fly at 50 or 100 feet, skipping over the treetops, struggling for control against the buffeting of the wind pockets and the thermals, flying so low you can almost reach out and scratch the footprints in the sand, buzzing along the beaches so low you can see the algae on the turtles' shells, and dipping your wings at people waving from the scrub.

The Gammon Aire planes are sitting almost directly behind each other, about 15 metres apart. Between them, Mango and Coop stand in the sun, planning a minor detour. They're going to try a formation take-off and then swing north for a thrill-seeking slide through The Hole In the Wall, a treacherous gap between Raragala and Guluwuru islands in the Wessels. It's a tight one, so narrow that the water rushes through in powerful waves, smashing anything in its way against the sheer sandstone cliffs.

Sailors working on naval patrol boats up this way tell of trips through the Hole, unauthorised hell rides guaranteed to chop a couple of hours off their schedules and years off their lives. Patrol boats are so wide and the alley so narrow that they ride straight through, clinging to the bulkheads with a prayer and a grin, shooting a wave to the other side.

Which is precisely what the boys from Gammon Aire are intent on doing this morning: heading up the coast to the Wessels and bridging the gap, rolling the Cherokees over and slipping through sideways, right foot jammed to the floor, left hand pulled right down, screaming through the gap with little hope of pulling out . . .

Hardie climbs into the first plane after Captain Coop. Gary Morris straps into the second with Mango. Over on the sidelines, Cookie strikes a match to his cigarette. 'The 1st of the 9th,' he drawls through the smoke, 'was an old cavalry division that had cashed in its horses for choppers and gone tear assin' around Nam looking for the shit. They'd given Charlie a few surprises in their time here, but they were mopping up now; it hadn't even happened yet an hour ago.'

It's a chunk of Michael Herr's narration from *Apocalypse Now*, an old favourite that's got him through many a tour, and upon delivery he laughs and shakes his head. But the laugh is bitter, echoing out of some place too tired to smile.

The props are spinning and red dust rises like a mist from the strip. When Mango sees Coop lurch away, he hits the throttle and chases him down the strip, hauling back on the joystick and dragging the beast into the air.

At 100 feet something's amiss. The plane's handling is sluggish and the air is bad. He's caught in the slipstream. He glances at his instruments, but they're all going haywire. The air speed reading's too low, the controls are slack and the whole ship shudders like it's about to stall. He jams the controls forward, nose-diving towards the strip, fighting for clean air. He's on full flaps, but still he's going too fast for a safe landing. He hits the runway, flaps up, hurtling towards the end of the strip. A barbed-wire fence looms through the plexiglass. He jams the brakes on, a tyre explodes and the whole aircraft slews through the dust.

Beside him, Gary Morris remains motionless. 'Well that,' he says as the propeller slows, 'was pretty good.' He pulls on the door and bails out, leaving Mango to catch his breath.

'Morris had had a pretty good day for himself,' I recited, taking up the Apocalyptic theme. 'Well, he wasn't a bad officer, I guess. He loved his boys and they felt safe with him. He was one of those guys that had that weird light around him; he just knew he wasn't going to get so much as a scratch here.'

Cookie laughed again. A dry hollow laugh that said, 'Yeah, but he'll break us all in the process.'

With the Cherokee crippled at the end of the strip, Peter Gifford walks up to the Oils' pilot and says, 'Okay, let's see what this piece of tin and perspex on radials can do.'

The Oils' aircraft is a King Air, the flashiest plane in the squadron. It's an executive twin prop with everything but a toilet on board. The pilot's an amiable 25-year-old named Charlie who doesn't mind teaching them all to fly.

In the air, the Oils sit chatting quietly, engaging in the small talk of a band on the road. They've spent so much time couped up in hire cars that the pressurised confines of a small plane are far from being a big deal. Even if they are barrelling over country that, forty years ago, was marked as Hostile Territory. (American pilots at the time were warned that, on bailing out, they'd be at the mercy of spear-throwing natives.)

Below them lie rivers and the creeks that snake across the country, dumping so much silt from their estuaries that the seawater is milky rather than clear. Along the shore lie the mudflats and the mangrove swamps, home territory for the big saltwater crocodiles that bask on the banks. Further inland, the country is covered with eucalypts, stumpy old cycads and big red anthills that jut from the earth. Further east lie the great red scars of the bauxite mines that have been bulldozed from the bush around Gove.

The biggest airport in the region, Gove was named after Sergeant William Julius Henderson Gove, a pilot who was wiped out in a mid-air collision over Milingimbi in April 1943.

He was with the 13th Squadron, an RAAF mob who flew sorties in Hudsons and Venturas and shared the strip with the Boomerangs of 83 Squadron.

The Oils are buckling up for the landing when the King Air's radio crackles and a report comes through that a light plane has just gone down in the Torres Strait, the stretch of water separating Australia from New Guinea. While the band disembarks, a Coastwatch Nomad lumbers down the tarmac and struggles for altitude.

Minutes later, a couple of Ansett aircraft roar in from Townsville or Darwin, and above the whine of their jets an argument breaks out on the tarmac. The Oils are safely away in the terminal, and now the Blackfella-Whitefella pilots are establishing their ground. The Sydney pilots – long socks and bared shoulders to a man – are secure in the knowledge that they're flying *the personnel* around on this trip, and *not* the black boxes, which are the lowly domain of the Gammon Aire cowboys from Darwin.

Well they've blown it now, those Top End sky jockeys. All their showing off and egalitarian swagging it with the band has come to nought. They've still got a plane full of gear sitting like a lame duck on Elcho. And it's gotta be here for the show tonight.

The Sydney boys crowd around the scruffy Captain Coop and tell him, in no uncertain terms, to hop into his Cherokee, fly back to Elcho, pick up the rest of his mate's gear and bring it over to Gove. But Coop just stands there grinning. His hands are plunged deep into the baggy pockets of his pants, and all he needs to cap off the hillbilly image is some straw sticking out of his mouth.

He shuffles and shrugs and then fixes them with a couple of evil red eyes, road map eyes, so red they're glowing like the ashes after a bushfire. He's just indulged in post-flying pleasures and, as he works his brain around the alternatives, claims to be in no fit state to pilot an aircraft.

The twin-engine boys, who've spent the last two nights relaxing at the Hideaway Motel here in Gove, argue that since they've already done the trip to Elcho and back today, they don't need to tackle it again. Besides, none of them wants to climb into a tinny single-engine Cherokee for a couple of hours when it could be better spent at the bar.

Captain Coop shakes his head and walks away, leaving his colleagues to argue among themselves. He retrieves his can of beer, jumps into a waiting hire car, and powers down the road to Nhulunbuy for a quiet gin and tonic by the pool at the Walkabout Hotel.

The last time I hit the Walkabout, about fourteen months ago, the idea of settling down to a quiet G and T was out of the question. The bar was bristling with lunatics with wild, dilated pupils, vicious grins and concentration spans so short they couldn't even remember who they were fighting. There was a pile of bad speed in town that night, and a lot of mean and ugly drunks. When I suggested to Neil Murray that we stick around to check out the action, he just gave one of his customary grunts and glanced around the room. The level of nervous energy was so high and unpredictable, and relations between the white majority and the black minority so strained that I think he was tempted to leave the gear there and flee.

'Places like this,' he muttered, 'are full of mongrels and itinerants. The desert weeds people out. Up here, they're all blow-ins. Come up here for a few months, make some bucks, and nick off. But the desert's like a screen. You find characters down there, real characters.'

Which is true to a point, because the whites of Nhulunbuy have got it pretty easy. It's a strange place. An urban satellite that's been plonked in the jungle, it's a company town with a population of 3,000 and all mod cons like kerbing and guttering and fluorescent lights. It's a lush tropical paradise with a hospital and schools and elaborate churches, a supermarket, a coffee shop and a newsagency, clubs and pubs and parks, grassy football fields, basketball courts, a golf course, swimming pools and bowling greens; dropped on to the end of the Gove Peninsula in the early 1970s at a cost of 35 million dollars.

Step right up, everything you desire. A close-knit community, social clubs, ample work, good money, a neat and tidy town, good education and health facilities for the kids, 38,000 dollars a year. 'A well-organised town' say the locals, a company town with a forty-two-year lifespan and then the jungles can get into the concrete and the steel and the glass and the stamp of Nabalco.

It's a town with too much money and not enough to do; a town with booze and speed and smack where a night's not tops at the Walkabout unless there's two good blues at the end of it.

The flashpoints of excessive behaviour among the white community can be partially explained by the town's isolation. A permit from the Northern Land Council is required to drive out because the only road traverses great chunks of Aboriginal land. And a flight to Darwin or Cairns for the weekend can set you back 500 dollars or more.

It's almost like being on a desert island. People seek recreation in fishing trips, but there the crocodiles lurk – huge, fast, saltwater reptiles that play hell with one's sense of relaxation. And even the fish can't be relied upon, due to the prevalence of ciguatera poison in their flesh, which, according to a local cabbie, 'is caused by the smaller fish eating the weeds on the wharves'. Swimming is out of the question for much of the year because of deadly marine stingers like the Portuguese Man-o'-War, and trips into the bush are limited by the fact that all land surrounding the town is under Aboriginal (or Yolngu) control and is, therefore, impassable without a permit, and preferably a guide.

Nhulunbuy itself is built on land traditionally owned by the Rirratjingu clan. The bauxite mines that justify its existence are gouging land owned by the Gumatj clan.

Twenty Ks south of Nhulunbuy, the Aboriginal community of Yirrkala, home to 1,200 people, overlooks a series of fantastic beaches. Because of its history as a mission, its close proximity to a large white town and the experience of the land battles of the early 1970s, Yirrkala is arguably the most sophisticated of the Top End communities.

Nowhere else on the trip have we come across two such different settlements sitting side by side. It seems appropriate that just a few kilometres to the south, down in a creek that flows into the bay at Birany Birany, crocodiles are said to have been created.

In 1935, around the time five Japanese beche-de-mer fishermen and three whites were killed in the neighbouring Caledon Bay area, Yirrkala was established by the Methodist Overseas Mission. Control of the mission was later handed over to the Uniting Church of Northern Australia.

During the war, the RAAF base was established a couple of kilometres to the south carved out of the glowing red earth that would later yield huge quantities of bauxite, a mineral used chiefly in the production of aluminium.

In 1949, small deposits of high-grade bauxite were discovered to the north of Yirrkala, on Marchinbar Island in the Wessels. Further mineral exploration of the region in 1952 revealed the bauxite deposits on the Gove Peninsula. By 1965, mining interests were ready to turn the peninsula into a bleeding hole in the ground. Much to the consternation of the local Aborigines, whose spirits dwelt in that earth, they weren't consulted.

June 1965 saw the formation of Nabalco (Northern Australian Bauxite and Alumina Company), an amalgamation of the Swiss Aluminium Limited (Alusuisse), CSR, AMP, MLC, The Bank of New South Wales, Peko Wallsend, CBC of Sydney and Elder Smith Goldsborough Mort. The company pledged a development budget of 100 million dollars, promising to build an alumina processor, a town and a port.

Three years later, Nabalco and the Australian Government signed an agreement granting the company a forty-two year lease to develop the mine. (Though the traditional owners weren't consulted, the Federal Government's consent was required because the area was part of the Arnhem Land Aboriginal Reserve.)

The cards were in place for a ding-dong brawl.

The first significant Aboriginal land claim was written on bark and presented to the politicians in Canberra. It was prepared by Mungurrawuy Yunupingu, head of the Gumatj clan (with assistance from his son Galarrwuy).

A year later, in 1969, the Rirratjingu and Gumatj people of Yirrkala took out a Northern Territory Supreme Court writ in an effort to save their land. In 1971, the case was rejected when the court ruled that Aboriginal people didn't own the Arnhem Land Reserve.

Mining began, and in July 1971 the first bauxite was exported.

The battle of the people of Yirrkala to retain control over their land led to the Woodward Royal Commission, which resulted in the *Land Rights Act* (NT) of 1976.

Meanwhile, the Aborigines were still trying to find a way around the powers of the mining companies. The result was the start of the out-stations or homelands movement.

The Yirrkala Council wrote to the Council of Aboriginal Affairs saying they wanted to move out of the mission and back to their traditional lands. 'Our sacred places must be protected,' they wrote, 'and only Aboriginal people allowed there ... We want to have land to ourselves that the mining company or its workers can't come on without permission ... We want a lot of land left so that we can go hunting there and no one else can go there.'

The Council of Aboriginal Affairs recommended that, in order to gain some legal standing, the Yirrkala community be incorporated. It was a recommendation that set the pace for communities throughout the Territory.

The Federal Government also gave some recognition to the Aborigines' claim to spiritual links with the land. In view of the loss of hunting grounds and the probable destruction of sacred sites, the Federal Government recommended that the people of

Yirrkala be paid compensation in the form of mining royalties. The locals, however, were left out of the negotiations. Under the arrangement, the Rirratjingu clan gets royalties from the alumina processor on their land in Nhulunbuy, and the Gumatj clan are paid for the use of their land for the mining of the raw materials.

In Western Australia, the Ngaatjatjarra and Ngaanyatjarra people have found a solution to the problem of protecting sacred sites. In Western Australia, the Aboriginal people have a different mode of land tenure from that now enjoyed by some of their neighbours in the Northern Territory. Because of the conservative nature of the State Government, Aborigines have not been given inalienable freehold title to their land. Instead, they're given the opportunity to negotiate ninety-nine-year leases which don't give them the same control over mining as that enjoyed by people whose land fell under the *Land Rights Act* (NT) of 1976.

While they can't control mining interests on their land, the Ngaatjatjarra people of Warakurna have developed a strategy to protect their sacred sites and their links with the Dreaming while, at the same time, allowing mining companies to explore their land. Because the integrity of their sacred sites is so important that even to disclose where those sites are would be an infringement of their religious lore, the Ngaatjatjarra have preserved the secrecy of the sites by showing seismic teams from the Shell Company where the sites are not situated, thereby allowing the teams to conduct tests in areas that do not present major cultural problems.

> 'You see this watch? It cost seven hundred dollar. My father buy it for me. Mining royalty!'
>
> GEORGE RURRAMBU, GUMATJ CLAN

Each year, Nabalco pays out royalties of 1.3 million dollars. Of that, around 1,000 traditional owners in the region receive a 30 per cent split (around 390 dollars per person). Forty per cent goes to the Land Council that administers the land, and the other 30 per cent is set aside for the Aboriginal Benefits Trust Account, which distributes funds in the form of special grants to Aboriginal projects.

It's interesting to note that the traditional Aboriginal lands that were originally set aside as reserves because the whites had no use for them – they being, by and large, useless for pastoral ventures – are now yielding about 92 per cent of the Territory's mineral resources.

With the establishment of the Northern and Central Land Councils in 1976, control over mining interests fell to those bodies. Under the CLC's jurisdiction lie the oil and natural gas wells at Palm Valley and Mereenie, and the gold mine at The Granites in the Tanami Desert. The NLC receives royalties from the manganese mines on Groote Eylandt (worth 2.4 million dollars per year), the uranium mines at Jabiru and Narbelek (12 million dollars and 1.5 million dollars respectively), and the bauxite mines on the Gove Peninsula.

Aboriginal groups also have land claims pending on places such as Coronation Hill. There, the Jawoyn people are concerned about miners destroying the sacred sites associated with the Dreaming of Bula, a spirit so powerful, it is said, that if he's disturbed it will mean the end of the world. Bula, as luck would have it, sits on incredibly rich uranium deposits.

Since the advent of mining on their lands, and the sudden influx of thousands of whites, the people of Yirrkala have sought to gain an equal footing in the modern world. Unlike those remote communities that, as yet, have been untouched by such large-scale development, the people of Yirrkala have had to adapt quickly. So with the royalties from mining in their region, they've invested in a series of ambitious projects. Royalties from the alumina processor are put straight into a trust fund for future generations, those who will come after the mining leases expire. Royalties from the mines have gone into the establishment of incorporated companies like Yirrkala Business Enterprises (YBE) and Yunupingu Industries which, between them, contract trucks to Nabalco, build houses and run repair workshops. In the spirit of self-determination and self-management, the community now runs its own store, offices, health clinic and craft shop. They're also in the process of taking over the school, setting up a cable TV network to service Yirrkala and Nhulunbuy, and buying a fuel station in the mining town.

INVITATION FROM DHANBUL ASSOCIATION

It was with interest we read of the Invitation of the Dhanbul Association, for the residents of Nhulunbuy to attend an evening of entertainment on Monday night at YIRRKALA, which will feature two bands – MIDNIGHT OIL and the WARUMPI BAND. Permits are not necessary but it is requested that alcohol not be brought to the concert. We hope there will be a good representation from Nhulunbuy.

ARNHEM COURIER, VOL. 3 NO. 102

The invitation is a rare one designed to break the stigma of black drunks at the Walkabout, and many of the other problems of having an Aboriginal settlement so close to a get-rich-quick mining town.

There are a couple of thousand people at the show, the whites from Nhulunbuy reclining by their eskies in deck-chairs at the front or on their feet by the stage. The local Aborigines sit in the shadows on the hill behind.

The stage setting is perfect. Out in the open air, a couple of semi-trailers have been pulled together to form a stage beneath a magnificent eucalypt and a massive fan palm. The front of the stage has been decked out with palm fronds.

The Warumpis turn in a great performance; the merchandising manager hangs a couple of t-shirts over a billboard proclaiming WORKING WITH CHRIST, and suddenly he's besieged by whites wanting t-shirts. Reinforcements appear and 170 t-shirts are sold in about fifteen minutes. The Aboriginal people, hanging back in the shadows, don't have a chance.

And then the Oils come on, delivering their hottest set since Mutitjulu, powering through with dynamism and passion, a strong and humorous performance.

It's a beautiful night. People are responding – they're calling out for songs! Clapping! Cheering! Slapping palm fronds against the stage! Hurling the fronds, wrenching them off the side of the semi and spearing them on to the stage.

The band is charged, flailing through the set, ripping out the jams and just going for it. Giffo, cigarette hanging from his lip, webbing belt over his shoulder, holds it all down while Rotsey chops through the rhythm and Moginie peels off the melody. Garrett dances like a dervish, crashing all over the narrow stage, all colour and movement and dripping sweat. Hirst, hammering his kit, aglow with sweat, bouncing and rolling, an athlete on the blocks, is unerring in his accuracy and his pace.

His boom mike slips out of vocal reach, and Lippold, behind the foldback desk, tense and ready to go, launches himself on to the stage, dashing across to get the mike back into position. Half-way to the kit, his foot slips on a palm frond and he loses his balance, his legs shooting straight out, his hands going to the deck, his bum crashing into the metal bars where the trailers join.

He crawls back to the fold-back desk, buckled over in pain, unable to sit up, unable to move. There are five songs to go so he crouches there silently screaming, operating the desk with his teeth.

Despite Lippold's injuries, the show has been an outstanding success, for the people of Nhulunbuy are rarely allowed into the Aboriginal community and, despite fears to the contrary, there's been little friction. The whole show has gone off in the spirit of the Blackfella-Whitefella expedition, with people of both races, who would rarely congregate in the same area, getting together in a 'dry' community for a night of spirited entertainment. The people of Yirrkala have invited those from Nhulunbuy into their community and, with the television cameras rolling, the hope is that the event will lead to better relations between the two.

Some observers, such as Richard Geeves, a white teacher working with Aboriginal trainees in the region, see the people of Yirrkala as deft politicians, public relations practitioners par excellence.

'Their sense of important people is much more refined than in a lot of other communities. They'll know who's coming in and who's going to be worthwhile and they'll pick them out and give them a show. They'll put on a show.

'I don't want to devalue what they're doing, but they'll give that person the impression that they're being taken on board and it's 'very important', and there's a bit of brotherhood happening here, and they're going to tell them a lot of very . . . the deep information and a few tribal secrets and so on.

'Now they don't, 'cos they know all Europeans are transients, especially these propagandists; it's unlikely that they'd come back.

'But they're very good at giving the impression that they're taking that person and they're going to slip them a bit of the good oil.

'Those people have had a lot of contact with Commonwealth agencies, governmental agencies. They've had a lot of researchers here; they know what people like Peter Garrett wanna hear. They know that those people want to hear stories about the land and the spirit of the land. They know that! And they'll do a good show.'

And sometimes, the local politicking gets even stickier than that. When tenders were called for Nhulunbuy's bus service in 1985, the previous contractors, Yunupingu Transport, put in a bid. When it was rejected in favour of a Darwin-based company, Yunupingu Transport boss Galarrwuy Yunupingu (Yirrkala resident, head of the Gumatj clan and chairman of the Northern Land Council) instructed his solicitors to revoke the permits allowing the rival bus company to use the Central Arnhem Road. The only road out of Nhulunbuy, the only thoroughfare between the town and the mines and the airport and all points beyond, it's on Aboriginal land.

The dispute was soon settled (Yunupingu backed off), but not before hackles had been raised on both sides.

After the Blackfella-Whitefella gig, a few of the crew head down to the Hideaway Motel for a couple of beers in the garden. The place is managed by a bloke who, back in the 1960s, was 'a traveller' who 'covered 40,000 miles every year' on a run around the cattle stations of the Northern Territory.

Early one Tuesday morning, so his story goes, he drops into Murray Neck's Retravision Store in Todd Street, Alice Springs, only to find that the blokes minding the store have got severe hangovers on account of a Lions Club meeting or some such do the night before.

In walks Charlie Perkins (now Head of the Department of Aboriginal Affairs). He wants half-a-dozen washing-machines for Yuendumu. The bloke behind the counter points him in the direction of a bunch of Westinghouse machines and goes back to nursing his hangover. Charlie checks out the washing-machines for a couple of minutes and returns to the desk.

'They're no good,' he says. 'They're all white.'

'Yeah, but look inside,' says the salesman. 'The agitators are all black!'

CHAPTER TWELVE
GROOTE EYLANDT

About twelve hours after Lippold did his back in, he was cranked full of painkillers, taken to the airport in a waiting hire car and shunted into a plane. But by that stage of the game he was anybody's, so full of dope we could've been shipping him anywhere.

When he finally came to, 16,000 feet above Caledon Bay, there was a warped and twisted voice hammering at the back of his head.

'Hey Cap'n! Don' look now . . . but down there's Caledon Bay.'

Lippold kept his eyes locked up tight. He cringed and moaned and lapsed back into blissful unconsciousness, struggling to blot out the voice that kept twisting in his brain like a blunt and rusty blade.

'Yo! Dig it, man. Jus' down here's where them Japfellas got it in '33 . . . five of 'em. Fishin' for trepang right down there in the bay, a couple of luggers, just about there I'd reckon, and bingo! It's all over. Five of 'em with spears hangin' outa their bellies.

'Yo, wild season that one. This mob, Caledon Bay mob, Blue Mud Bay mob wild eh?! Killed two whitefellas on Woodah Island, down south, and then spear copper, Constable McColl, same place.

'Mission mob, Groote Eylandt, where we're goin', they thought them Balamumu was gonna attack 'em, 'cross the water 'n' all. So they stuck broken glass 'round all them buildings!'

The next time Lippold opened his glassy eyes, the aircraft was swinging low over the dense semi-tropical scrub of Groote Eylandt. Great bunches of long, slender eucalyptus leaves explode in the prop wash. Towering, craggy anthills and the tough leathery fronds of prehistoric cycads swish past the left wing. Erupting from the bush, rugged grey ridges lurch toward the plexiglass, suddenly giving way to bleeding black scars, a legacy of years of manganese strip mining.

The King Air completes its incoming circuit, sweeping over the mines, over the tarred road to Alyangula, the telegraph lines strung from their termite-proof steel poles and the mining road with its huge rumbling trucks, skipping across the tarmac.

A sign looms into view:

> THIS AIRPORT FORMS PART OF
> THE GROOTE EYLANDT MINING
> COMPANY'S LEASE.
> THE ADJOINING LAND, PAST THE
> ROAD IS ABORIGINAL LAND.
> ANY PERSON WISHING TO ENTER ABORIGINAL LAND
> WILL REQUIRE A PERMIT

Within a couple of minutes of each other, three of the aircraft drift on to the strip, disgorging little collections of people and swags and bags. Transport arrives in the form of a tip truck, the tray of which has been lined with mattresses. Swags, guitars, briefcases, bags and packs are thrown in and people scramble over the top, dropping into the back for the dusty 50-kilometre journey across the island.

The north-eastern side of Groote Eylandt has seen a lot of activity in its time. At some stage over the last 300 or 400 years – possibly as late at 1644 when Abel Tasman sailed into the Gulf of Carpentaria and passed Groote Eylandt – the Macassans started venturing into the Gulf in search of the sea cucumber beche-de-mer. It's a species of holothurian echinoderm, with a warty skin and a sluggish disposition, but when boiled and dried and smoked it's considered a delicacy in soups.

The Macassans established a camp at the place called Tjarrakpi on the north-eastern coast of Groote, and every Wet season they'd arrive, anchor the proas off the beach and get down to the business of curing the beche-de-mer they'd plucked from the waters of the Gulf.

According to anthropologist Donald Thomson, the contact with the Macassans had some interesting effects on the local Aboriginal population. In order to conceal themselves from the visitors, the women would carry stitched tea-tree screens to hide either under or behind.

In 1921 the Anglican Church Missionary Society established a mission on the south-western side of the island on the Emerald River. A year before the outbreak of World War II, QANTAS set up a flying boat base in Port Langdon, a bay on the north-eastern coast. It was a base that, like all other trading posts and missions on the coasts of Arnhem Land, was destined to attract the curiosity of the surrounding Aborigines. With that in mind, Thomson recommended that the Aborigines be kept away from the flying boat base. Trading such things as tobacco for artefacts was subsequently banned.

Across the lagoon from the QANTAS base, which was subsequently taken over by the RAAF for Catalina flying boat operations during the war, a settlement called Umbakumba was established by an Englishman named Fred Gray to keep the Mamarika away from the base.

In 1958 it, like Emerald River, fell under the jurisdiction of the Church Missionary Society, which maintained control until 1966.

Today, Umbakumba is still dominated by the Mamarika. Other clans include the Bara, Bara Bara, Jaraglia, Mamanyamanja, Wanambi and the Wurrawilya. Servicing five out-stations, the community includes a school, health centre, out-stations resource centre, council offices, community store, powerhouse, mechanics' workshop, building workshop and housing. Its population of 250–300 includes twenty Europeans, half of whom are teachers.

Across the island, GEMCO P/L (a wholly owned subsidiary of BHP) operates the world's largest manganese mine, gouging away great strips of land in search of a metal used for the hardening of steel.

While none of the people from Umbakumba actually works on the mining operation, they reap the benefits through lucrative royalties. 'Maybe,' an Aborigine from the Medical Centre surmises, 'they don't like the work.'

Or maybe it's the 50-kilometre drive to the office that puts them off.

> *MIDNIGHT OIL BAND.*
> A BUS WILL BE DEPARTING
> FROM THE TOWN MESS AT
> 5.30pm TUESDAY 22/7/86
> FOR THE SHOW AT UMBAKUMBA.
> RESIDENTS WITH THEIR OWN
> VEHICLES ARE URGED TO TAKE
> THEM AS SEATS WILL BE
> LIMITED. THANKS MUST GO TO
> GEMCO FOR THE BUS & HARRY
> MUSGRAVE AS THE DRIVER.
> 'STRICTLY NO LIQUOR'

Since the local Aborigines are allowed access to beer on Mondays, Wednesdays and Fridays, the Council in Unibakumba have booked the show for the Tuesday night because it's a grog-free evening. Posters have been erected by the Public Affairs Officer in the mining town of Alyangula, and cars are starting to roll in for the gig.

But the Oils aren't sure whether they can get their equipment in. With the Queen Air still sitting on the strip at Tindal and a Cherokee 6 immobile on Elcho, the logistics are falling apart. Even with back-up flights there's no chance of getting the gig underway before 9 pm.

After a meeting in the teachers' staff room at the Umbakumba school, where holidaying students have prepared plates of sandwiches and biscuits for the bands, the show is abandoned, and the boys head down to the wharf for a spot of fishing.

There's an old bulldozer on the beach, red with rust in about half a metre of water. The brave desert warriors of the Warumpi Band sit at the end of the concrete jetty, tossing lines in and dragging them back out. Kumanjayi Rurrambu stalks knee deep through the water with a rock in his hand, adopting a traditional method of fishing. He comes up with a beche-de-mer that, much to their desert-bred discomfort, he flops at his comrades' feet.

Back in the teachers' staff room, one of the 'Big Country' crew answers a bleating telephone. The Council President, comes the message, has been going around telling everyone the show's going ahead as planned tonight. 'Can't leave it 'til tomorrow – big mob grog problem . . .'

Plans for a relaxing night off are shelved and activities frantically switch to the gig. The set-up is a frenzied affair. The crew rush through their paces under the glare of the Mulphase lights strung from the branches of the trees.

Lippold, dosed up with assorted painkillers and determined to pull his weight, is back throwing boxes around. As he passes one of the PA bins to the Warumpis' crew, they start jabbering and lose it. The 120-kilogram box slips back, and Lippold tries simultaneously to catch it and dodge it. As he grabs it and twists away, the pain of torn muscles rips across his back.

In screaming agony, Lippold is carted off to the staff room, and his place in the road crew is taken by band members chipping in to help.

The site for the show is beneath trees in the schoolyard and is surrounded by deep white sand. The stage is a concrete slab that's backed by a workshop and tales of a 2 metre king brown snake that lurks within.

The Warumpis front up first, and during 'Breadline' Glad Reed makes a guest appearance blowing trombone. Later, Jim Moginie plays keyboards in 'My Island Home', a number Neil Murray wrote for Rurrambu after the period spent at Fourth Creek in 1985. Again, it's a responsive audience.

The significance of this show, and last night's at Yirrkala, is that in each case the Aboriginal communities have invited in the whites from neighbouring mining towns (Nhulunbuy and Alyangula). By doing so, they've given whites – who normally wouldn't dream of coming in (and probably refer to the places with a fair degree of mockery or derision) – the opportunity to visit and take part in the activities without the need for permits.

In Yirrkala, the visitors swamped the locals, taking up the closest vantage points with rows of deck-chairs and blankets . . . while the Yolngu people of Yirrkala hung back in the shadows on the hill. In Umbakumba the mix is less clearly defined. People perch in the trees and sit on the sand, crowding around the makeshift stage.

The Oils kick off with a bang, but during their second number, 'Dead Heart', Rob Hirst starts lagging and the whole band begin to lose it badly. Gary Morris, who's standing in front of the mixing desk, shakes his head. 'Bloody Hirst, he's way out. Just falling behind. I had a talk to 'em before, and Hirst was real pissed off . . .'

But the problem is hardly psychological. Rob's busted the skin on his snare drum, and Lippold, his guardian angel whose dedication dictates that he must still operate the fold-back desk, is barely able to function.

The aura of the pampered rock star is suddenly stripped away as Hirst rises from his kit and stalks off towards the workshop with his snare drum.

Since the band's inception, Rob has been known as the friendliest and most outgoing of the Oils, a man who thrives on the joy of being in the band. Like all musicians, he's best avoided immediately before a show, but afterwards he invariably has an amiable ear for the fans. It's fair to say that he's more relaxed than his colleagues, a man who can be relied on for a smile, a firm handshake and a warm word. Of all the Oils, it's Rob who consciously cherishes and nurtures the band, its fans and its position.

There are those rare times, however, when depression sets in, for reasons unfathomable to anyone outside the tight inner circle. A former Oils record producer, Nick Launay, once said of Rob that 'his gloominess is like an English summer' – a description that's not out of place tonight.

It seems to have been bubbling for the last few days, this squalid air of discomfort. Hirst puts it down to the need to restrain himself on stage, the discipline of having to lay back when he'd rather be thrashing the kit. But he's afraid that if he plays in his usual tempestuous style, he'll drown everyone else out or drive people away from the noise. For the first time in his life, he's having to deliberately play under par, having to think about what he's doing before he does it, and for Hirst that's a horrible experience. It is, he feels, the antithesis of what great Midnight Oil music is.

An obsessive Beatles fan as a child, he 'coerced' his mother into buying a pair of drumsticks for his seventh birthday. Later, he got into Creedence Clearwater Revival. And then, when he was given a copy of *Live at Leeds* he discovered The Who and became so fanatical he was wild that no one had ever introduced their music to him before. He started emulating Keith Moon's style of drumming, but never, oddly enough, his style of living. Moon had the rock 'n' roll lifestyle down pat: he trashed hotel rooms, blew doors off their hinges with cherry bombs, drove his Roller into swimming pools, got drunker and louder and crazier than any star before him, and spent his money on huge houses and equally huge damages bills. Hirst loved every moment of it, but when his own time came, his off-stage antics were so respectable you'd never have picked him for a pop star, for an absolute maniac behind the kit. He took another road altogether. He developed an interest in botany.

His first drumkit, bought at the age of 15, was 'an ugly volcanic lava-green through red number, just a simple jazz kit with two cymbals and a hi-hat'. He bought it to play in his first band, Schwampy Moose, with Jim Moginie.

Sixteen years later, that kit sits silently in the sand in the Umbakumba schoolyard, and the rest of the band stand around wondering what to do. It's probably the first time the Oils have had to deal with being on stage without Hirst.

Garrett fills in with some banter and the rest of the band slip into a country and western rave-up with Garrett improvising lyrics about the influence of the Murdoch press in the Territory. And then, with no sign of Hirst, it's down to brownie points.

'Lose three points,' Garrett explains, 'and you've got to sit in the back of the hire car all the way from Melbourne to Sydney.'

So the guys swing into Rotsey's instrumental, 'Wedding Cake Island', and Garrett hunkers down behind the kit, pounding out a surf beat on the toms. He looks clumsier than usual, head down in concentration, arms tense, listening and hitting. For Pete, instruments don't come so easily as speeches.

When Hirst returns for 'Only the Strong', sits down and clips the snare drum back on to its stand, the strain shows in his face, etched by the glare of the Mulphases; lights so powerful that they blaze forth like headlamps on high beam screaming straight into a rear view mirror.

So powerful that they drive most of the audiences back into the seclusion of the shadows, encroaching on the shyness, the reserve of a people more accustomed to firelight.

But the gig, like the lights, is a scorcher. The guys are starting to loosen up, starting to smile and to jam and to cook. It's rough ... but it's fantastic as it soars along, bordering on absolute liver-rumbling chaos.

And Rob's back on top, so spirited, so carried away during 'The Power and the Passion' that his whole body starts steaming, cooling off only when his obligatory drum solo dips into a piece of cool after-dinner swing.

After the show, Lippold and the crew retire to the teachers' staff room, lounging around on plastic bucket seats and dipping into bowls of spaghetti. Lippold cringes in a corner, recounting tales about such notorious special effects roadies as 'Heart Attack Jack' and spearing the pain in his back with rib-crunching bouts of laughter. And then, utterly exhausted, he retires to his swag on the verandah with a body full of Serepax and other assorted painkillers.

Off in the darkness, sitting cross-legged over the ashes of a fire, Garrett and Richard Geeves talk over old times. A friendly redheaded bloke, Richard's been living and teaching in eastern Arnhem Land since 1981. He went through Sydney's Barker College a year ahead of Garrett and remembers him as a 'big, tall blond streak, really skinny with white hair'.

'I knew of him because he used to play full-back for one of the football teams, and he was one of those players who always gets injured whenever they play. And we all thought he was putting it on.

'The other reason we knew him,' he later recalled, 'was 'cos he was in the cadets. I don't know whether it was because he was very tall and susceptible to sunlight or something, but he was one of the first guys who always dropped when we had a parade or something. You'd always look for Garrett and if he was swaying you'd know that a few people were about to keel over. He was the one, the reference point, the barometer, the big timber.'

A couple of years later, the pair met up at the Australian National University in Canberra.

'Burgman, the hall of residence Pete was in, was full of private school people with lots of money; hedonistic, immature, lots of silly games around the place, driving around on bikes at midnight, all this sort of stuff.'

Garrett, it seems, had little time for such pranks. Having to earn enough to pay his own fees, he held down a variety of jobs including college barman, truck driver, cleaner and labourer.

At ANU, Garrett studied law and sang with a uni band, Devil's Breakfast, before teaming up with Richard on drums in Rock Island Line in 1974. Five years later, Richard took over as the Oils' bus driver for a New Zealand tour. Months later, he started teaching in the Top End.

In 1983 he was responsible for the Oils doing a show in Numbulwar. Their first in an Aboriginal community, it was a night that inspired the Blackfella-Whitefella Tour.

Sitting by the fire, Pete takes Richard's tobacco and rolls himself a smoke. 'This is one of the very rare occasions when I'll have a smoke,' he says quietly. 'When I'm with an old friend I haven't seen for years.'

One of the glories of this tour is that it's being conducted during the Dry season.

You can slip into your swag beneath the stars at midnight, smiling quietly at the brilliance of a full moon suspended like a silver disk in the clearest skies you've ever seen.

But the weather's been strange this year. The mangoes have started blooming a couple of months early. It's been snowing in Sydney and Melbourne, and there've been frosts in the desert.

Within a couple hours, those sleeping in the open are scrambling for shelter as massive raindrops pummel their swags, beating a tattoo on the canvas. Brief showers that retreat as quickly as they pounced.

Towards dawn, Lippold rolls out of his swag and across the verandah. When he comes to, he realises he can't move. He's paralysed. With a feeble croak, he cries for help. The ABC's sound engineer, Johnny Garwood, hears him and hauls him back into his swag. 'Big Country' director Rob Stewart comes to his aid.

Lippold lies in the darkness, tears hanging from his eyes, unable to speak. Garwood heads off to alert tour manager Martin Hardie who, ignoring the request for assistance, promptly rolls over and goes back to sleep.

By mid-morning, Lippold is flat on his back on a door. It takes six people to carry the door from the verandah to the back of a Nissan Patrol four-wheel-drive that serves as the ambulance for the Umbakumba Medical Centre.

'If you drop me,' Lippold croaks, 'I'll drop all your amps *and* your guitars.'

The Alyangula Medical Centre is over 70 Ks away, at least 50 of them over corrugated, spine-jangling, head-banging, axle-cracking dirt. In the back of the Patrol, Lippold's held in position by a couple of swags and covered with a blanket. The back doors won't close because of the length of the 'stretcher' so they're tied together with string, and swag canvas is gaffed over the back to eliminate the dust.

With a towel for a pillow and a foam swag mattress cushioning the ride of the door, Lippold sets out for the hospital. As the Nissan negotiates the corrugations, he winces and motions for another Camel. The driver's an Aboriginal bloke called Warren who comes from Umbakumba and works in the medical centre. The most common problems he's faced with are chest infections and malnutrition. Before the makeshift ambulance climbs on to the bitumen at Angurugu, Lippold loses a pair of tears.

'Just get a gun and shoot me,' he moans.

At the air-strip, Richard Geeves bails out. 'Good luck!' he calls through the window. 'We'll probably see you in Sydney in about six months.'

'Nah, you'll see me in Numbulwar tomorrow!'

At the single-storey medical centre in Alyangula, a nurse is called and Lippold's door is transferred to a bed.

Lippold's in luck. If he'd done his back in almost anywhere else on the tour, he would've been right up the creek. Half-decent field hospitals are a rarity in the bush, and the only reason Groote Eylandt has one is because of the size of the white population in the mining town. So it's better serviced than any other community we've been through, bar Yirrkala which also has the advantage of being near a mining town.

Alyangula's resident doctor is a thin chap with a bushy beard and gold-rimmed spectacles who seems more concerned about catching the gig in Numbulwar than in assessing the patient's condition.

'Where does it hurt?' he asks.

'Aaagh!' comes Lippold's reply.

'Do you think you'll be able to put the Numbulwar show forward to two o'clock tomorrow? I'll be over there then.'

'Aaagh!'

'I went over to Umbakumba last night, but I missed the band 'cos some bastard dislocated his shoulder.'

'Aaagh!'

'When do you need to go?'

'When does the pub open?'

'Nurse, could you open the drugs cabinet?'

'That's a good idea . . . But don't I get to see the menu first?'

The doctor gives him a cursory examination, diagnoses a torn muscle, explains that the rest of the back muscles have locked up to hold the injured one in place, and recommends physiotherapy.

The physiotherapist flies in once a fortnight, he explains. By sheer good fortune, he's due in tomorrow – on his way to Numbulwar with the doctor. He'll see what he can sort out. Meanwhile, Lippold is given a bed, a can of Coke and a sandwich.

'You might be out of action for a while,' says the doctor.

'I'm beginning to get that impression.'

The extremes of health care facilities in the Territory are extraordinary. At the top of the range sits Royal Darwin Hospital, a multi-storey building that was erected during the Fraser years. Rather than wasting money on a new design, they simply copied the plans of a hospital in Canberra, right down to the central heating and the snow guards over the windows. A stay there is enough to freak most bush Aborigines right out: for people used to sleeping on the ground, being put in a bed two or three floors above the earth is enough to generate serious trauma.

At the other extreme are the independent health services, which often operate out of a caravan in the scrub. In Papunya, for instance, the Lyappa Congress Health Service is run independently of the Northern Territory Department of Health.

'The role of the local health services,' as Charlie McMahon explained it, 'is to run the health system with as much local (Aboriginal) involvement as possible. And basically, that's the only way people are going to get better health. You help yourself to health. In the case of infant mortality, the areas that have had the greatest decline in infant mortality are those that have established strong independent health services.'

A quick scan of the Northern Territory Department of Health's annual report for 1984/85 presents some frightening statistics on the state of Aboriginal health.

Infant mortality among Northern Territory Aborigines, for instance, is almost five times higher than among non-Aborigines. In 1984, approximately 15.3 per cent of the 866 Aboriginal births were not delivered in hospitals. There were twenty-seven stillbirths, ten deaths of children under the age of four weeks and another thirteen who died in their first year.

According to the report, hepatitis B 'is hyperendemic in rural Aboriginal communities and ... infection is contracted early in life'. From that same report comes the information that '73% of new cases [of tuberculosis] in 1984 were detected in the Aboriginal population'.

There were 884 cases of syphilis detected among Aborigines, compared with sixty-eight in non-Aborigines. Sexually transmitted diseases had a bearing on the extent of such problems as trachoma (preventable blindness) and otitis media (preventable deafness).

Otitis media among Aboriginal children is a severe problem: '25% of the Territory's 12,000 Aboriginal school children have an educationally handicapping hearing loss in one or both ears, caused by chronic middle ear disease ... An interesting finding in rural Aboriginal community screening was the decrease in hearing problems in one community in the Alice Springs region where children had access to a well maintained swimming pool.'

Malnutrition, according to the report, 'is comparable to that found in developing countries'.

At present, the Federal government is trying to meet the problem with funding of 4.8 million dollars per year.

The answer, though, would appear to lie with a better standard of education, providing knowledge about nutrition, general hygiene, and establishing the ground for the Aboriginal health workers of the future, for people who can work in their own communities and communicate effectively with their own people.

For a company town, Alyangula's not a bad place. It's got a pub and a bowling green, a golf course and a pool, and stacks of prefab houses behind lush tropical gardens. There's heaps of money – so much that even the most chronic dope smokers and drinkers can save 20,000 dollars in six months. There are boats in backyards and sprinklers out the front and, down by the waterfront, blacks and whites sharing the facilities of the pub.

Alyangula also has serious social problems. Marriage break-ups are common, and apparently exacerbated by the absence of hairdressers and social workers. In their place is the single men's hostel, a building with fibro walls and lino floors and a TV room. It's to that little establishment that Gary Morris, Pat Pickett, David Cooke and the pilots have retired with a couple of cases of beer. The bands have flown on to Numbulwar, so tonight's the first opportunity for the crew to get a bit loose.

With a beer in his hand and money in his shorts, Gary sits at the table holding court. He's about to hit 30: a man full of energy and dreams; a man with an impulsive nature and clear-sighted visions of the future; a man who, at this moment, has a 2-metre python writhing and wrapping itself around his torso.

He heard the stories about it in Umbakumba last night; the tales about how it had been speared once and hit with a waddy, and how it had hidden in the shed behind the stage. What could a poor boy do but bag himself a pet?

Since the beginning of the tour Gary's been having serpentine dreams. Almost every night since he toyed with the snake on the road to Uluru, the reptiles have slithered through his sleep. The rivers flowing from beneath the Rock . . . the serpents painted on the rock faces south of Kintore . . . the tales of the king browns in the Top End.

The temptation was too much, the Biblical connotations too great, so this morning Gary couldn't resist bagging himself a Joe Blake. He hunted around in the darkness of the shed behind the stage while the blackfellas clustered at the door, not quite believing that this mad man was poking around between the crates.

Him loopy, boss.

He's found an old Globite school case for the snake, but before putting it away for the evening, it graces his shoulders, rolling down his arms, coiling around his chest, enhancing the centre of attention.

The pilots sink cans of beer and watch with grins on their faces and wary looks in their eyes. Pat Pickett raves about assuming control. Now that Lippold's out of action, it's Pickett's responsibility to ensure that everything goes smoothly. And in a nutshell, the way Pickett sees it, that means he's responsible for ensuring that Martin 'It's in the Queen Air' Hardie goes smoothly. Horizontally, preferably.

Lippold has a strict rule that if anyone disturbs his crew so much that they deserve punching out, then he, the fastest stage roadie in town, has the privilege of doing it. It's a rule that's even saved Gary from being decked by other crew members a couple of times. But now Lippold's flat on his back and Pickett's in charge of the crew.

'Look Gary,' he argues, 'gimme twenty minutes with Hardie on me Pat Malone and there won't be anymore stuff ups. I just want to ask him some questions. I want some straight answers. He either pulls his weight or he doesn't finish this tour.'

Gary goes on tempting the snake.

In the morning the pilots visit Lippold. He's bed-ridden in Ward 2 at the Alyangula Medical Centre, just near the sign saying NO PARKING – MORTUARY ACCESS ROAD.

'People die in hospitals,' he moans.

He gave up lifting boxes two years ago, figured he'd let the younger blokes do it . . . but then decided he'd tackle it one more time, just for this tour.

'I think this might be the end of a good career.'

CHAPTER THIRTEEN
NUMBULWAR

If there is an experience, a place to which the origins of this tour can be traced, it is Numbulwar.

Midnight Oil did forty-seven shows in 1983. A *Stop the Drop* show in Melbourne in January raised about 50,000 dollars for the People for Nuclear Disarmament. A *Jobs – Every Home Should Have One* show in Sydney in May raised 51,339 dollars for a range of selected youth refuges and resource centres for the unemployed in the western suburbs. A CND benefit in London later that month saw the band sharing the stage with anti-nuclear activist E.P. Thompson and raising funds for the Community for Nuclear Disarmament. A show in Numbulwar in August saw the band making its first contact with an Aboriginal community.

Numbulwar's a quiet place. The mail plane comes in twice a week and the barge once a fortnight. *Kava*'s been banned and so has booze. If a drink's what you want it'll cost 350 dollars to charter a plane to someplace like Borroloola, Mataranka or Groote, someplace with a pub.

The settlement, at the mouth of the Rose River, was established by the Anglican Church Missionary Society in 1951. A spin-off from the Roper River Mission, it's populated by about 400 Nunggumaijbarr clanspeople of the Nunggubuyu language group.

'There are a few outsiders chucked in,' says Richard Geeves. 'A lot from Groote (Anindilyakwa) 'cos there's big marriage lines across there, and some, from down south of Roper (Alawa and Ngalakan) 'cos marriage lines run down that way too.'

There are also some Ritharrngu people from the Lake Evella region further north who've stayed on since the mission system was abandoned and self-determination was pursued.

For the Oils, getting to Numbulwar in 1983 was a gruelling trip. It took them two days to drive from Mount Isa to Katherine, a distance of some 1,200 Ks across flat grey country littered with dead tyres and dead kangaroos, dead cattle and dead cars. It was a journey that took them through the occasional town like Camooweal with its sign over the roadhouse counter 'You Are In the Sticks Now So Don't Expect City Prices', through the Barry Caves roadhouse ('Cafe Closes 8 pm/Truckies Served Anybloodytime') and on to Three Ways, one of the loneliest junctions in the country, a corner that's earned a place in the phraseology of hitch-hiking mythology: *Three Days At Three Ways*.

The Oils stopped for the night at Tennant Creek, 26 Ks down the track, and then pushed on north to Katherine. From Katherine they chartered a couple of light aircraft and headed out over Arnhem Land, over the ruined city, over Flying Fox Creek and the Jalboi and the Wilton and Phelp rivers and down over the Rose and on to the red dirt strip at Numbulwar.

'The town,' as Richard Geeves recalls it, 'was terribly excited that the Oils were coming. We'd had country and western acts through there before, but this was the first real rock act.'

The Oils' fourth album, *10, 9, 8, 7, 6, 5, 4, 3, 2, 1*, had been in the national top twenty for nine months and was on its way to triple platinum status.

Earlier that year, the community had been switched into the outside world when a satellite dish was installed. For the first time the ABC-TV could be picked up through Intelsat.

'People here,' says Richard, 'had no idea that the Oils were well known, because they weren't on 'Countdown', and 'Countdown' was the barometer of acceptability.

'But all the same it was a rock band, and they were coming, and they were going to play in Darwin and people were terribly excited.'

Like the majority of Australians, the Oils had never been into an Aboriginal community before. They were met at the air-strip and given a quick tour of the settlement, riding around in the back of a truck while kids jumped about on the sides of the red dirt roads, cheering and yahooing and running along behind.

'They were so excited that this band had come,' Richard remembers, 'and when they saw Pete and the head they thought "this is just fantastic!"'

Tickets had been printed and flown in from Darwin, and the gig was staged on the sand behind a shed overlooking a dry billabong.

'The Darwin promoter,' Richard grins, 'was paranoid about security. He was paranoid that all these people were going to break into the gig, crash the gig, and he was paranoid that they were going to sneak up with spears at night and spear people through the floor.

'Anyway, there was no security at all; no fences, no bouncers, nothing. We set up a car with a cash box on the bonnet and everybody dutifully filed past, and if they had their ticket they gave it to me or bought one. They were just packed in there, old and young, really old people. Everybody was there. We had 350 people.'

As Rob Hirst remembered it in an interview shortly afterwards, 'They didn't really react in a Western way by clapping or raging. They laughed a lot, particularly when Peter started dancing, they rolled around in the dust

'It was an incredible experience for us, hopefully it was an experience for them. It was probably one of the most memorable shows we've done.'

Within twenty-four hours of their arrival in Numbulwar the Oils were playing to 10,000 people at the Darwin Amphitheatre.

A month later, they played to home-town crowds of 36,000 at the Sydney Entertainment Centre.

'When the Oils left,' says Richard Geeves, 'everybody wanted the *10-1* cassette. You'd walk around town and you'd hear the songs coming out.

"Short Memory' was the one they really liked. When you heard them singing the verses, all that business about 'lonely man Afghanistan' they didn't know what it was about and they had other words that fitted in. They loved it. It just stuck and stuck and stuck, and everytime we had a disco at school they wanted 'Short Memory'.'

NUMBULWAR NUMBURINDI COUNCIL INC.

Under the provision of Section 17 (1) of the Social Welfare Ordinance 1964-1972, the Numbulwar Numburindi Council has agreed to allow:

MIDNIGHT OIL & WARUMPI BAND

to visit Numbulwar for a period from: 23rd July 1986.

Mr/Mrs/Miss JONAH MANGGURRA COUNCIL PRESIDENT will be responsible for the person/s named above for the duration of this permit. This permit may be revoked at any time by the Numbulwar Numburindi Council Inc. It is a condition of this permit that no photos will be taken of the village without permission of the Council.

The Oils have been looking forward to this one for weeks. Since the tour was first mooted there's been an edge of excitement about getting back to Numbulwar, back to the gig that inspired the whole trip.

But on the ground the action is subdued. Their concerns, in no particular order, are fourfold.

Michael Lippold, the man who's been beside them for every gig in the last five years, a bloke who's been looking forward to returning to Numbulwar as enthusiastically as anyone in the band, is laid up in a field hospital in some town the name of which he can't even pronounce.

The ABC crew have been banned from Numbulwar because their permit applications weren't lodged soon enough.

The Numbulwar Store – an essential supply depot for an airborne team that's travelling as lightly as possible, and therefore isn't carrying food – has been shut for two days because of a break-in. The European owner isn't about to make any exceptions to his decision to shut up shop, and says he won't open again until the offenders are caught and punished.

And to top things off, rather than being greeted by streets filled with squealing kids, feted with the fanfare of home-coming heroes, welcomed back with something akin to a ticker-tape parade with shredded palm fronds fluttering across the sky, the reception is almost nonchalant. Walk down the street and people carry on with the business at hand.

Perhaps, Richard Geeves surmises, it's because the band's been to other communities and Numbulwar is no longer exclusive. Or maybe they're just jaded: 'Oh yeah, you again.' Or maybe it's 'You guys still trying?! It's been three years and you ain't even been on 'Countdown' yet! Must be really down on your luck though. Last time you came through we had to pay you. Now you're playing for free.'

The Warumpis aren't too excited by the reception either. Throughout the trip they've camped away from the rest of the party. In the desert they stayed in the settlements, visiting relatives and friends. In the Top End, away from the country they know, they've continued to maintain their distance, huddling around convenient kitchens or video machines with people they've met before. But having never been here, they've got no friends in Numbulwar, in this place of fish eaters, so they retreat to a camp with the Oils.

The bands retire to the school, laying their swags on classroom floors and foraging around for food. During the evening, the two bands get together for their first impromptu jam session for the tour, hunkering down over a piano, swapping instruments and songs; ten musicians having a quiet hoot on their night off in a strange town.

In the morning, while the bands are still in their swags, three teenagers who've been found guilty of breaking into the shop are subjected to the public humiliation of a beating by their elders.

'The beating,' Richard explains, 'is organised by the Community Council, and the idea is that the families of the wrong-doers are responsible for seeing that their relatives are punished for their part in the break-in.

'But the beatings look more spectacular than they actually are. I think the idea is not so much to inflict pain as to inflict shame.

'An older brother or an uncle or some responsible person will get the miscreant and pull them out of the crowd, and either have a fist fight with them or hit them with a bit of stick or hose pipe or something like that. The idea is not to bash the person senseless, but just to show them in front of all the other people in town that they've been indulging in some anti-social behaviour and that the rest of the community don't think too much of them.

'The police would far rather the Community Council take responsibility for the maintenance of law and order than for it to become a police matter. I think most of the coppers who work out here agree in principle with communities being responsible for maintaining their own security and their own order.'

In the wake of the morning's entertainment, the equipment, the managers and the rest of crew arrive. The planes, with the exception of the Gammon Aire Cherokees, fly back to the hostel on Groote.

As the afternoon swells, warm and bright, a Dry season's day that seems to linger and bask in its own reflection, half of the Oils pile into a truck and head off to a local billabong for a swim. But concern about crocodiles leaves them paddling on the water's edge. 'Normally I'd chuck the dogs in first,' Captain Coop yells. 'Crocs love dogs.'

The only person twisted enough to plunge in is Gary Morris. Irrepressible, he does his Tarzan act from the bough of an overhanging tree.

Within a couple of hours, the store re-opens for the first time in three days. It's a cause for celebration, and the building is immediately swamped. People crowd the shelves, grabbing armloads of flour and tea and sugar, cigarettes and cans of food. Kids cluster outside, sucking on cans of soft drinks and chewing lollies, catching up on the sugar hit they've been denied.

Meanwhile, with the assistance of a couple of the Oils and the Warumpis' crew, Pat Pickett's setting up the gear on the oval. They unload it from the back of a big white caged truck and, under Pat's watchful eye, arrange it on the football field. There's no power outlet within cooee, so a local electrician 'hard wires' into the power lines, climbing a light pole in the street and tapping straight in. It's a mains earth electrical circuit and Pat, worried about safety, argues with the bloke, insisting that he climb back up the pole and patch in a neutral wire.

During the Warumpis' soundcheck, at about the same time that the street lights start to glow, Sammy Butcher complains that he's getting shocks off his bass guitar. Pat races across and checks the three-phase plug with his voltage meter. The red warning light's bleating, there's juice running straight down the earth line and Pat freaks. He kills the power and goes hunting for the guy who wired him in.

To make Pat's first day as head roadie even more traumatic, the whole sound system's starting to pack up. The cooling fans in the amps are so clogged with dust that they're on the verge of blowing up. Switches on the mixing desk are jammed with dust, and the plugs pulling the whole system together are so full of the stuff that establishing an electrical contact is dodgy.

By the time the Oils come on, after sets by the Warumpis and a local act, the PA is farting and screaming, making hideous noises. The vocals are distorted and cracking up badly.

Most people sit back out of the area of the Mulphases, so there's an unbridgeable gap of about 30 metres between the audience and the band. Three girls, reeking of petrol fumes, get up and dance for a couple of minutes and then retire to their place in the shadows. It's the first sign of an audience reaction all night. Well out of range of the fumes, Garrett promises to dance with them if they'll get up again. A couple of songs later they do and he does, stomping through the dust with all the grace of a marionette duelling with a cattle prod . . . until his nostrils tweak to the smell and he retreats to the sanctity of the stage.

The gig the Oils have been so looking forward to has turned out to be a total anti-climax, an absolute bummer, and in its wake they retire to the school in a moody silence.

But first, they give Pat a hand with the gear, dragging bass bins through the dust and heaving them into the truck. Pat's so astonished, he grabs his camera and captures the sight for posterity. Garrett feigns disappointment. He helped unload the gear from the planes when they arrived this morning and now, when photographic evidence of his labour could be caught by the flash of a bulb, he's got nothing in his hands. The photo is duly retaken.

But it's not just the Oils who are having a hard time tonight. After the show, a disgruntled Neil Murray wanders up. 'Whaddya do with a band that won't even play their next single?'

He's talking about 'Siddown Money'. A number about the convenience of welfare cheques, it was co-written by himself and Sammy Butcher, and recorded during the sessions for *Big Name No Blankets* well over a year ago. Now Neil's hoping to release it as a post-tour single, so every night, he's stuck it in the song list, and every night the band has skipped over it. They don't like playing it anymore.

Early the next morning, Peter Garrett and Richard Geeves bail out, hopping into the teacher's Toyota for the nine-hour drive to Barunga. Pete wants to have a look at the sights from ground level, and Richard's promised a scenic trip.

At the age of 30, with a BA and an MA in history, Richard started looking for a job. With the aim of landing a teaching position in New Guinea, he tackled a Dip Ed. 'I thought Dip Eds were a wank, so I decided if I was going to do one I might as well do it somewhere interesting. I went to Darwin. When I was there, I got interested in Aboriginal education and development, community development. They sent me out to Numbulwar to do a teaching practice and I've been here ever since. It satisfied every reason I wanted to go to New Guinea: get away from city living, another culture, become a real learner again.

'It's an immensely enjoyable environment to work in. Endlessly fascinating. Lots of questions to think about and try to answer, very stimulating mentally, exotic, different.

'I can't understand why lots of teachers don't come here. It's so rewarding and satisfying being out here in this countryside. It's clean. You're always walking sand through your house, so it always seems to me to be like a holiday place. You feel as though you're living at the beach, which you are. It's one of the great undiscovered travel bargains of all time!'

And one of the great challenges. Since 1980 only six Aborigines in the Northern Territory have successfully completed studies to Year 12 – a figure disputed by the Northern Territory Teachers Federation, who claim there has been none.

The education of the young has always been a fairly brutal affair in the Territory. Until twenty years ago, it was not uncommon for Aboriginal children to be taken from their families 'for a holiday' and shipped to missions in places like Croker Island. There, too young to know who their parents were or where they came from, they'd be given a rudimentary white primary education and then trucked off to Darwin or Adelaide for secondary schooling. If they were lucky, the children would find out where they hailed from by the time they were 30 or 40 years old.

Today, the emphasis has shifted towards educating the young so they can gain the skills necessary to help their home communities achieve a degree of self-determination.

'Most of the older people I've spoken to,' says Richard, 'define their aims in very broad terms, and they'll say things like 'We want our children to speak and write English and be able to do maths to a level that'll get them a good job.' By a 'good job' they mean school teaching at a fully qualified level, employment with the Public Service as a Field Officer with DAA; or the ability to work in, say, Numbulwar Council at a level where they can read incoming stuff from Darwin or Canberra and make sense of it, discuss it with local people, write a reasonable response and send it off so they've got the responsibility of running the affairs of the place, not just at the policy level but at the administrative level.'

Each of the communities we've travelled through is equipped with a rudimentary primary school, some of which offer bilingual programs. In the desert, the schoolrooms tended to be metal demountables and old caravans. Up here, they're more elaborate. In the bilingual schools, the walls are plastered with visual aids depicting a campfire or a humpy where, in a standard state school, you'd see a stove or a house. The pictures are accompanied by, for example, the Luritja word *waru* and the English word 'fire'. The most essential skills taught in such places are a rudimentary grasp of the English language, maths and sciences, and critical lifestyle subjects such as hygiene and nutrition.

The gaining of a European education has never been a high priority among Aboriginal communities. For a start, the curriculum has often been irrelevant to the needs and aspirations of the students and their home community. Until recently, the curriculum has been biased towards the English language, a foreign language in most communities. When the kids go home to their parents, they converse in Pitjantjatjara or Gumatj, or whatever their traditional language is. It's only recently that bilingual education – in which children learn in their traditional language and are then given the English translation – has been introduced.

The study environment at home is hardly ideal. With English as a second or foreign language, the kids often don't have the opportunity to practise their skills. In many cases, their parents have little idea of what the kids are learning. The home is often overcrowded and conditions squalid. Their parents can't read or write, and therefore outside help with school problems is restricted.

After a basic primary level of education, some communities offer a post-primary course that's designed to prepare students for secondary education.

'In theory,' says Richard, 'the kids going into post primary have finished their primary education, so they should be at Year 6 or 7 level. Everybody knows that they're not. The ones who can perform the best in a range of subjects would probably be performing at Year 3 or 4 level, so that's a 14- or 15-year-old kid performing to the level that you'd get at the end of Year 4 in a mainstream Territory primary school.'

Poor attendance records among Aboriginal students, according to Mark Crossin, Liaison Officer for the Northern Territory Teachers Federation, are of major concern. He cites as reasons for the poor attendance: 'Little curriculum relevance, including no recognition of Aboriginal education and knowledge as being valuable; large teacher turnover in remote communities; social obligations of traditional Aboriginal students; cultural reasons including ceremonies and various kinship obligations; teachers lacking an empathy with community / parental aspirations and philosophies of self-management; little or no intrinsic value of European-style education for human development; poor support structures to cater for Aboriginal students in predominantly non-Aboriginal urban schools; and institutionalised racism.'

In white society we at least have the opportunity to gain an education. Whether we want to take advantage of it or not is another matter entirely. Out here, kids often don't have that choice.

The only two opportunities for traditional (or bush) Aboriginal students to acquire a post primary education tailored to their needs (and therefore preparing them for secondary school) are two boarding colleges – Kormilda in Darwin and Yirara in Alice Springs. To study there, the children must spend a lot of time hundreds of kilometres away from their families, a situation that presents their parents and their communities with a burden they could well do without. For the teenagers, there's also the added culture shock of mixing with kids from a variety of language groups and tribal backgrounds, and the loneliness of being separated from their land and their family.

The Department of Aboriginal Affairs has argued that over 90 per cent of students who have attended Kormilda and Yirara and returned home have ended up unemployed. According to the Select Committee Report, 'They can then become restless and petty offences can occur and they can have problems such as petrol sniffing and anti-community feelings'. Many former students, according to the DAA, 'appear to be in a situation where they are caught between two worlds and belong to neither'.

But, as Mark Crossin is keen to point out, 'Yirara and Kormilda Colleges have, over a number of years, produced the teachers, policemen, nurses, book-keepers, store managers, bank clerks, labourers, skilled tradespeople and community leaders among the majority of Northern Territory Aboriginal communities.'

To gain a matriculation level education, the students have to attend an urban high school, an environment that doesn't provide the support facilities necessary for kids who are hundreds of kilometres from home. According to the findings of a House of Representatives Select Committee on Aboriginal Education, 'Many Aboriginal children who were academically bright could not cope with the social problems of an urban high school.'

Even those communities close to an urban high school experience major problems. Yirrkala is a fine example. The Aboriginal-run school at Yirrkala is a bilingual one with a large post primary section. The school also provides on-site teacher education programs for Aboriginal teachers working in the community or on out-stations as well as adult education programs (in which people learn such practical skills as elementary carpentry, plumbing, welding and electrical skills). However, the post primary section fails to provide qualifications that would give Aboriginal children a fighting chance in the European world – if indeed that was what they were after.

Unlike most communities, however, Yirrkala has the benefit of a white high school just a few kilometres up the road in Nhulunbuy. But over the past six years, only three Aborigines have attended the school, and their success has been minimal. According to Mark Crossin, who spent five years teaching at Yirrkala, 'The high school, not unlike most urban schools, has failed to provide the necessary support programs needed to ensure success for traditional Aboriginal students. As a result, students have returned to their communities.'

The other alternative is to send the students interstate. Says Richard Geeves, 'Some of the families (from Numbulwar, Groote Eylandt and Roper River) have started sending their children to boarding schools in Queensland, assisted by fairly substantial amounts of money from the Commonwealth Department of Education who pay the students' travel expenses and fees.

'Some of the Queensland schools that operate a full secondary program for them say they prefer the kids to come across when they're 13 and finished their primary schooling, and start them at Year 8. Of course, these children don't perform at the level of a lot of other kids at school. But there's no doubt that by the time they've done two or three years there, the levels at which they're performing in written English, mathematics, science and so on is far higher than they'll ever achieve at post primary grades in their home communities. For a start, they're living in a [boarding] community in which English is the dominant language and they're having to speak it a lot. They're fairly disciplined environments. The schools operate with what they get.'

While the Blackfella-Whitefella Tour was moving through the Top End, Mandawuy Yunupingu, a Gumatj clansman from Yirrkala, was at Batchelor College, down the track from Darwin, studying for his Bachelor of Education degree through Deakin University. Although he'd left school at a young age, he was accepted into Deakin as a mature age student. In July 1987, he became the first Northern Territory full blood Aborigine to earn a university degree. Mandawuy is now taking over as headmaster of the Yirrkala school and is overseeing the school's radical transition to a curriculum that merges white (or *Balanda*) and black (*Yolngu*) modes of thinking.

The transition is radical because what Mandawuy calls 'both ways' education hasn't been tried on this level before. For example, the school is developing a mathematics program called *Ganma* (literally the point at which saltwater and freshwater meet). 'This mathematics project,' says Mandawuy, 'is really centred on *Yolngu* thinking, so it doesn't focus on one particular area. It focuses on language, art, all those things that are formal in the *Yolngu* way of living, culturally: how we pinpoint just where we are as far as formal understanding in the *Yolngu* world view. The relationship between maths and art is the formal high level thinking that's required: deep thought, analysing . . . you've got to be exact where you put that line, where you put this. That's part of mathematics in art. Even going back and identifying this space within time, when you're doing that painting your mind travels, always travels. And if you know that Dreaming story that you're painting, you can go deep, deep down into the land, the songs, *yidaki* [didgeridoo], the body clay and the ochre, and that's when it locks into the musics of our world. If you could utilise that skill when you go and do mathematics at a *Balanda* school, you can get into it straight away.'

Mandawuy's aim is to attract the children of the community and the neighbouring out-stations to come to the school. 'Where we're at is developing the kind of curriculum that will allow parents and children to be interested (in the school's activities), so that when they come to school they enjoy it, there's something meaningful for them. That's why we're giving the kind of atmosphere in the school where there's lots of *Yolngu* things happening there: dancing, art, going food gathering, knowledge about the environment, land, kinship, all those things that need to be happening in a school situation.

'When I was teaching post primary, it seemed to be always directed to the formal *Balanda* understanding of things. The main thing that *Yolngu* communities should be doing is working out how the *Yolngu* curriculum level will be interpreted, motivating kids to come to school because it's their culture that they're learning. The thing about *Balanda* and *Yolngu* teachers doing it together is that *Balanda* are giving their input, informing children about their culture, which should be relevant for *Yolngu* to use when they're in a *Balanda* situation, similar to the *Yolngu* informing children about their cultural values and beliefs. By doing that both-ways education, we're explaining this is what *Balandas* talk about, this is how they live, how you can use this *Yolngu* thinking to come in here, be comfortable here but still be able to maintain that relationship.

'It's a good challenge for the *Yolngu*, the teachers in particular. I see a lot of changes happening within the classroom, among the teachers themselves, through community input and community awareness. It's a slow process, at the *Yolngu* pace, but it's happening. It's great stuff.'

If it's difficult for the students to cope with an alien environment, it doesn't appear to be much easier for the white teachers working in remote communities.

Richard Geeves arrived in Numbulwar late in 1981.

'Here you are in a house. There are 350 Aboriginal people around you and thirty or forty Europeans. How are you going to organise your social life in a place like this? Where are you going to go? What are you going to do? Do you become a sort of all things to all men and be a hypocrite in the interests of easing into the white community? Because a lot of them are very strange ... or do you spend a lot of time down in the village with Aboriginal people?

'Initially I was fortunate because I got on very well with three or four of the other eight teachers. That was pre-TV, pre-radio. We used to play cards, play all the games people played before television. There were lots of darts championships and silly games of spoons to amuse yourself.

'And then I was lucky because I met an Aboriginal bloke who was in his mid-twenties and was married with four children. He really took me on as a friend and introduced me to his family and made me feel a part of the place. We used to go out fishing a lot. I'd go down there and sit round with him or he'd come and sit with me; more him visiting me. It was probably two years before I ever really felt that it was all right for me just to walk into the village and sit down on the sand outside his house and talk with the family.'

When the rest of the crew arrive at the Numbulwar strip for the flight to Barunga, Michael Lippold is found buckled over in the shadow of a refuelling shed. The pilots dropped into the Alyangula Medical Centre this morning to say goodbye, and Lippold insisted on checking out. If he didn't go with them, he figured, he'd be forgotten and left there forever. It wasn't an appealing idea. 'I really wanted to do that show last night,' he tells Hirst.

'Mate, you didn't miss anything.'

CHAPTER FOURTEEN
BARUNGA

Sunlight glints off the chrome, glares at you from the red dirt strip. Up in the cockpit of the Queen Air, the pilot sweats. He hates this gig.

He's the biggest of the pilots, a Bunteresque character with short black hair and glowing red pimples erupting on his neck above the collar. To cope with the heat, he wears white short-sleeved shirts, singlets, shorts and long socks, but he never looks comfortable.

He isn't so gregarious as the others. He isn't a talker, he rarely comes into the camps and though he has a spare seat, he refuses to carry passengers. He always travels alone, just him and the cargo and a hammer. He's carrying amps and racks, big black boxes full of magnets that play hell with the compass. Some of those boxes weigh upwards of 240 kilograms, and their balance in the plane is crucial. The Queen Air's only got one exit, and that's about half way down the fuselage. It's through that door that the boxes are shunted and wedged.

The pilot always get in first. He sits in the cabin, sweating, his ruddy face peering out of the darkness while the crew curse and grunt and jam boxes into the back of his seat. No, he doesn't like this gig. With all that gear stacked behind him, if he goes in there's no way he'll be able to make it to the door. Which is why he carries the hammer – to bash his way free through the windscreen.

When he takes off, rumbling down the strip and wobbling into the air, the rest of the aircraft follow through. We're on a course heading due west from Numbulwar to the air-strips at either Barunga or Tindal. It's a journey of 350 kilometres, and as rain clouds move up and blanket the skies, the compasses start swinging wildly and the planes wander off course.

The pilot of Gammon Aire Two, a young bloke from Darwin who's flown in to replace Chuck Mango, is getting edgy. Visibility is only marginally shorter than the fuel gauge, and with neither maps nor reliable navigation aids, he starts looking for the highway, or someplace flat enough to set the craft down. But the country out this way is pretty rough. Huge boulders climb out of the scrub and towering cliff faces threaten to turn the plane into a rock painting. Fumbling for a cigarette, I ask about parachutes. 'No worries,' says the pilot in his best bedside manner. 'There's one in the nose locker.'

'Uhuh . . . Um, how do we get into the nose locker?'

'Ah, that's a problem.'

'You mean, we're in here and the nose locker's *out* there?'

'In a nutshell . . .'

When you're laughing into the drone of a Cherokee 6, no one can hear you scream. Ahead lies Katherine. No one can hear you scream out there either.

Katherine's got a reputation as a mean and ugly town where the beer coolers are decorated with buffalo horns. It's 341 kilometres south of Darwin and, because of its strategic position – giving access to the Gulf of Carpentaria to the east, Joseph Bonaparte Gulf to the west, and the coast of Arnhem Land to the north – its population has almost doubled in the last two years.

Since the RAAF announced it was building a major air base for the F-18 jet fighters at Tindal, just 10 kilometres out of town, people have been arriving in search of work. There are rumours that the Army wants to station a cavalry battalion in the area, the economy's booming, real estate values are going through the roof and the housing shortage is chronic. At the same time, the number of local Aborigines living in and around the town has dropped by 14 per cent.

Real redneck country, Katherine's long had a history of poor racial relations. In the mid-'70s, a local policeman, Dave Jennings, was forced to resign after admitting that he'd started up a chapter of the Ku Klux Klan.

In 1981, the local Aborigines – the Jawoyn – lodged a land claim for the Katherine Gorge, 29 kilometres north-east of the town. It's a region that attracts about 90,000 tourists a year.

In response to the Jawoyn Land Claim, a *Rights For Whites* campaign was launched in Katherine. The blacks, the whites argued, would cut Katherine's water supply and make the Gorge off limits to tourists. Neither argument was valid, but up here that sort of gibberish gets a lot of coverage.

The ranks of the *Rights For Whites* campaign have now been bolstered by a group calling themselves SPONGE. There have also been reports of renewed activity from the KKK. Aboriginal people claim they've been chased by men in black hoods. Tape recordings of the Grand Dragon addressing rallies in the scrub around Katherine have found their way to the Aboriginal communities around Darwin, and a certain level of paranoia is beginning to creep in.

The safest place for Aborigines around Katherine, it seems, is Barunga, a community 80 kilometres to the south. Originally known as Bamyily, Barunga was established in the '50s as a government settlement after Beswick, 30 kilometres away, was abandoned because of bad water.

During and after World War II, a lot of Aboriginal people were shifted into the Katherine region. So although the traditional owners of the area are the Jawoyn, they now share it with the Ngalkbon, Mangarrayi, Yangman, Alawa, Rembarrnga and others.

According to the NLC, the common language 'is known as *kriol*, a language incorporating some of the English lexicon as well as traditional grammatical structures. Although there is a superficial 'pidgin' sound to the language, be wary of trying to think of *kriol* as English.' Such is the widespread use of the language that a *kriol* edition of the Bible is now being translated.

It was in Barunga that white musicians like Redgum's Stephen Cooney and, later, Neil Murray, learnt to play the didgeridoo. On his way to Barunga in 1978 to find David Blanatji Bangadi, the maker of a didgeridoo he'd been given in Melbourne, Neil stopped at a roadhouse on the Stuart Highway. Seeing a car-load of blacks, he took the log out. One of them called him over and started blowing it through the window. 'The world stopped,' says Neil. 'Just this sound. There was this Aboriginal bloke on one end, me on the other, and the bowser attendant standing there with petrol gushing all over the place!'

In Barunga, the Oils crash at the school, setting up a kitchen in the home economics room and rolling their swags out for a bit of kip in the library. The air-conditioning wheezes incessantly, maintaining the temperature and safeguarding the computers that line one of the walls.

The Blackfella-Whitefella show has probably inspired the biggest influx of people since the community staged the annual Barunga Sport and Culture Festival. Held early in the Dry season, it attracts people from communities right across the Top End.

Among the first to arrive are the Swamp Jockeys, one of the Northern Territory's most celebrated bands. They've driven down from Humpty Doo, keen to open the show with a dose of their mango madness. Gary Morris likes the idea and they're added to the bill.

Cookie, however, has serious objections. He figures they're a bunch of rich white boys cashing in on a free gig. He argues that they've nothing whatsoever to do with the tour and therefore don't deserve to play. When he's told that it's got nothing to do with him, that they are playing, he lobbies to have their set reduced to twenty minutes.

Pat Pickett also lodges an objection. He hasn't been consulted, or warned, about having to make room for another band and he doesn't like the idea one bit. Objection over-ruled.

At dusk, the 'Big Country' crew films the Swamps miming to 'Cast Iron Motive' on the first floor of an abandoned weatherboard house. Below them, huge black pigs amble across the lawn as carloads of people roll into town from Katherine, where the streets have been plastered with posters, and Darwin where news of the gig has spread by word of mouth.

To celebrate the event, Barunga is raging. The bar – a small shuttered window at the end of the store – is open for business. You can get half-a-dozen green cans for $8.40, and trade is swift. There's a long line of people, black and white, shuffling towards the window, in Tiwi t-shirts and grubby green shorts, football jumpers and thongs; a Rainbow serpent of colour snaking its way down the queue.

After spending three weeks in predominantly dry communities where the abuse of alcohol is strictly discouraged, it comes as something of a shock to hit one in which a truckload of grog is foaming for all comers.

Alcohol has long been recognised as one of the greatest contributing factors to the destruction of Aboriginal culture. Consequently, in order to protect them from the evils of grog, Northern Territory full blood blacks were, until the late '60s, prohibited from drinking.

Until a referendum in 1967, Aborigines weren't even considered to be Australians. They weren't counted in the census, they weren't allowed to vote and their freedom of movement was restricted severely to the point where people had to apply for special permission to travel interstate.

A case in point is that of Albert Namatjira, the famous Aranda artist whose Western-styled landscapes of Central Australia were hung in the most prestgious galleries in the country. As a Northern Territory full blood Aborigine, he was considered to be a 'ward of the State' rather than a citizen of the Commonwealth of Australia. A successful artist whose work was in demand right across the country, Namatjira had to pay taxes but wasn't permitted to vote. Nor could he build a home in Alice Springs or apply for a grazier's licence. If he wanted to leave the Northern Territory for an exhibition of his works in Sydney or Melbourne, he had to apply to the Minister for Territories and the Administrator of the Northern Territory for permission to travel. Because of his high profile, Namatjira was granted full citizenship rights in 1957. He was taken off the register of 'wards', given the vote, allowed to move out of the Northern Territory without seeking special permission, and permitted to live with the whites in Alice Springs.

His relatives and children were still 'wards of the State', however, and were not allowed to remain in Alice after sunset – an anomaly that flagrantly disregarded the traditional bonds of kinship. His citizenship also entailed the right to buy and consume alcohol. In 1958, Namatjira was jailed for – under traditional obligation – sharing a bottle of rum with one of his tribal brothers.

Permission to drink, when granted to Aborigines in the late '60s, led to a period of unprecedented slaughter. One of the worst affected communities was Papunya. Much of the alcohol was brought in from the pub at Glen Helen, a tourist spot about an hour and a half's drive south of the settlement.

'When the grog shop was running at Glen Helen,' Neil Murray recalls, 'it was carnage. About fourteen people a year used to die through grog-related things: violent death, fighting with their brothers and fathers or killing their wives or whatever, cars tipping over, y'know, young blokes driving back.'

'At the Glen Helen pub,' says Charlie McMahon, 'I think half of their sales were fortified wines during the bad grog days.'

In the mid-'70s a law was passed allowing Aboriginal people to appeal against the granting of take-away liquor licences in their vicinity. The Papunya Council appealed, the grog was cut off and the carnage cut back.

Elsewhere, other means of controlling the flow of grog have been tried. The Warmun community of Turkey Creek in Western Australia have taken an enterprising approach to the problem.

Amid fears that Harry's Place, a roadhouse a kilometre down the highway, would win a liquor licence, the community did a secret deal with a fuel company to buy the property. With assistance from the Aboriginal Development Commission and the Western Australian Aboriginal Enterprise Company, they've blocked anyone from applying for a liquor licence for the roadhouse by taking it over.

Other attempts to beat the trauma of grog have led to enthusiasm for the out-stations movement; people trying to get their families away from the liquor outlets have headed into the bush and established dry communities. Many of the early out-stations were established by women tiring of their menfolk's alcoholic behaviour.

Through the tyranny of distance, people like the Pintupi of Kintore are now equipped to deal with the problem.

'The thing that the people of Kintore have,' says Charlie, 'is that they are one people living on one land, their land, and consequently they have much stronger lore. Also, they don't have any through traffic. They don't have much interference. They've also had a taste of the horrors of alcohol. In a way they're protected by their isolation because they're 500 kilometres from the nearest pub. The Kintore people might go into town and have a few beers, but by jeeze it won't last 500 kilometres on a hot dry road.'

Territorians are rated as the third greatest drinkers in the world, consuming 21 litres of pure alcohol per person each year, 56 per cent more than in any other area of Australia. Significantly, the homicide rate in the Territory is between five and six times higher than the national average.

In urban centres like Katherine, Alice Springs and Darwin, the drinking problem has reached major proportions, largely due to the remarkable availability of take-away booze. You can buy it in the supermarket or the corner store. Alice, for example, has two-and-a-half times the number of take-away licences per head of population than does Western Australia, and four times more than Queensland. In all, there are sixty-two liquor outlets, including thirteen shops, to service a population of 23,000.

Statistics from the Northern Territory Department Of Law and the New South Wales Bureau of Criminal Statistics show that Alice Springs has six times the number of drink-driving offences than do similar-sized towns in New South Wales.

People found drinking on the streets are liable to be taken into protective custody. In 1984–5, police in the Alice Springs region took 9,750 people into protective custody. (In a 1987 interview with the *Sydney Morning Herald*, Alice Springs Police Superintendent Jack Ilett reported that 'between 85% and 90% of the protective custody cases involved Aborigines'.)

In Darwin and Tennant Creek there are Sobering Up Shelters run by the Salvation Army and regional drug and alcohol groups. Fifty per cent of protective custody cases are delivered to these shelters, as an alternative to holding them in police cells.

Since the introduction of the '2 Kilometre Law' a couple of years ago – legislation prohibiting the public consumption of liquor within 2 kilometres of licensed premises – the incidence of Aborigines openly drinking in front of tourists has been reduced. The law has taken the problem off the streets and pushed it into the riverbeds and the fringe camps on the outskirts of each town.

The one bar in which Aborigines were allowed to drink in Alice has been pulled down, which has done little to alleviate the problem and which raises the question of discrimination. It's not that Aborigines are not allowed to drink in other bars, it's just that they have introduced such stringent dress regulations that, in most cases, entry is prohibited. It's supposed to apply equally to blacks and whites, so if you're a young white wearing jeans, you're unlikely to find an open bar either.

Such policies encourage the purchase of take-away liquor, which is fine for the whites who have houses and caravans in which to do their drinking. It's not so easy for the blacks who are restricted to town camps that frown on the consumption of alcohol.

In an effort to remedy the situation, the Tangentyere Liquor Committee in Alice has been trying to set up four licensed clubs which would provide 'food and recreational facilities to discourage dangerous binge drinking habits' and give 'access to health and welfare services so that drinking problems can be addressed when they occur'. The reason the committee wants to set up a total of four licensed clubs is 'to prevent fights and tensions arising from people from separate language groups mixing in one place.'

Another approach to the problem has been the introduction of the *Beat the Grog* campaign, a move specifically aimed at Aboriginal people. It has parallels in Territory-wide campaigns like *Let's Beat Alcohol Together*, *Alcohol Action Week* and *Boozers Are Losers*.

Essentially an educational push, the *Beat the Grog* campaign includes the production of radio programs, video programs and posters. By focusing on the family rather than the individual, the people behind the anti-grog movement are aiming 'at renewing cohesion and unity within the group (the positive and strong aspects of Aboriginal community life which are broken down by widespread alcohol and substance abuse)'.

Turn on the radio and you'll hear ads stressing the dangers of drink driving: '*Billy Jones lost it down the track. Rolled the car eight times. Real mess it was. But Billy died happy. When we cut him out of the wreck he still had a can of beer in his hand.*'

It's an uphill battle though. The Territory, after all, is a region in which distance is measured by the amount of beer you can drink between points A and B. ('Darwin to Katherine? Oh, that's a carton. Katherine to Barunga? Three green cans should get you there.')

Beer drinking is such an integral part of the mythology of the Territory that the place wouldn't be the same without it. Even the survival of tourism seems to hinge on it. Where else could you get a beer bottle like the Darwin stubby, a receptacle that holds 2.5 litres of the amber fluid? Where else but Darwin would you find a major event on the social calendar like the annual Beer Can Regatta, a boat race in which the competing vessels are all built with empty tinnies?

Even government elections have been moulded to suit the amber lifestyle. At the Northern Territory polls you can bet on the outcome with the TAB, and then retire to get smashed at the bar in the tally room where you can 'see your favorite politician weeping, crying, smiling or whatever while sitting in the most comfortable seats in town'.

Such is the cultural acceptance of drinking in a society that seems ill-equipped to get its brain around a four-syllable word like 'moderation'. Stan Stockton from the Swamp Jockeys, though, seems to have developed a sensible attitude. 'Do you remember that Dustin Hoffman movie *Little Big Man*?' he asks. 'There's a line in that when Custer's looking down at Hoffman grovelling in the dirt: "Anyone can be a drunk".'

Back at the ranch, Barunga's getting loose.

The bar, run by the community, has had its licence extended until midnight. And being the only watering hole within an hour's drive, it's doing splendid business. At 5 pm, the price for half-a-dozen cans jumps to 10 dollars.

Gary Williams turns up and strikes himself off the AWOL list. After getting off at Maningrida, he's spent the last few days hanging around Darwin. Now he wants to get back on the bus.

The gig is being held in the community hall, a vast concrete-floored, Bessabrick building with shattering acoustics. As the squeals and burps of the soundcheck erupt from within, most people hang around outside, drinking.

A road block has been set up outside the hall and the three-phase powerlines fed through PVC pipes that run from a workshop across the road. When Pat checks the distribution board in the workshop, he finds it's been overtaken by an ants nest.

As darkness sets in, people start filing into the hall, standing around the sides, waiting for the Swamp Jockeys to unleash a bit of their celebrated Humpty Doo dreaming. In recent months, Midnight Oil have heard a fair bit about the Swamps, so when they start playing, the Oils wander in.

For the Swamps, it's a rough and invigorating performance. Like most Swamps shows, it's sloppy and highly entertaining.

Though not everyone seems to think so. David Cooke shows his frustration by repeatedly throwing vocalist Stan Stockton's dog, Goysha, off stage.

The Oils stick around for the entire set and then wait on for the Warumpis.

But the Warumpis are a mess. Rurrambu's been drinking again and his delivery is so woeful that even Pat Pickett walks out, realising there's nothing he can do to save the sound.

During the set, most people shift outside, leaning against utes and Toyotas and battered HQs, sharing bottles and smokes and dreams, getting primed for the onslaught of the Oils.

By the time the Oils come on, the crowd's cooking. It's happening. The pressure's on. It's an open gig with grog; the first Blackfella-Whitefella wet gig of the tour. And the crowd is raging. But the Oils don't know how to deal with it.

They kick off with 'Some Kids (Got No Time For Games)', and when some kid down the front holds a green can up to Garrett, he takes it, literally swiping it away, and places it at the side of the stage.

When a local Aborigine leaps up and starts dancing on the stage around Garrett and Moginie and Rotsey and Gifford, flailing arms and shaking legs, careening across the boards, they look at each other in disbelief. The floor is packed. There are people *standing*, *DANCING*. And the Oils look as though they don't know what the hell to do. They can't cope. They're lost.

And then, finally, they start to rage. They suddenly seem to realise that this gig is happening! It's familiar! People are *responding*, clapping and cheering and whistling and dancing. They can relate to this crowd. It's a pub gig. The Mulphase lights are glaring down, there's a seething mass of people, black and white, dancing across the floor. For the first time on the tour there are more people down the front than up the back. They're drinking and dancing and yahooing and having a great time.

Even Lippold's back in action. From his position by the side of the stage, he sends Hardie out as a drums roadie to retrieve the snare drum during 'Short Memory' so it can be repaired before the next song.

And at the end of it all, Pat Pickett walks up and says, 'Pat Pickett just turned it down 'cos he couldn't stand the acoustics of the hideous hall.'

The next morning, the Warumpis leave early for the airport at Tindal. In the first vehicle, Gary Williams is travelling with Neil Murray, Cookie and Rurrambu. Sammy Butcher and the rest of the band are following in the truck behind.

Along the road, Cookie and Rurrambu keep sniping at each other over the singer's drinking. Rurrambu calls Neil out, Williams tells them all to shut up, and before he knows it the vehicle pulls off the road and into the scrub. The time has come to take care of Rurrambu. He's brought shame on the band through his drinking and none of them are impressed. Discipline is called for, and in the ensuing debate Rurrambu is punched out by Sammy Butcher.

When they arrive at the airport, Gary Williams demands that his bags be pulled off the plane. After the episode in the scrub, he decides he isn't going any further. After just one night back on the tour, he's seen enough. George might be magic man, he thinks, but he's a spoiled creature from the Top End, and that's what they all are up here. The desert people are just the opposite of that; they're very inward. George was in the wrong 'cos he was talkin' drunk and talkin' out and Gary doesn't need any of it ever again.

When Sammy is seen a couple of hours later, he's got a piece of sticking plaster on his cheek. And George Rurrambu is very, very quiet.

CHAPTER FIFTEEN
WADEYE

Inside the airport terminal at Tindal, the Blackfella-Whitefella entourage hangs around, waiting for the morning's rain to ease.

The mood among the whitefellas is light. People tinker with the soft-drink vending machine, trace their travels on the faded tourist map on the wall, and poke around the unmanned flight booking desks. In their midst, Gary Morris is bounding on the balls of his feet. He's assumed control of the tour management, and now it's time to get the show in the air.

'Okay!' he grins. 'Pilots! What are we doing? Are we flying or not? We are?'

'Some are,' says Garrett, ever the happy mediator. 'Some aren't.' He's standing in the middle of the room, smiling broadly as the rain rattles the roof. 'No risk-taking on the Midnight Oil tour,' he cautions. 'Remember, rock bands: there's only two things that bring them down – overdoses of drugs and plane crashes.'

Around him, the room breaks into nervous laughter.

'There are no drugs around here,' he adds, 'so let's get down to the pub before it's too late.' For a man who rarely drinks, his sense of humour is tuned.

Ahead, 300 kilometres to the west, lies the Daly River Reserve, an area of over 6,000 square kilometres proclaimed as Aboriginal land in 1923. On its western coast lies Wadeye (formerly Port Keats), an inlet on the Joseph Bonaparte Gulf that was discovered by Captain Phillip Parker King in 1819 and originally named after Vice Admiral Sir Richard G. Keats.

In 1932, the Daly River Reserve hit the headlines when three Japanese fishermen from the lugger *Ouida* were killed by a group of Aborigines on Injin Beach. The blacks were led by a wild warrior called Nemarluk. Chief of the Chul a mar (Red Band of Killers), he's reputed to have been over 2 metres tall and to have had five wives. In the early '30s, faced with the prospect of increasing intrusion by white prospectors, cattlemen, and the crews of Japanese luggers plying the coastal waters, Nemarluk and other tribal leaders chose to protect their country by repelling any unwanted visitors. After the killings of the *Ouida* crew, Nemarluk managed to evade capture for a couple of years. When he was finally caught by a tracker named Bul Bul, he ended his days in Darwin's Fannie Bay Prison.

Three years after the *Ouida* killings, Port Keats was established as a Roman Catholic mission. The history of the missions shows that people drifted towards them because they were inspired by tales of regular food – flour, tea, sugar and tobacco. They were intrigued, apparently, by stories about tractors and machinery. But they were less inclined to take an interest in other aspects of the missions: religious instruction and work.

The missionaries, naturally enough, were keen to stamp out what they saw as 'pagan' rituals. The idea of a man taking more than one wife was frowned upon, as was the adherence to traditional religious ceremonies.

Life at the Sacred Heart Mission, as the Aboriginal elders recall, was tough. Minor offences were punished by the withdrawal of such luxuries as tobacco rations. More serious matters were handled with a stock whip.

But if that seemed a harsh way of instilling discipline, then some of the Aborigines' practices sound rather brutal, too. The initiation ceremonies of the region were particularly harsh. In his booklet *The Port Keats Story*, Brother John Pye MSC wrote: 'The actual ceremony ... was ghastly. No one was ever heard to complain or make a sound. No wonder, rags or leaves were pushed into the mouth. The victim was sat on and arms and legs held and a yell like Yarr Yarr was set up. The doctor, Wagon, used a piece of broken bottle to circumcise the patient.'

Wagon, as he was called by the whites, must have been a powerful old man. The spears in this area are either shovel-nosed or barbed and less than a metre long. Wagon is reputed to have been in hundreds of spear fights without ever being hit. He was also renowned for being able to kill people by taking their kidney fat without leaving a scar. Unable to visit Daly River because of tribal death threats, he was still living in and around the Port Keats mission in the 1960s.

Now known as Wadeye (the 'e's being pronounced as in *yet* rather than *eye*) the old mission is a community of 1,200–1,500 people. It's owned by the Murinnhpatha people, but settled by people from at least seven other clans as well.

The Wet season lasts for up to five months of the year, and during much of that time Wadeye is impossible to reach by road. The barge only calls in once a month. It's such an isolated place that, even in the late '80s, Darwin police trying to make contact have had to patch in through ham radio operators in Perth, 2,700 kilometres to the south-west. The only other way of assuring contact is to fly in.

Carved out of the jungle in 1939, the air-strip is marked with 44-gallon drums that have been sliced in half and painted white. Trees bank up all around it, and if you miss the strip you end up in the swamps, struggling through the mangroves that grow thick as a beard, fighting off the sandflies, the mosquitoes and the saltwater crocodiles.

As the aircraft taxi off the runway and swing towards town, a large crowd gathers behind the fence, standing and chattering and watching the new arrivals. Clusters of teenage youths in jeans and

Rambo t-shirts, camouflage gear and combat fatigues introduce themselves as members of one of the local gangs, the Sea Spray Mob, and help to load the gear onto utes and Toyotas for the trip into town. It's the first time on the tour that the bands have been given such a reception.

The bands are met by the Town Clerk, a whitefella named Jon Blewitt who lives with his wife and kids in a modest house. He invites the visitors to use his home for showers and ablutions, and throws it open for food and refreshments.

The local people, he says, went out and shot a couple of bullocks yesterday, and a post-gig feast is planned. Between the hours of 5 and 7, activity in Wadeye is focused on the Murinnhpatha Social Club. It's a big Bessabrick building surrounded by freshly cut lawns and fine young palm trees. The complex is enclosed by cyclone-mesh fencing topped with barbed wire.

At 4 pm groups of men start gathering on the grass within the enclosure. By 4.30 they're jockeying for positions at the gate. Strict rules apply. Tickets have to be purchased on entry, and each person is limited to four cans of beer at 6 dollars.

The bar, lit by fluorescent tubes, is inside the building. It's the kind of place that's so sparse you can wash out the dregs with fire hoses at the end of a session. At one end of the room there's the high counter that serves as the bar. The rest is just concrete and a couple of pool tables so frayed that the green felt has given way to patches of black slate.

The old men are given their tickets first, either out of respect or a fear that they'll be trampled in the rush.

By 5 pm, there are a couple of hundred people milling around, popping inside for beers and a game of pool or sitting on the grass beneath the palms. The whites working in the community sit in little groups on the grass, and outside the kids cling to the fence, peering in and giggling. By the front gate, keeping watch over the proceedings, stand a white constable and a black police aide.

The introduction of police officers to Aboriginal communities is a delicate process. According to Assistant Commissioner A. Grant of Darwin, 'The best of suitable applicants are chosen for the positions. They are assessed on their field performance and ability to work successfully with Aborigines. All recruits in training, and members receiving refresher training, undergo intensive instruction and exposure to Aboriginal culture. Most sessions are conducted by outside experts, including traditional Aborigines.'

Aboriginal police aides are only posted to communities who request them. Following a request for a police aide, the community is asked to recommend candidates who undergo the following assessment: standing in the community; acceptability to clan groups and sections within the local kinship structure; ability to speak the language(s) spoken by the local Aborigines; character; and ability to perform the duties. Their training consists of an induction course and annual three- or four-week training courses. The few instances in which aides from other language groups have been put into communities have met with 'mixed success'.

'The biggest problem faced by police officers,' says Grant, 'is community apathy. If the people are interested in stopping anti-social behaviour then the problems diminish.'

'Police,' he adds, 'get much more support from locals [Aborigines] in an Aboriginal community than they ever get in the white community.'

This can be explained by the traditional nature of discipline in tribal communities whereby if someone breaks the law or indulges in anti-social behaviour, the responsibility of meting out punishment lies with the offender's family. With a resident policeman to call, the onus is shifted away from the relatives.

In Wadeye, the police like to keep an eye on the activities at the social club. Despite the effects of fifty years of Christianity, inter-tribal fighting continues to plague the settlement. According to Grant, 'There is an ongoing dispute over a ceremony which flares up between two tribes when liquor is involved. The young men throw rocks and the old men grab their spears.'

This afternoon, though, everything seems calm.

Gary Morris is waltzing through the crowd and no one knows what to make of him. He's got the snake out again. Draped around his neck, the python is wrapping itself around his arms, its head vacillating between his nipples. As he steps through the crowd, people make way. That fella, he gone troppo!

For the Oils, the place has an oddly familiar feeling: people milling around in the late afternoon, sinking cans before the gig; groups of men inside playing pool by the bar; women congregating at tables and chairs outside. Morris recognises it as the beer garden of the Royal Antler, the Narrabeen pub that was the Oils' stronghold in the late '70s and early '80s, a place where the surfers and footballers of the Northern Beaches would get out of their minds before the gig and then cram into the sweatbox to dance and rage and drink.

Among the Blackfella-Whitefella party, a mild form of combat fatigue is beginning to settle in. There are just three gigs to go, and there's an edge of stir-craziness in the air. 'Have you noticed,' Rob Hirst observes as he sips on a can of Four Kisses, 'how everyone's starting to smoke more? Even the non-smokers?'

At 6 o'clock the Warumpis wander in. In the wake of Rurrambu's performance at Barunga they've instituted strict rules of their own. No one in the band or their crew is permitted to drink. As they sip on a round of soft drinks, Rurrambu is uncharacteristically humble – a man who's brought shame on his friends and has, in turn, been shamed by them.

As the sun drops over the waters of the Joseph Bonaparte Gulf, the boys from Gammon Aire decide to pull another stunt, taking off in the Cherokee and climbing out over the swamps. The plane circles lazily above the community. People around the social club look up, wondering what the plane's doing there at this time of day.

Suddenly there's a collective gasp that rips attention away from Gary and the snake. Through the encroaching darkness, Chuck Mango tumbles towards the earth, collapsing his chute, spinning around in circles, drifting towards the open-air stage and finally touching down within about 12 metres of the crew, while the assembled crowd roars and shrieks with delight.

Having dispensed with his chute, Chuck strolls into the social club for a beer. It's right on closing time, people are being ushered out, and this man wants his first drink for the day. On the way to the bar, he's collared by another pilot who's evidently flown in to see the show.

'Did you see that jump?' the other pilot asks.

'What jump?' says Mango with a quizzical look. 'No, I've been over that house there. Somebody jump, did they?'

'Yeah, no permit, nothin'. Don't know who it was, do ya?'

'Dunno who it was. Must've been one of that Katherine mob. I saw a few of them up here.'

There's an old song that Jim Moginie wrote and the Oils recorded in 1980. It's called 'I'm the Cure', and when it was released on the *Bird Noises* EP it was greatly overshadowed by 'Wedding Cake Island' and 'No Time For Games'. The lyrics are poor, the melody's suspect and the only point of interest is the use of a vibrator in the bridge. It's one of the band's more forgettable recordings. But there's a guy at Wadeye who really wants to hear it, and before the Oils take to the stage he asks them to include it in the set.

Tonight's backdrop is a deep black sky against which the bands are silhouetted sharply.

People sit politely on the ground while Pete introduces the songs, and as soon as the drums or the guitars kick in, the dust billows and everyone leaps up and starts dancing. There are a couple of hundred people down the front and they're going for it, adopting an aggressive form of dancing, just cutting loose. The men dance with each other, all flailing arms and legs and leading jaws. Over on the other side of the stage, the women do the same.

About a third of the way through the set, the Oils slam into 'I'm the Cure' for the first time in maybe five years. And suddenly this kid hits the stage, bouncing across the concrete slab in a pure white jumpsuit, shimmying up to the drums, sliding towards the amps, leaping and jumping and jiving and singing along with Pete, so high on the experience and the colour and the noise there's nothing that can let him down. The crowd love it. Tuned on their four cans of beer, they're a wild and happy mob going crazy in the dust.

At the end of the gig, the Oils come off-stage looking forward to a sample of the local beef. But the bullocks have already been cooked and consumed by the crowd. There's nothing left for the entertainers, so they retire to Jon Blewitt's home for a hastily prepared supper of prawns.

Standing under the porch light, with an enamel mug reeking of rum in his hand, is a whitefella no one's seen before. He lobbed on to the tour today and claims to be a pilot, but no one can figure him out. What the hell's he doing here?

'Whaddya mean he's an ASIO plant?' Gary Morris and Chuck Mango are having a discussion in the kitchen. They're surrounded by the dirty plates and dishes that have been swept off the dining-room table. There are people bustling in and out hunting for cups of tea and coffee, and Chuck Mango has got the new bloke pegged as an ASIO operative.

The new bloke's come in without a permit, and in his kit he's got a bottle of overproof rum, a king hit spirit that you can't buy in the Northern Territory or Western Australia. Out here, it's the sort of contraband that could see a man facing the dawn with a brace of shovel-nosed spears in his back and the Av-gas exploding in his wing tanks.

It seems that he met up with one of the Sydney pilots in Katherine and figured that joining up with the tour for a few days might be a good lurk – sex and drugs and rock 'n' roll, a bottle of OP in the kit and a staggering onslaught of wild nights and wasted days. But this is an Oils tour, and as anyone who's ever travelled with the band knows, strict rules apply. The Oils, as Jim Moginie would say, 'are not very relaxed people'.

So this guy's lobbed on to the tour and thinks he's in for a rage. But pretty soon the boredom of it all starts to get him down. No one's talking to him, he can't find any action, and he's definitely feeling like an outsider.

After dinner, the Oils retire to a low camp fire and settle down to the serious 'band business' of selecting prospective producers and engineers, discussing recording budgets and studios for the next album, a subject that's been causing no end of concern in recent months.

They're sitting amid a sprawling pile of swags and bags, and by the flickering firelight they can make out segments of faces and elbows and knees propped in the darkness. Each of them speaks quietly and thoughtfully, mulling over ideas and introducing them for debate. They're a tight bunch who've been through a lot together, so they know each other well enough to be able to have a business meeting in the darkness without having to maintain eye contact.

But sitting just a short distance away, uncomfortably close, is an outsider. It's the new pilot, the ring-in, and while he's being reasonably quiet his presence is given away by the sickly sweet fumes that waft from his chipped enamel mug.

'What's that you're drinking?' Garrett asks, with an air of hostility in his voice.

'Overproof Rum! Want some?'

'No thanks.' The disapproval in his voice is unmistakable, to anyone whose sensibilities haven't been bashed stupid by OP rum. 'I thought this was a restricted area.'

The intruder lies back against a swag, unable to believe just how bloody boring this mob is. A few minutes later, as the ideas and assessments of producers circulate among the band members, another slug of rum surges through the intruder's system, prompting him to butt in with a new, far more interesting subject. 'Have you still got any political ambitions?' he asks.

'Not that I'm going to talk about,' comes Garrett's annoyed reply.

From the other side of the fire, Gary Morris explains that they'd like some privacy.

'Okay, I'll keep quiet,' says the pilot.

By morning, he's been thrown off the tour.

•

It being a Sunday, Garrett rises early enough to attend his first mass in a Roman Catholic church. Against the backdrop of a reredos of traditional Aboriginal design, the candles are modelled on barbed spears and the altar panel features crucifixes and a variety of traditional totemic symbols.

A couple of hours later, Jon Blewitt takes the Oils to the bottom camp to meet with some of the elders. Their interpreter is an old man named Felix whose father attended to the task before him. His father, he explains, was a bushman 'when people were hunting around and fighting each other'. Shaded by pandanus and ferns and sitting by the creek, the meeting is filmed by the 'Big Country' crew.

Garrett assumes the role of interviewer, probing for questions and answers.

Felix explains that during the days of the mission, school was compulsory for the children. Today, it's up to the parents' discretion. The kids, he says, go to school and listen to rock 'n' roll. The community wants to keep the kids 'out of mischief'. Petrol sniffing has been cut right down. Because it's an isolated community, there's a greater chance of retaining control. Essentially, they 'want to get it fixed'. The ceremonies are still strong, and the council now runs the town, 'doing part of the government job'.

The community wants 'fair talk' from the politicians. 'The politicians don't come out here, so there's not much money for roads or education.'

'Land, it is very important to us,' Felix says. At present, there's a lot of interest in exploration. The mining companies want to come in to lay seismic lines, testing for oil.

The community wants to set up an arts and crafts centre. A proposal was sent off last year, but they haven't heard back yet. Jon Blewitt promises to look into it.

It's obvious that these blokes are treating Garrett as a potential lobbyist, but when he turns the tables by lobbying for an up-coming Labor candidate, his comments are met with an inscrutable stare. (Interestingly, when votes were counted in the 1987 Federal election, over 90 per cent of votes registered in Wadeye favoured the ALP candidate, former Central Land Council worker Warren Snowdon.)

Within hours of Midnight Oil leaving Port Keats, 200 people were involved in a tribal brawl.

The settlement's police force of two constables and an Aboriginal police aide were unable to contain the situation. One of the policemen was later treated for head injuries.

According to Assistant Commissioner Grant, 'As a result of an incident that occurred on that settlement, one Police Officer did receive medical attention that required stitches to a head wound.

'No one was charged as according to the member he got too close to the fight, which could never be contained by police employees.

'Police employees who have to respond to these types of confrontations are all too frequently unintentionally injured.'

Four months later, in early November 1986, heavily armed police reinforcements were airlifted into Port Keats in an effort to stop tribal fighting that had raged uncontrollably for two nights. In the fighting a police aide was injured and another man evacuated by an aero medical team to Royal Darwin Hospital with three stab wounds to his back.

Early reports of the fighting – channelled through a ham radio operator in Perth – maintained that the Murinnhpatha Social Club had been over-run, houses broken into, shotguns fired, and rocks and spears thrown as fifty Aborigines engaged in a running battle.

Two days later, police task force members returned to Darwin. Northern Command Assistant Commissioner Bill Goedegebuure later issued a statement saying, 'It's all quiet. We went over there, helped restore order and came back.'

In January 1987, as a result of that incident, seven members of the Sea Spray Mob fronted the courts in Darwin. Three were committed to the Supreme Court on charges of attempted murder.

CHAPTER SIXTEEN
NGUIU

On the ground outside Nguiu on Bathurst Island, 70 kilometres north-west of Darwin, Hardie shoulders his bag and ambles across the air-strip. 'This country,' he says, referring to Bathurst and Melville islands, 'is the home of the Tiwi people. The Tiwis have got this dance called "The Bombing of Darwin". The old men are the Japanese planes and they run around with their arms outstretched. The young men hold their hands over their eyes like binoculars, watching out for the planes, and then their hands become anti-aircraft guns and they shoot the planes down. And the dance finishes with the old men crashing to the ground.'

To support the story, he points out a small, hand-carved and ochre-painted *pukamani* pole that's stuck in a patch of grass in front of the tiny shed that serves as the Bathurst Island airport terminal.

The short pole is a memorial to Matthias Ulunguru, 1921–1980, who, according to the inscribed plaque, 'unarmed, on 19 Feb '42 on Melville Island captured the first Japanese prisoner of war (a Zero pilot) to be taken on Australian soil'.

Contemporary newspaper reports note that Matthias snuck up on the pilot, pinched his revolver, and ordered him to 'Stick 'em up allasame Opperlong Casserty!'

From all accounts, it was a memorable day for the Tiwi. Right in front of the Sacred Heart mission station, clan groups were sorting out a tribal conflict when suddenly the wobbling spears were superceded by half-a-dozen Japanese fighters strafing the air-strip and the church. The warring Tiwi panicked and took off, and the Japanese aircraft flew on to wreak havoc over Darwin.

Official accounts reveal that at 9.35 that morning, Father John McGrath hit the radio at the mission and bounced a message across the Beagle Gulf to the Amalgamated Wireless station in Darwin. He warned that a big mob of aircraft was heading towards the city. The RAAF operations room got the message at 9.37 and, figuring it was a false alarm, sat on it for twenty-one minutes. As the first of the Japanese bombs started falling on Darwin, the air-raid sirens finally rang out. In the ensuing carnage, at least 238 people died.

Covering 8,000 square kilometres, Bathurst and Melville islands lie in the Timor Sea. Bordered by swamps, the islands are covered with scrub and small idyllic patches of rainforest. The settlements on each of the islands are shaded by towering palms and tamarind trees planted by the voyaging Macassans.

The strategic value of the islands was first recognised by whites in 1824 when an outpost, Fort Dundas, was established on Melville Island. To support the settlement, the first water buffalo and Bantang cattle were introduced from Timor. When Fort Dundas was abandoned five years later, so too were the animals.

In 1910, the Order of the Sacred Heart began its work on Bathurst Island, establishing a Roman Catholic mission at Nguiu in 1911. Two years later, the island was proclaimed an Aboriginal reserve. Set among coconut palms, mango trees and the huge fruitbearing tamarinds, Nguiu nudges the treacherous Apsley Strait which divides the islands.

The Tiwi people are as different from the people of the mainland as Top Enders are from those of the desert. Cut off by 40 kilometres of water, they traditionally believed the mainland to be 'the home of the spirit of the dead'. Consequently, although they clung to their own perception of the Dreamtime, their culture developed independently of that of the mainland tribes. Today, their culture shows strong Macassan and European influences, and reveals a far more sophisticated (in Western terms) outlook on life.

Perhaps because of their close proximity to Darwin and the fact that European influence extends back over seventy years, the Tiwi people are well advanced in terms of tourism, trade and local politics. Political development was encouraged by the missionaries, who set up a local Tiwi-run council to oversee the affairs of the islands. Further development was assured with the establishment of the Tiwi Land Council, which operates on the same criteria (but independently of) the Northern and Central Land Councils.

In recent years, the Tiwi have established a number of facilities to take advantage of Western interest in aspects of Aboriginal culture. Among the enterprises that have been developed in Nguiu are Tiwi Pottery; Tiwi Pima Art (a resource centre and distribution outlet for local arts and crafts); two screenprinting workshops – the independent Tiwi Designs (which was set up in 1969 by Bede Tangutalum and Giovanni Tipungwuti), and the church-run Bima Fashion (which employs seventeen local seamstresses in its 300,000-dollar factory); Tiwi Tours (a tourist minibus service conducting half-day, full-day and two-day tours of the islands for which entry permits are not required); and a restaurant for tourists.

They're also building a motel; and over the last three decades or so, the Tiwi have developed an extensive reafforestation and wood-chipping industry, working with termite-resistant cypress pines.

Since the modern world moved in on them, tribal Aboriginal people throughout the Territory (and indeed throughout the country) have had to make the transition to the Western economic system. Because their traditional food resources have been depleted, they need money to buy food and to pay for essential services. An unavoidable reliance on 'siddown money' has developed: welfare cheques, pensions and children's benefits, and sickness and unemployment benefits. Along with that has come criticism of 'the Federal government's paternalistic hand-outs'.

Some communities, including the Tiwi, have tried to develop pastoral interests in order to survive. But these have rarely met with success. Where once Aboriginal people worked on cattle stations for payments of flour and clothing and a place to camp, some tribes (such as the Gurindji) are now buying those properties. Trying to make a go of them, however, is difficult; previously the properties were able to support a white family who would give meagre rations to the blacks in return for their toil, but they now have to support the 200–300 Aboriginal people living on them.

Other communities have tried pastoral ventures in order to keep their people occupied. South of Warakurna, at Warburton, the people have tried running cattle, but the distance from the markets has made that an unviable proposition. A scheme at Docker River to sell feral camels to the Arabs has run into difficulties for the same reasons. They're too remote to be viable. Transport costs are too high and the ventures are therefore not cost-effective.

Many other communities have now developed arts and crafts enterprises which, because of their low overheads and increasingly high demand, are proving to be profitable. They keep people occupied (enhancing their connection with the land through traditional artistic activities) and bring in a reasonable return, which in turn gives people a sense of pride. (A sense of pride, as any social worker dealing with chronically unemployed people will confirm, is the first step in improving the quality of life.)

The people around Warakurna have taken another approach altogether, one which avoids the pitfalls of primary production and will, they hope, lead to economic self-sufficiency. There are 1,200 Aboriginal people living in the region, 85 per cent of whom receive social security benefits. In order to gain economic self-sufficiency and therefore a greater influence on their own struggle for self-determination, most of the people contribute between 5 and 15 dollars each week to the Ngaanyatjarra Council. Since 1982 the Council has been buying businesses at the rate of one each year.

They now own a trucking company and a buying agency in Perth, two single-engined and one twin-engined aircraft for their own airline, Ngaanyatjarra Air, and have recently spent 500,000 dollars building a hangar and maintenance workshop for the aircraft in Alice Springs.

The Ngaanyatjarra Council has also purchased the Central Australian Ampol Dealership, which now allows them to control petrol supplies throughout the region.

The dealership stretches from Tennant Creek in the north to Warburton in the west and the Flinders Ranges in the south. During negotiations for that deal, the Ngaanyatjarra Council worked with Ampol's chemists to have additives put into the petrol to make it unpalatable to the sniffers. (Not an entirely successful move, going on past experiences on Elcho Island where sniffers found that if the fuel was left in a dish in the sun for a couple of days, the additives would evaporate.)

When that deal went through, it made the front page of the *Centralian Advocate* under the headline 'Aborigines Buy Ampol Agency: Dole Pumped Into Petrol Deal'.

The article quoted the Council's Project Officer Chris Duff as saying, 'Even the pensioners put in their ten bucks. There's no government money involved.' (A debatable point, but I guess that once the dollars leave the Department of Social Security and land in a person's pocket they become 'private money' rather than government money.) 'The transaction was based, to an extent, on financial necessity. The community lives in country which may be beautiful but which is no good for running cattle.'

The *Centralian Advocate* went on: 'The community had been advised that within twenty years the Government would not have enough money to be paying out welfare money. It was a question of these people looking out for themselves. The way the Australian economy is going, it looks like anyone dependent on welfare will soon be up the creek.'

The idea of a community taking advantage of its isolation to buy up a trucking company, an airline, and a fuel depot – all services that it and other similarly disadvantaged communities need access to in the modern world – is brilliant. Similarly, the

Tiwi of the Bathurst and Melville islands using their idyllic tropical location and exotic arts and crafts to lure the tourists is a move that can't be beaten.

There's a degree of civic pride here that extends far beyond that of other settlements. But it seems that some tourists are treated with more deference than others. Aware that the Oils and the ABC's cameras were coming to town, the Nguiu Council had a 'dog out' last week, shooting all the mangy mutts that were detracting from the beauty of the place.

The only Aboriginal community that's actively embraced the concepts of tourism and production line crafts industries, Nguiu is a hive of activity for much of the year. During July, though, the settlement's population vanishes as everyone heads out for 'bush holidays'.

They're off living on out-stations in the scrub, getting back to their country and the traditional ways, hunting and fishing and teaching the kids the ancient crafts. During these breaks, the men spend their time hunting for wallabies and wild cattle, turtles and fish, geese and pigs. The women, while looking after the children, scour the scrub for possums and bandicoots and carpet snakes, and collect wild honey and berries and yams. Along the coast they gather crabs, cockles, oysters, mussels and a local delicacy, the mangrove worm *yuwurli*.

On the eve of the school's resumption, the Tiwi will break camp and the town will once again swell with people.

Having a day off, the Blackfella-Whitefella party is split between Darwin and Nguiu. Those who've elected to spend the day on the island lie around reading comics, playing cards 'for free', and swimming in a local billabong.

Gary Morris leaves his snake in its Globite case and goes in search of larger reptiles. He spends the afternoon wading up a creek in the mangroves, looking for saltwater crocodiles. Ignorant of just how quickly the beasts can move – far quicker than a man kneedeep in mud – he is, fortunately, unsuccessful in his quest.

Martin Hardie, a less adventurous type, scours the town for action. He has an uncanny ability in any settlement to find the one white advisor's house with a television (preferably tuned to the cricket) and a fridge full of beer.

Locking yourself indoors in a place as pleasant as Nguiu, though, is a silly proposition. The streets are wide and clean, towering palms line the waterfront and huge groves of tamarind trees shelter the grassy parks. Many of the houses are simple two-room affairs divided by a verandah, shaded by sprawling frangipani trees and surrounded by lawns.

From the beach you can look across the swiftly flowing Apsley Strait to the scrub on Melville Island, scrub that gives way to the refreshing beauty of Turacumbie Falls and the delightful waterfront settlement of Milikapiti.

Behind the stony beach at Nguiu there's a white statue of the Virgin Mary that stands against the palms. At its base is a plaque:

> *Christopher John Tipiloura*
> *(John Boy)*
> *Born 27th October 1963*
> *Drowned in Strait 26th June 1982*
> *Aged 18 years*
> *Ngajiti ngimpangi pungintayi*
> *Ngiya waya nguwujingimuwu kapi ngawa rringani*
> *Ngiya waya kuriyuwu kapi ngiya ngilipi*
> *Ngiya waya awungarra ngimanuwun jirramukuriga.*

On the southern edge of town there's a Christian cemetery. Each grave bears a white wooden cross marked with black Texta showing date of birth, name, date of death, and rest in peace over a mound of gravel strewn with shells.

Further out in the scrub are the weathered *pukamani* poles of the traditional funeral ceremonies which are conducted within one to four months of a death. The poles, cut from bloodwood or ironwood trees, are individually carved and painted with local red and yellow and white ochres and chunks of black charcoal.

After dark, those members of the Blackfella-Whitefella party who are on the island are invited to visit the white's house that Hardie's found. Because it's a whitefella's place, the Warumpis choose to stay behind. The rest of the crew pile into the back of a Toyota for the trip to the shack on the outskirts of town.

It's a weatherboard house, the character of which is brightened by a complete set of early Mental As Anything *Egypt* posters, circa 1977. The vibe of the place, though, predates the Mentals. There's soporific hippy music on the stereo and a general air of decadence. On the table sits a dying bottle of Bundaberg rum. None of those present seems capable of conducting an intelligible conversation.

A seedy anachronism on the edge of a pretty town in the tropics, it's not the sort of place any of the Oils crew feels like hanging around. So when our host offers to run a couple of people back to town, the entire Blackfella-Whitefella party, with the exception of Hardie, piles out of the house.

Miffed that there's a general rush to escape, the somewhat inebriated host says he'll take a short-cut . . . plunging the Toyota through huge puddles, boring straight through so that muddy red water showers over the cabin and sprays those riding on the tray. It's a long short-cut, barrelling down dirt tracks, rolling through the scrub, turning corners and swiping trees in the dead of night, grinding on through the darkness until finally he pulls into a compound enclosed by a cyclone-wire fence.

The driver jumps out and stands unsteadily in the wash of the headlights, pointing to the town's lockup. It's a small Bessabrick building and its barred door is ajar. He stands there slurring, 'I heard about youse Midnight Oil blokes. We know you're all degenerates so you gotta get out now and stay here! Out ya's get, c'mon!'

The 'Oils Vibe' is a curious experience, a stone walling block of defiant solidarity that's drawn upon whenever circumstances warrant it. It's a negotiating technique that's been developed over the years to such a fine point that record company executives, television producers and rock 'n' roll promoters throughout the world have quickly learnt that it cannot be shaken. It's such a sobering, silent experience that even the driver soon realises that no one's in the mood to play his game.

Back at the hall, the party sits around a campfire, boiling the billy, chatting to a pair of young Tiwi women, and trying to gnaw through rubbery steaks. When the Tiwi women leave, those sitting around the fire are joined by a young white woman who's been getting into the downers and the rum on the other side of town.

She's a couple of sangas short of a picnic, and has one of those strident voices that screeches like a rusty Hills hoist. A real charmer, she epitomises the proposition that there's something so inherently sordid about the rock 'n' roll touring exercise that it attracts the most vacuous personalities in every town – even up here.

In the morning, truckloads of people roll into town, and so does the rest of the tour party.

Plans to hold the gig outside are shelved when it becomes apparent that the threatening grey skies aren't going to clear, and the venue for the show is changed to the booming community hall.

At midday, the crew finish setting up the gear, and the Warumpis swing through their first decent rehearsal and soundcheck for the tour, creeping through new songs like 'No Fear' and 'Falling Down'.

Under fluorescent lights, the louvred Bessabrick hall gives the snare drum so much brightness it sounds like sheets of fibreglass being smashed in your eardrums. It doesn't bode well for a pleasant afternoon gig.

By 3 pm, the concrete floor is covered with blankets and dogs and people in Ford and Holden windcheaters, camouflage shirts, Northern Territory footy shorts in brown and gold or black and white, bare feet, RMs, combat boots, work boots, VFL footy jumpers, jeans and shirts and knee-length skirts, and wonderful, colourful blouses.

When the Oils hit the stage, the sound gets even louder, so loud that by the time they get to 'Hercules' people are streaming out, heading home. They've seen and heard enough of this attraction.

Outside, the old men sit around the campfire. A couple of metres away, Gary Morris, who's spent the morning entertaining the incoming kids with his snake, sleeps on the ground, blissfully unaware of the noise.

Inside, kids are running around yelling 'Deaf! Too deaf!' while halfway down the hall, an old Tiwi woman sits with tears dribbling down her cheeks. She's got a few jagged teeth, gnarled hands, silver hair and bare feet, and she's wearing a pink skirt, an iridescent red jumper and an old brown cardigan. During the 'Dead Heart' she just sits, smiling with joy while the tears roll down her cheeks.

After 'Kosciusko', Garrett says, 'Are people going to dance today? Are you allowed to dance? You can, now okay!' And the women pick up their kids and head outside as if a call to dance is a call to riot, to go wild and trash the joint. No one dances. They don't care if it is 'The Power and the Passion', they're not having any of that violence around here.

CHAPTER SEVENTEEN
COOINDA

Sometimes you'd wake with eyes so bright and a head so clear you could almost see for days.

But the last date of the tour, twenty-five days in, was heralded by the glare of a feeble sun clashing with a dozen hangovers trying desperately to come to grips with the orange curtains and lime-green furniture in a gaudy string of Darwin hotel rooms. It wasn't a pretty sight.

Twenty-five days on the road can take the stuffing out of anyone, especially when that time's been spent bouncing through places in which you can't even find a postcard.

Each night I'd hit the swag, snuggling in beneath a bright new sky, and try to recall the day's activities. But by the time I got past breakfast I'd be asleep, clobbered by the exhaustion of the travelling and the air, the meetings and the glare. I don't think I ever had trouble getting to sleep out there. Even a reeling brain was no match for the physical drain.

There's a point at which fatigue slips into the realms of hysteria, when you just want to sit and stare at a wall for a few days, bolted into a chair by the chains of gravity. Cookie was close. I think most of us were. In a couple of days he'd be back in Alice, so far up the wall he'd be evicted by his girlfriend, seeking solace with a yard full of fellow veterans who'd wish only for silence and a wall without any shadows.

But that was still a day or two off, and until then, even those who were susceptible to such breakdowns were determined to hang on for at least another show, to keep it together and see it through. Planes were refuelled at Darwin airport and cans of 'headcrack' soothing beer secured for the short hop to Cooinda.

The last date of the tour, it's being staged in the middle of a tourist complex in Kakadu National Park.

Drifting in over the paper bark swamps of Yellow Waters, all heads are diverted to the windows, scanning the glistening waterways for crocodiles. On the ground, out under a blazing sun, attention is turned to more hedonistic pursuits. If there's been an edge of stir-craziness in recent days, it's on for young and old at Cooinda.

The venue is the grassy beer garden of the Cooinda Motel, an establishment with a palm-shaded kidney-shaped swimming pool, a bank of pool tables and enough refreshments to sink the average supertanker. It's owned by the Gagudju Association and managed by Four Seasons, a by-product of the royalties from the uranium mines at Jabiru. The Gagudju, of whom 400 live in the national park, bought the complex in 1979. Having extended it, it's now worth about 7 million dollars.

Rather than wasting the royalties (of which they receive some 3.6 million dollars of the 12 million dollars issued annually by the Ranger mine), the Gagudju Association gives each of the traditional owners 1,000 dollars and spends the rest on projects to ensure self-sufficiency. They own some 200 vehicles, from four-wheel-drives to heavy earth-moving equipment that's hired out for use in the national park. They've started two cross-cultural schools, built their own mechanical repair shop, set up a sight-seeing tourist operation and are now building a 13-million-dollar crocodile-shaped motel.

Their traditional lands are among the most beautiful and most ecologically significant wetlands and escarpment in the world. They're also a magnet for tourists.

Throughout the day, carloads of people roll in from Darwin and the neighbouring uranium mine at Jabiru. Many have been drawn by the Oils.

As Garrett sits down to a beer and a sandwich for lunch, a miner from Jabiru walks up and tells him he needs a haircut. Garrett smiles back and gets on with his lunch. Okay, well if that's the way this one's going to be played, then let's have some fun.

The Swamp Jockeys turn up again and land a gig opening the show late in the afternoon. Jim Moginie, impressed by their performance at Barunga, offers to do their front of house mix.

As the sun sinks over the South Alligator River, the Warumpis take to the grass stage. Hilary Wirri turns up unannounced, making a welcome return to the fold, and the yellow and green fluorescent lights above the bar add to the party atmosphere. (That it's the second last time the band's most durable line-up will play together is something that hasn't been foreshadowed.)

During the Warumpis' 'Blackfella Whitefella', the Oils sidle on to the stage area, providing backing vocals and handclaps, systematically taking up their instruments and joining in. On cue, Rob Hirst slips on to the drum stool as a beaming Gordon Butcher vacates it. He holds the beat, flailing away in his customary exuberant style. Without missing a beat, the song slips, almost imperceptibly, into 'Dead Heart', the first active changeover of the tour and, in retrospect, one of its musical highlights.

The Oils' is a funny and appropriate set punctuated by power failures. Rob covers the black-outs with ad-libbed drum solos while hundreds of tourists dance on the grass and respond with a level of enthusiasm that's rarely been a feature of the tour.

In a celebratory mood at the end of the gig, Gary Morris hosts a dinner party in the motel's restaurant, a bunfight that bubbles along into the early hours of the morning when the staff show far greater signs of fatigue and frustration than the revellers. The pressure is finally off and now everyone's ready to party.

The tour may have started off with a degree of tension and apprehension, but by the end, the relationships between the two bands are as strong as they're ever likely to be. The tour has gone smoothly, under the circumstances, and while it's been hard work for both bands and road crews, people boast that if it were possible to launch into it again tomorrow, they would ...

But they won't. In the morning, Gary Morris will release the python he's been carrying for a week into the wetlands of the National Park. And then he and the Oils will return to Sydney.

Pat Pickett will return to his regular gig of mixing Spy V Spy; Michael Lippold will sign back on as Midnight Oil's stage manager and continue to live on his out-station in the bush; Martin Hardie will become a Northern Territory Aboriginal Community Arts Officer; Gary Williams will find his way back to Sydney and start working with an Aboriginal land council in New South Wales; Stephanie Lewis will resign from the Oils' office, spend a few months recovering, and then return to the media, taking a gig as the Sydney reporter for an ABC TV rock show 'The Factory'; trombonist Glad Reed will continue to tour with the Oils and form a new band, Red Ochre.

A 'Warumpi Band' line-up will record the album *Go Bush!* which will continue to reflect the wealth of Neil Murray's experiences in the outback. While George Rurrambu will continue with the Warumpis, both Gordon and Sammy Butcher will elect to stay in the desert, declining opportunities to record and tour with the band. On *Go Bush!*, the Oils' Jim Moginie and Peter Gifford will appear as guest musicians under the names of Tjapanangka and Bulangi respectively. David Cooke will manage the Warumpi Band for another couple of months, come to his senses, and look for a less traumatic occupation.

Midnight Oil's 'Dead Heart', the song that initiated the tour, will become a top five single within weeks of the tour's completion. Royalties from 'Dead Heart' will be channelled into special projects being set up in some of the Aboriginal communities we've visited.

The Oils will go on to record *Diesel and Dust,* a superb album owing much to their experiences in the desert. The album will top the Australian charts within a week of its release, becoming the fastest-selling record in the history of CBS Records Australia.

From that album, one track, 'Bullroarer', will cause some consternation among Aboriginal people. Although the Pintupi elders of Kintore will grant the band permission to use a sound similar to that produced by the swinging of the sacred bullroarer, the Sacred Sites Authority in Darwin will object to its use. A damaging three-day media beat-up will develop out of the issue, but no contact will be made with Midnight Oil by those allegedly offended by its use.

But all that lies in the future, far away from the starry skies of Kakadu. In the wee hours, campfires blaze and swags are rolled out for the last time. As flames lick the sky, groups of us sit around singing 'Knocking on Heaven's Door' and 'Blackfella Whitefella', high on the experience that we've come through.

With us sits a beautiful old woman of about 60. Her name's Ruby and she's one of the traditional owners of this country, one of the people who ensured that the environmental and spiritual integrity of what we call Kakadu was preserved, long before it was proclaimed a national park. She's frail but strong and she sits up 'til dawn, listening to whitefellas and singing along, so happy that there are people from the city who care, who have demonstrated a desire to learn and share and experience the country.

It's only in recent years that non-Aboriginal Australians have begun to realise, as Peter Garrett puts it, just 'how incredibly precious, and of what extraordinary depth and age, Aboriginal culture is'.

It's only now that we're beginning to comprehend how crucial land tenure is to the spiritual survival of the traditional owners of this vast country. And yet, many of those people – people who have survived the last 200 years; not to mention the last 40 or 50,000 – don't have the right to say *this is my land.*

That there still exist Aboriginal people who are living on their grandfathers' lands, who have retained their traditional languages, who are still committed to the stories and the lore of their Dreaming and their culture is to be celebrated. We can be thankful that all has not yet been lost, grateful that there are people who have survived, people who still have the keys to unlock a land the secrets of which may not be exposed for another two or three or four generations – until we develop the faculties to comprehend the thought processes that have taken them so long to develop and tune.

As Garrett told the 'Big Country' crew during his last interview, 'Some of the things we see with Aboriginal people we might find a bit difficult to understand, [but] that's just our own cultural values. The truth of the matter is that back down that end of the sticks [the cities] is not like this end of the sticks. That's a simple version of it, but I think that that sort of thing's very important.'

That the policies of the past 200 years have, in many parts of the country, led to the widespread disintegration and outright destruction of languages, families and spiritual and political aspects of the oldest culture in the world is to be deeply regretted.

Those policies have led to the dispossession of people from their land and their countrymen. Babies have been kidnapped and sent to mission stations for a 'proper' European upbringing. Young children have been taken away from their parents, taken away on 'holidays' from which they never returned, removed from their birthplaces and never told where or who they came from.

Our cultural values have not prepared us for the understanding that, at the age of 40, someone like Gary Williams can be thrown into a state of confusion and displacement by learning that his grandmother came from the Gulf of Carpentaria, and that therefore there are spiritual land-based connections that he hasn't tapped into.

It may seem insignificant to white Australians brought up in a society of decreasingly nuclear families and the goal of owning a 40-square home and a couple of cars, but to Aboriginal Australians, those aspects of family and country are crucial to their survival.

The genealogy of Aboriginal culture is its lynch pin, a concept so complex that it'll take anthropologists another 40,000 years to unravel. It's the relationship between father and son and aunt and uncle and grandparents and cousins. It's the protection of the family, the concept that each person is responsible for the well-being of all others. The concept that each person is part of a skin group and has a totem, and that it's their responsibility to ensure that their totem – that animal, that Dreaming, that site – is protected forever.

Through our education system, we have learned to speak of Aboriginal culture in the past tense. For generations, the school curriculum suggested that these 'primitive natives' had no culture to speak of, that they simply ran around with spears and boomerangs donging each other on the head. We were given to understand that they had no culture because they hadn't even reached the most basic level of farming. That they harvest and replenish and cultivate in a manner that is in absolute sympathy with the land was too subtle a concept for European minds. They had no leaders, we were told, and therefore no viable system of government. What we couldn't see was the highly developed organisational structure in which everyone participates in the decision making process, a structure that carries on through a complex network of inter-linking tribes.

'One thing that's come home to us when we've come out here,' says Garrett, 'is that unless all Australians come to terms with the fact that there are Aboriginal people who were Australians and are part of this country, an essential part of it – have been, are now, and will continue to be – then we can't call ourselves a nation because we came in and jumped on this other nation.'

Almost eighteen months later I was sitting at a desk in Sydney surrounded by coffee cups and newspapers. The Oils were on the radio, winding through 'Beds Are Burning', and out in the street they were – though the effect was hardly what the band was after. The 200th anniversary of the landing of the first convicts was still a week away, but the scene was being set for a violent confrontation between protesting Aborigines and partying whites. As more attention was paid to the rights of Aborigines, a level of hysteria seemed to be rising in the press.

On page one of the *Sydney Morning Herald*, Charlie Perkins, Permanent Head of the Department of Aboriginal Affairs, was calling for a review of Asian immigration. On page three, the police in Bourke were being issued with riot gear to deal with black troublemakers. The Western Aboriginal Legal Service claimed there's a 'considered policy on the part of senior NSW police involving the use of large scale displays of force against Aboriginal people in situations where it is clear to those police that the force is not justifiable on any grounds other than a cautionary show of strength'. Further down the page, BARK (the Bicentennial Australian Revolutionary Kommandos) claimed responsibility for attacks on the Tranby Aboriginal College and the home of the New South Wales Minister for Aboriginal Affairs. On page eight, a reader suggested that to give Aborigines management control of national parks in New South Wales 'is verging on outright insanity' and would create 'a civil war, with whites held firmly to the coastline and unable to enter inland without black permission'. Another reader argued that 'The Aborigines kept this land . . . in pristine condition for 40,000 years. Look around at what we've done to it in 200 years' and asked, 'Why are we congratulating ourselves?' Page nine saw columnist and former cabinet minister James McClelland saying that he can 'understand the rage and frustration which must well up in the breast of an Aboriginal person at the raw deal which his people have received at the hands of ALL governments and ALL (political) parties.'

Up the road, black vigilantes were standing guard outside the home of a lawyer from the Redfern Legal Service who'd received threats on his life from white supremacists.

Across the harbour, the Aboriginal Arts Board's answering machine was being jammed with calls recommending that 'the government should give every black a bottle of scotch and an axe so you can all kill each other'.

The rumour mill was turning with reports that somewhere between 10,000 – 30,000 blacks were about to descend on Sydney to protest against the bicentenary. They were on the road, winding in from Queensland and Western Australia, the Northern Territory, South Australia and Victoria, rolling down the highways in convoys of beaten-up cars and trucks and buses, gathering around campfires on the side of the road, streaming towards Sydney on the Long March For Justice, Freedom and Hope.

Police throughout the country were on alert, and if you believed the stories coming out of Redfern, Rights For Whites groups were hell-bent on hostility.

Over the next few days, huge camps were set up at La Perouse on Botany Bay, accommodating the thousands of bush people who'd drifted in.

On 24 January, the Bicentennial Protest Group staged a fundraising concert at the Bondi Pavilion. The line-up for the show included a series of bands: Yothu Yindi from Yirrkala, the Swamp Jockeys from Darwin, Brown Sugar from Western Australia, Black Lace, Nukkanya and Roger Knox, Bobby McLeod and Robin Green. Speakers included the Aboriginal poet Oodgeroo Noonuccal, Jim McClelland, the anti-nuclear Senator Jo Valentine, and Northern Land Council chairman Galarrwuy Yunupingu. Sharing the stage as comperes for the event were Gary Foley and Peter Garrett.

That a whitefella like Garrett should be asked to play such a role is evidence of the links he's established with the Aboriginal community as a result of the Blackfella-Whitefella Tour.

The turnout that afternoon was extraordinary; 4,000 people gathered on the grass to take part in the event. But it wasn't just the numbers that were encouraging. It was the mixture of people, the mingling of blacks and whites. Moving through the crowd I came to realise that there'd be no trouble at the protest marches on Australia Day. For there, sitting together on the grass, wrapped in dusty cardigans and old bush store dresses, were groups of women from the scrub, transplanted from the desert to the sea. Elsewhere, groups of tribal men from the bush stood in clusters, nodding to old friends and talking quietly among themselves. Many of them had never been to the city before, but the vibe they put out was one of absolute calm. They were there to partake in the protests and the meetings that would go long into the night. They were there to represent the people from the bush, the communities we'd travelled through. Standing in their midst I could feel the spiritual power of these people. I knew there wouldn't be any trouble because their presence precluded it. By merely being there they had everything under control. For these were the people who embodied the spirit of the land, and there was no way any short-fused hot heads from the city could spoil it.

As Garrett moved around that afternoon, he connected with the elders from Wadeye and Maningrida, Galiwinku, Papunya and Yuendumu. He too could sense the warmth and the peace.

The blackfella-whitefella spirit was spreading.

EPILOGUE

Midnight Oil met Andrew McMillan around 1978, not long after he arrived in Sydney from Brisbane to try to break into music journalism. A chain-smoking night dweller, with a talent for gonzo-style, highly evocative prose, McMillan was soon filing stories for magazines like *RAM* and *Rolling Stone*.

He was one of the first in the rock press to take the band seriously; diving into the burgeoning punk-fuelled inner-city music scene that spawned a new generation of independent bands in the early years. As the music spilled out to beachside suburbs, whose clubs and pubs became the unlikely breeding ground for the great Oz rock explosion of the time, he was there, chronicling the journey.

Still, it was a big jump from stream-of-consciousness reports of wild gigs and critiques of contemporary Australian music to penning his first book. Yet with *Strict Rules* it is fair to say he pulled it off. McMillan's account of the Blackfella-Whitefella tour, across the western desert and the Top End of the Northern Territory we undertook with the Warumpi Band way back in 1986, still hums with the fevered atmosphere of the time.

This crazed journey of good intentions to very distant places, where audiences encountered sights and sounds unlike anything they had seen or heard before, was as audacious an undertaking as his effort to produce a book that both described the ride and provided a context for the rapid-fire events in black white-relations that followed.

Strict Rules, as well as describing the ride, also includes the corollary experience of a bunch of semi-naïve white fellas, heading out where history's scars were still fresh and finding that their world had also been turned upside down.

Our goal was pretty straightforward: we wanted to discover and better understand the lives of that group of Australia's first peoples who lived in a remote, nether region that had never featured in our education, a place almost beyond imagination. As *Strict Rules* lays out, we were able to enter this world, but at the same time the experience forced us to reevaluate our country, our way of seeing, and how we made music.

So taken was McMillan with the experience that he subsequently moved to Darwin, where he continued writing books, including the fine *An Intruder's Guide to East Arnhem Land*, poems and later on songs, until his death in 2012.

This first encounter has rolled on in fits and starts to the present day, with members of the band making return visits to touch base with the people we first played to decades earlier, and, in my case, as a government minister, promoting specific programs and getting around to visit as many Aboriginal communities as possible. The intertwining of two cultures, and the desert in particular, has stuck to the Oils throughout.

It is a connection that any person can make be they student, tourist, businessperson, retiree – in fact, in any capacity at all. Reaching out, as many Australian musicians subsequently have done, even taking a small step, is a practical way for someone growing up today to cross the bridge to Indigenous Australia.

As a writer Andrew McMillan brought a journalist's unflinching eye to proceedings. He was close enough to the day-to-day action to provide a vivid account of the stumbling, soaring experiment in advancing black/white relations that was at the heart of the tour.

He travelled with the road crew, which accounts for the entertaining sketches of some of those now legendary figures (at least in our small circle) and explains his occasional speculations about what the band thought and felt about the situation we found ourselves in.

We all had much to learn. The summaries of the history of places and the descriptions of the personalities we encountered that set up each chapter still provide a sound footing for anyone interested in this part of the country, and why it has such a hold on those who live and visit there.

At first glance little has changed since we rumbled over rutted, red earth tracks, setting up on make-shift stages – and sometimes in the dirt – to play fast and loud rock music.

The overwhelming presence of the natural landscape is a constant. Its features, incorporated into Aboriginal belief systems, mean that most of what the visitor sees is infused with a sacred dimension, even if you don't fully comprehend this at the time.

You only ever scrape the surface of a person's worldview in a land so different to the big cities most of us live in. Still even these glimpses get the head spinning, as does the proximity to space and a crystal-clear sky chock full of stars, and the occasional flashing meteorite.

Of the recurring motifs in the book, this palpable sense of an environment full of meaning – living, breathing – is still there for anyone who travels these parts. But so too are the equally visible, multiple challenges that people face in putting their lives back together, and building prosperous and healthy communities.

As this account shows, until very recently people were living undisturbed on their country, in the western desert as hunters and gatherers, across the whole of the Top End as traders, custodians and educators. In a split second Aboriginal people were hard up against the incoming dominant, Western juggernaut and the incompatibilities and effects of that collision are legion.

It is the various attempts to close the yawning gap of disadvantage that many first peoples still bear that linger in the mind once you finish reading *Strict Rules*. There has been vigorous debate, usually emanating from Canberra, about the capacity of small bush communities to last the distance, and a raft of policies and promises designed to rectify the statistical chasm in wellbeing have been advanced, but so far with little success.

John Howard's conservative government introduced a quasi-police state in the Northern Territory – the Intervention of 2007 – ostensibly to lessen the impact of alcohol and minimise domestic violence. Still the generic, top-down, one-size-fits-all approach was bound to founder. Whilst initially welcomed in some quarters, in other locations it was bitterly resented and resisted. Critically, this sledgehammer policy failed to rectify any of the alleged problems it was designed to address.

The West Australian state government recently proposed shutting down some 'unsustainable' remote communities altogether, despite evidence that the health of people living out bush is often better than those who reside in towns. Former Prime Minister Tony Abbott infamously described people living on their ancestral lands as exercising 'lifestyle choices', whilst his government systematically removed support from a number of key Aboriginal organisations and programs.

The Rudd–Gillard Labor governments, of which I was a member, tried successive measures to encourage economic activity and kick-start efforts to improve education and health, along with supporting cultural activities and Indigenous land management. Some actions bore fruit, such as expanding the Indigenous Rangers Program and providing more resources to the community art centres that have sprung up as vital centres of activity, which importantly provide independent sources of income in areas where high unemployment is the norm. Improved literacy in the primary years started to show through.

Yet despite the large levels of public investment the picture remains grim on many fronts: lower than average life expectancy, especially for males; high rates of incarceration, especially in the juvenile justice system, and generally poor levels of education attainment and participation in the mainstream economy. Infant mortality, and post- and antenatal health care have improved, as have some aspects of student literacy and school completion, but overall there is still a lot of ground to make up.

Which is not to say that we should read the current situation merely through the metric of the disadvantage that some Aboriginal and Islander peoples experience.

Just as the life force of individuals animates the pages of *Strict Rules*, so too Indigenous life force in action permeates the country. At the time we were crisscrossing the Top End there would likely have been no more than fifteen hundred Aboriginal and Islander university graduates in the country. There are now over thirty thousand, and this number continues to grow.

Aboriginal and Torres Strait Islander people are prominent in the arts and sport, active in local and, increasingly, state and federal politics, and a growing Indigenous middle class has emerged to take its place in business, academia and other areas of national life.

Strict Rules gives a unique insight into an earlier era, and reminds us that we shouldn't be surprised at how difficult it is to reconcile two cultures that collide with such force in the blink of an eye. The post-colonial legacy for indigenous people that *Strict Rules* explores in the course of following the tour has repeated itself in the histories of other countries like Canada and the USA, and with many similar results.

What has been missing up to now is the continuation of focused political will which listens clearly to what Aboriginal and Torres Strait Islander people are saying, and in concert with them commits to the necessary next steps: infrastructure development, intensive training, locally supported-delivered health programs, evidence-based welfare reform, the list is a long one, but above all with a bipartisan approach that is dedicated to enduring action over the long term.

In the symbolic arena, constitutional recognition as the next step before consideration of a treaty or compact is needed. In the practical arena, focusing on the things that work, hand in hand with communities, encouraging, and supporting, as partners not prescribers, but with high expectations, must become the new operating system.

Today, a traveller following the same path we took in *Strict Rules* would witness communities, albeit slowly, picking themselves up, taking charge of their destiny.

In Kintore (now Walungurru), where Midnight Oil had the rare experience of sharing local sacred law objects with traditional owners and elders, a community-based and locally driven health initiative is mounting a substantial response to the persistent problem of kidney disease.

Ironically, in the absence of any external help, the program was initially financed by Pintupi artists specifically producing paintings specifically for that purpose. The program, Western Desert Dialysis (Western Desert Nganampa Walytja Palyantjaku Tjutaku Aboriginal Corporation), provides a 'Purple Truck', which visits outlying communities, as well as a 'Purple House' in Alice Springs, for people to access primary health care. Now in its twelfth year, it is widely acknowledged as a success.

Closer to Alice, Papunya has grown in confidence. Sammy Butcher, the Warumpi band guitarist, is now chairman. There is a new store (always the epicentre of community life), additional housing and more local people are employed in the town than ever before. The scent of resilient purpose hangs in the air. In the north there is a raft of activity across the region. Wadeye is now one of the fastest growing towns in the Territory, and has covered a huge amount of ground since our visit. New schools and a large housing development are evidence of a community on the move, driven in part by the local Indigenous corporation, and leaders determined to improve opportunities for the rapidly growing numbers of young people.

Of the strong Aboriginal characters that populate *Strict Rules* a number are no longer with us. This is another reminder, if one was needed, of Indigenous Australians' poor health prospects. George Rrurrambu, the Warumpis' lead singer, and Mandawuy

(Backamana) Yunupingu from Yothu Yindi, were giants of their time and their legacy is significant. In Yunupingu's case the success of Yothu Yindi and the wide broadcast of the song 'Treaty' are ample evidence of the capacity and reach of Indigenous culture that continues to this day. Both men were close friends, younger than me, and I think of them often.

The big quiet still blankets the western desert and clammy tropical air still wafts through the Top End. The pulse of a growing, more assertive Indigenous population reaching out, adjusting and rubbing up against the invaders, the settlers, the proselytisers and profiteers, is getting stronger.

The flux and familiar crashing of clan culture against Western strictures is morphing, as communities continue to evolve, respond, absorb and/or push back against the European tide. The cultural economy – visual art, music and dance, traditional and modern – is healthy, and there are numerous opportunities for local communities to benefit from sharing the beauty of natural land and seascapes, and the mineral riches that lie beneath the ground.

There are shards of bright light that relieve the gloom, wisps of hope as people rise up, kick off the weight of recent history and step into the future, taking the deep wealth of their culture, learning, and fused connection to land – land that is everywhere and always present – as armory and inspiration for a better life ahead.

Peter Garrett
Sydney, 2016

ACKNOWLEDGMENTS

For their assistance in the preparation of this book, the author would like to thank Bill Searle, Mark Crossin, Christopher Lee, Alan James, 'Rock', 'The Waas', Robert Angus Gosford, Charlie McMahon, David Cooke, Gary Williams, Matt Peacock and Marie Bennett, Martin Hardie, Bakamana Yunupingu, the Oils, Tom Marinucci, the Warumpi Band, Phil Stafford and T.V. Browne.

For their patience and support, I am also indebted to Christine Cherry, Glen Woodward, Lisa Paddison, Paul Kelly, Jenny Groves, the Elands mob, Judith Alison, Anthony O'Grady, Helen Dickensen, Greg Taylor, Frances Law, Bert Hingley, Denise Officer-Brewster and Christopher Kirkbright.

Acknowledgement is made to RESOURCE MANAGERS PTY LTD for kind permission to reprint lines from the book *Australia's Kakadu Man* by Bill Neidjie.

Acknowledgement is made to the INSTITUTE FOR ABORIGINAL DEVELOPMENT for kind permission to reprint paragraphs from *Current Distribution of Central Australian Languages* by John Hobson.

The publisher would like to thank Denise Officer, Simon Niblock, John Watson and Toni Tapp Coutts for their assistance in the publication of this new edition, and Rob Hirst and Peter Garrett for their wonderful contributions.

ABOUT THE AUTHOR

Andrew McMillan was a Darwin-based writer who started freelancing for the national rock music magazine *RAM* as a Brisbane schoolboy. During eleven years in Sydney he freelanced for *The Australian*, *Sydney Morning Herald*, *The Age* and *Sunday Telegraph*. He also wrote for dozens of magazines in Australia and the UK before 'retiring' to Darwin in late 1988. *Strict Rules*, his first book, was initially published in hardback in 1988 and in paperback in 1992. His other non-fiction books include *Death In Dili* (1992), *Catalina Dreaming* (2002), *An Intruder's Guide To East Arnhem Land* (2001, updated in 2007) and *Tiwi Footy* (2008).

In 2001 his first one-act play, *Dingo Calling*, enjoyed a 3-week season in Darwin. In 2003 he wrote and produced 25 radio specials on remote NT roadhouses for the ABC after a 3-week, 8,000 kilometre pub crawl with a mate, Chips Mackinolty. In 2004 he updated the 'Darwin, Top End & Kimberley' sections of the US-based *Fodor's Australia* guidebook.

He won awards for essays, short stories and poetry and earned royalties for songs he co-wrote with Neil Murray ('Coolamon Moon') and Kitto, an Aussie singer based in Sweden. He had essays published in *The Monthly*, *Griffith Review* and *Meanjin* and spent time as (acting) Chief of Staff for the occasional 'rock journalism' typewriter act Darwin's 4th Estate. He barracked for Collingwood in the Dry and bred frogs in the Wet.

Andrew McMillan died in 2012.

www.ingramcontent.com/pod-product-compliance
Ingram Content Group UK Ltd.
Pitfield, Milton Keynes, MK11 3LW, UK
UKHW041300180426
11947UKWH00009B/584